OFTEN, HUNTERS THEMSELVES CANNOT DESCRIBE THE LOGIC OR CAUSALITY OF THESE THINGS. BUT I HAVE LEARNED THAT THE INTIMACY BETWEEN HUNTER AND PREY CREATES A TYPE OF KNOWLEDGE. IT'S NOT FACTUAL KNOWLEDGE, BUT IT'S A TYPE OF INSIGHT YOU COULDN'T GET WITHOUT THAT RELATIONSHIP.

Rane Willerslev

OUR MISSION

Modern Huntsman is a publication and media platform for like-minded conservationists, creatives and outdoor enthusiasts. Born out of frustration with the way hunting is often misrepresented in our culture, our objective is to shed light on a more honest side of the story. Told from the perspective of hunting purists and the diplomatically-minded, we present balanced narratives from diverse perspectives to bring about constructive conversations on otherwise controversial topics

For many of us, hunting is a way of life, a tradition passed down by our grandfathers, fathers and brave mothers. It's a way of staying connected to the land and harvesting wild food to sustain our families, and is a shared passion in most countries the world over. Hunting also plays a major role in conservation, which ensures that wildlife populations thrive and expanses of land stay untamed.

But this isn't just for hunters, and while we know that there will be opposition, we believe that through our collective words, photographs and films, we'll be able to educate some folks about overlooked realities and win the minds and hearts of those who still have them open. Through presenting stories based in virtue and ethics, as well as alternative perspectives on otherwise controversial topics, we aim to inspire, educate, challenge, and set the record straight in some cases.

Tired of being spoken against and labeled things we are not, it's time to write a new story about hunting. We created Modern Huntsman to be the banner under which those with common cause can gather, in hopes of bringing about constructive conversation and sensible solutions.

We hope you'll continue this journey with us.

IN THIS ISSUE

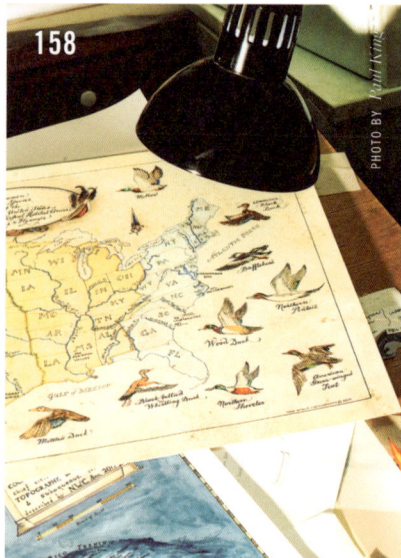

158

PHOTO BY Toni Kinn...

BUT IN THE END, WE ARE THE
AUTHORS OF OUR OWN STORY. AND
THE TRADITIONS WE PASS ON ARE
NOTHING MORE THAN WHAT WE MAKE
THEM. IT'S UP TO US TO DECIDE
WHAT THOSE TRADITIONS ARE.

Tito West

42

PHOTO BY *Jean-François Lagrot*

PHOTO BY *Robert Cabrera*

132

PHOTO BY *Jen Judge*

Sturgeon Spearing   Between icequakes, the sounds of chainsaws cutting through the 20" thick ice, and the last few trucks and ATVs leaving the lake there is an encompassing serenity of seeing the sunset reflecting on a freshly cut spearing hole. Before the shack is placed over the hole and well throughout the season, this window to the lake's hidden winter holds limitless potential. Every second spent looking into the depths feels as if a silent primordial fish might just make its way through and collide with our modern world in a flash of steel and excitement.

VOLUME FIVE

TRADITIONS

MODERN HUNTSMAN

CEO, EDITOR-IN-CHIEF
Tyler Sharp | *@tylersharpphoto*

CREATIVE DIRECTOR
Tito West | *@tito__west*

MANAGING EDITOR
Jens Heig | *@jensrheig*

INTERNATIONAL EDITOR
Byron Pace | *@byronjpace*

DIRECTOR OF OPERATIONS
Katie Clower | *@ktclower*

DESIGNER DIRECTOR
Elias Carlson | *@eliascarlson*

COVER PHOTO
Jen Judge | *@jenjudgephoto*

CONTRIBUTORS
Hans Berggren
Robert Cabrera
Danny Christensen
Mike Day
Chris Douglas
John Dunaway
Al Elliott
Guillermo Fernandez
Della Frederickson
Gloria Goni
Gunnar Guðmundsson
Aaron Gulley
Holly Heyser
Rick Hutton
Daniela Ibarra-Howell
Jen Judge
Paul King
Jeremy Koreski
Jean-François Lagrot
Heidi Lender
Jillian Lukiwski
Shane Mahoney
Derek Malou
Phil Massaro
Jeff Moore
Justin Moore
Randy Newberg
Filip Örnerkrans
Jesse Perkins
Jonnah Perkins
Fabio Purroy
Elliott Ross
Sam Thompson
Dani Vergés
Kate Watson

CONTRIBUTING EDITORS
Jack Evans | *@jackevanswriter*
Katie Marchetti | *@katiecmarchetti*

CREATIVE ADVISOR
Chris Douglas | *@chrisdouglasphoto*

CONSERVATION ADVISOR
Simon Roosevelt

COPY EDITOR
Dylan Garity

EMAIL
info@modernhuntsman.com

WEB
www.modernhuntsman.com

SOCIAL MEDIA
@modernhuntsman

PRINTED IN LOS ANGELES
Red Car Media
www.redcar-media.com

RETAILERS
www.modernhuntsman.com/stockist

ADVERTISING
www.modernhuntsman.com/advertise

A LETTER FROM THE EDITOR-IN-CHIEF

Photo of Tyler by Danny Christensen during their red stag hunt in Transylvania.

As I write this letter, it's difficult to find words that sum up the first half of 2020, but it seems fair to assume that it caught us all by surprise.

These strange times have tested all of our limits, and for us it wasn't just as individuals, but as a company. We were forced to look inward and consider who we really are, and more importantly, who we want to be. When faced with unprecedented global challenges, do we feel that what we're saying, what we're doing, is meaningful, and worth laying it all on the line for despite the risk?

For us, the answer was yes, and I'm so incredibly proud of what we've been able to accomplish considering the circumstances. Beyond that, it was the bravery, tenacity, and integrity this team showed to stay the course, even when we were told it was a lost cause. In addition to keeping the lights on, we also managed to raise a meaningful amount of money for Bozeman medical workers, and for out-of-work freelancers. The fact that we were not only able to forge ahead with assignments and production, but continue that into a larger fundraising initiative is something that we're proud of and grateful for. Our intention is to grow this in momentum and scale as an ongoing grant program for independent artists affected by covid-19. More on that soon.

We could not have done any of this without continued support, as your purchases during the economic downturn allowed us to make those donations, and define a new direction for the company. We hope you'll continue the journey with us.

As we fought our way through production on this issue, each day was a new battle, many of which were lost. But we took it one day at a time, and got better, and braver, with each setting sun. We stuck to our promises, kept morale high, and as we talked with the 40 contributors spread all over the world, encouraged them to keep faith — that we had their backs. While it sometimes waned, this confidence, certainty and hopefulness was largely drawn from the theme of Volume Five, which could not have been more timely or appropriate: Traditions.

While that word can mean many things, for us, and in the pages that follow, it represents a deep and important connection to those who came before us, and the knowledge that they have passed on. Traditions tie us to our past, and in times of struggle or difficulty, remind us that the dynamic human spirit will endure, as it always has. To quote Joseph Campbell, who is a source of great inspiration for me, "We have not even to risk the adventure alone, for the heroes of all time have gone before us — the labyrinth is fully known."

Through these collected stories, you may find comfort in that concept: that the traditions we inherit remain a connection to our heritage, and often to the natural world. Whether related to hunting, cooking, survival, spirituality, or just keeping Grandpa's memory alive, they are the lessons we can lean on in hard times to provide a guiding light. Traditions are threads that tie us to our cultures, our humanity and our place within the natural order whether we know it or not.

Some traditions are more sustainable than others. Some are more socially acceptable. It's difficult to know where that distinction is, especially in a rapidly shifting world that is confining some to the pages of history, oftentimes when they don't fit the modern vision of

a "civilized urban society." While some should be left to die, other traditions can be updated, especially when viewed through a lens of conservation. Though most of us don't hunt to survive, there are many cultures who still rely on that, and beyond meat as sustenance, many hunt to keep their spirituality, their life source, alive. We felt it was important to highlight some of these stories, as they are more relevant than ever with the recent strain on our food-sourcing systems. Ancient hunting wisdom still serves us today.

While we do dive into the complexities and nuances of some particularly challenging topics, mostly, we dive into the purpose of traditions, which vary greatly between country, region or culture. It's also encouraging to think that you can pretty much join in at any time — unless tribal invitation is required. When circumstances call for adaptation, you can even start traditions of your own. For us, that meant pushing into new storytelling territory with a genre-bending publication, and now being on our fifth issue, we don't plan to stop that tradition anytime soon — we're not going anywhere.

For now, know that this book has a little something extra. We feel that these types of stories are more relevant than ever, so a little more love, and a little more blood, sweat and tears went into this one. We're damn proud of it, and hope that you can sense the difference. This is a new chapter, we are renewed in our mission, and more than ever we're thankful for your support.

I'd also like to personally thank our partners on this issue, because without their faith in our ability to pull this off, and their patience as we battled our way through the obstacles, this book would

not have made it to the finish line. A major heartfelt thank you to Ryan from Mystery Ranch, Bridget from First Lite, Ini from Purdey, Amanda from Tingley, Stuart from Hilleberg, Hope from EPIC, and Mason and Cheryl from Nosler. Thank you for believing in us, and for supporting this mission even during a global economic shutdown.

Now I'm very proud to present Volume Five: Traditions, and I hope you enjoy these stories that are as rich in lessons as they are in diversity. We all learned something through the process, and are better for it — may you find the same.

Whether in practice or purpose, aim true and shoot straight.

See you in the field,

TYLER SHARP
Editor-in-Chief | @tylersharpphoto

A LETTER FROM THE INTERNATIONAL EDITOR

Photo of Byron by Jo Stenerson

We must accept by being present in this life that we navigate our own purpose and meaning in the world. The notion of a preordained higher plan for our existence may provide a comforting backdrop to the often-mundane nature of our daily drudgery — bills, taxes, and the cyclical grind of waking, working, eating and sleeping — but we alone define why we are here. As the only species with the cognitive ability to contemplate our own evolution, we have a responsibility to determine our legacy.

Our experiences and relationships shape our sense of being: the vulnerability of love, the profundity of watching a life slip from this world, the biological brilliance of joining and replicating cells to create new life, all force an acknowledgement that nothing is constant. The 19th-century philosopher Kierkegaard observed that "human existence is an unfinished process where an individual takes responsibility for his choices." As we acknowledge a path determined by our decisions, we accept change as both inevitable and necessary. The legacy of the Anthropocene will be defined by actions borne from what we value as a society.

Our lives flow like the tumbling stream: cutting an ever-fluctuating path to an inevitable end at the ocean, as we write our story toward our final breath. Short or long, our stint on Earth is likely of fleeting individual insignificance across geological time. As our bodies break down, returning once more to the earth, what remains in the fabric of the culture we embodied are the traditions carried by those still on their journey through life. Like the single droplet of water, an individual doesn't have the power to sculpt a landscape, but the cumulative force of many over the years does. It is this persistent, determined direction of society that will create the collective architecture of our future.

Those who came before us gifted their knowledge to us, and as we embrace the traditions of our upbringing — or those we discover along the way — we hold them in trust for those who come after. Our challenge — yours and mine — is to maintain the importance and relevance of tradition within the construct of cultural heritage, as we grapple with the environmental degradation from anthropogenic effects. As we face down the looming, existential prospects of climate change, we have to ask ourselves if traditions really matter.

I am reminded of T.S Eliot's speech, "*After Strange Gods,*" as he reflects on traditions:

"*We become conscious of these items, or conscious of their importance, usually only after they have begun to fall into desuetude, as we are aware of the leaves of a tree when the autumn wind begins to blow them off — when they have separately ceased to be vital. Energy may be wasted at that point in a frantic endeavour to collect the leaves as they fall and gum them onto the branches: but the sound tree will put forth new leaves, and the dry tree should be put to the axe.*"

Consider the clean strike of a sharpened axe upon the *dry tree* in Eliot's passage. Society, like mountains rising from the shifting tectonics upon which we stand, may appear static through the vignette of the present but is ever-shifting through time. Even at its zenith, weather will re-shape these earth giants, and so too the depiction of what is ethically acceptable within societal norms also changes. The tree, as with tradition, sometimes has to fall,

while others are reborn in the warmth of spring.

To defend actions solely on the basis of tradition is never sufficient. Numerous pursuits in human history have thankfully slipped into obscurity: dogfighting, borne from the Roman invasion of Britain in 43 C.E. and continued until the 19th century; or the once widely practised 'sport' of cockfighting, adopted into Western culture from Persia before the Common Era.

Other traditions, often argued to be foundational by the cultures in which they developed — such as whale hunting in the Faroes described on page 178 — tread a precarious line drawn in the sand, with an incoming tide of global pressure ready to confine them to folklore.

The Western world riles with scorn and indignation at traditional Chinese medicine, as we vehemently recite scientific evidence in the face of dwindling rhino populations and the hundreds of thousands of pangolins being ripped from the wild every year. Yet the use of these animal products is part of a tradition deeply ingrained within a culture. The distinguishing element lies in the impact of the activity: not just taking, but contributing in a positive manner to the environment around us. It is this that defines the traditions which will stand the test of time; where we as humans stand as in awe of the life around us as we are of our own achievements.

Nothing depicts this with quite the gravity, or focus of mind, as a line highlighted in the King James Bible, brought to my attention by Oliver Sacks in his book, *A Leg to Stand On.*

"For that which befalleth the sons of men befalleth beasts; even one thing befalleth them: as the one dieth, so dieth the other; yea, they have all one breath; so that a man hath no preeminence above a beast."

We only truly comprehend what we have lost when it's gone, and oftentimes the remanence is only an irretrievable abyss of contemplation: what could have been, with more care, consideration, and reverence for the other wild beings of this planet? More than ever, we are understanding that indigenous knowledge, and the traditions inherent within these cultures, play a vital role alongside science in informing a future that sustains humans within natural ecological cycles — re-establishing these lost links with nature, not only for biological survival but for the very soul of humanity. To ignore the lessons evolved over thousands of years in the cradle of nature is to be indifferent to vicissitudes weighing on the only place we know to sustain life in the cosmos. Traditions transcend our individual existence, and as we build on the knowledge and lessons from the past, we have the opportunity to steer a course for the betterment of humanity: a future of equality among people and a respect for the natural world that fosters actions for the good of all living things.

Byron J. Pace

BYRON PACE
International Editor | *@byronjpace*

A LETTER FROM THE CONTRIBUTING EDITOR

As we were making this issue, I was hurting. In the winter, the days were tired and empty. I was struggling with personal loss, and probably also feeling our collective grief in these days of isolation and pandemic. Working on these articles was some respite, and the happiest I was all winter was when I was researching *Buffalo Country* (*pg. 94*), out on the Native hunting grounds in Montana, and on the Nez Perce Reservation in Lapwai, Idaho.

In one set of conversations, with Nakia Williamson, Tatlo Gregory and Josiah Blackeagle Pinkham, in Lapwai, I gathered a bit of sense and optimism back. We were just telling stories. Josiah told me the one about Buffalo sheltering the lost Nez Perce child, on some ancient night before time was measured. From this story, the Nez Perce know, still, that the buffalo will always provide for them.

I told him about the time I watched 20 different bears roam a heaven-spread valley in Alaska, and how since then, I've admired their way of journeying new trails, alone, as seekers.

Josiah said that one of the Nez Perce names for the bear is *Navigator*.

We were finding parallels in our vastly different learnings of the world, and all in our perceptions of nature. What I had sensed from animals in a lifetime of hunting no longer felt like my imagination alone.

The original Nez Perce stories often sound mystical, fantastical, like fables. But they're not meant to define the world literally. They're told for us to experience. Josiah described how intimately he knew those mythic fable-stories he was told over and over again as a kid. He's called up these tales throughout his life since, like they were his own history, and found greater and greater depth and nuance in them — degrees of meanings that were hidden from his younger mind.

To me, this speaks to the stories' quality of *existence*, their continuation — their impact beyond the first telling.

"We're trying to rejuvenate our relationships with stories," Josiah said. "And the ability to think and feel with them. What they do is display relationships, consequence, but also they help you deal with challenges in the way that people have dealt with challenges in the past."

Stories have that power. I think we only really believe in what we have experienced, but as readers or listeners we can take the tales of others into our own heads and hearts. We can *live more* through them.

In Lapwai, while researching the Nez Perces' grievously unjust modern experience, I was told over and over again: "We've been here for 16,000 years; we're not going anywhere." That was always said with a smile. Nakia explained later that his culture's resilience, that remarkable sense of firm, existential security in a people so materially oppressed, depends largely on the way they remember their truths through the generations.

It is harder to feel alone in a challenge when an elder tells you they've been there too. It is harder to be afraid, facing the mystery, when your ancestors have survived it before. This is all easy to remember when, as a community, you never forget to speak of your past.

In the face of a global pandemic and the social retrenchment that's followed, I have been thinking that my ancestors have lived through similar times of grief. I imagine that the pandemics and world wars they endured were at least as mind-changing, ominous and disturbing as what we face today. Unfortunately, I do not even know their names.

That doesn't condemn me, though. We have each other to talk to, and for all the difficulty of these times, it has been an absolute pleasure to assemble the honest tales of the hunting life in this Volume for you. Stories, told truly and heard in trust, are these validating reminders of the universality of even the most exquisite emotions, and the wildest. The telling is a tradition of collective exploration.

Hunting stories, whether they're humorous, historical, terrifying or revelatory, all tend to lead toward a sense of awe at what lies beyond our human experience. Our book stares into the place between human and animal life. The two stories I pursued for this volume — one based in an original American culture in Idaho, the other at an intersection of modern and ancient lifestyles in Eurasia — are both examples of the universal invigoration of spirit that we gain from nature. This is the invigoration that so often restores us.

It's always an effortful stretch to speak of the sensory world of the hunt in a modern, rationalist society — it usually makes for long stories. One of the best simplifications of it that I've ever heard, though, was this tale from Josiah that I think is relatable to any hunter:

"Explaining the spirit is like trying to explain the idea of water to a salmon that says it's thirsty," he said. "A salmon is swimming in water, with all these movements around it, currents and swirls. The water is *throughout* that

salmon. And yet, it's saying, 'I'm thirsty.'"

"Take it in?" I suggested.

"Take it in."

Hunting begins with that joyful exposure, and as the snow has melted around my home in Montana, I have healed from grief by heading to the mountains to take it in, and by writing about it.

This volume collects stories from our wild hunts, and I hope they will be good to think with in the field. Most important, though, is that they inspire you to tell your own, ever-worthy truths, large and small, visible and mythic. Stories are endless and essential, and the best tradition we can keep for each other as hunters.

JACK EVANS
Contributing Editor | *@jackevanswriter*

When you're coming apart at the seams, know that your pack won't.

From formidable load-haulers to functional daypacks, MYSTERY RANCH designs their products for men and women who have jobs to do, from the deep backcountry to the frontlines of foreign soil.

Dana Gleason, the godfather of pack design, and his partner Renee Sippel Baker have been working together for over 40 years to create a heritage of unmatched quality and durability in their packs. A distillation of time, space, and unwavering dedication to the task at hand, MYSTERY RANCH continues to be the standard of unprecedented strength and comfort today.

Designed in Bozeman, Montana to withstand the most arduous environments on the planet, these packs have been tested in the incinerating heat of raging wildfires, held their ground on the front lines, and tamed oppressive loads for the successful hunter.

True to their word when the world was upended by a pandemic, MYSTERY RANCH didn't have to be asked to enlist their textiles and time. Stitch by stitch, they were among the first to provide quality facemask protection for Bozeman medical workers on the front lines of the fight against COVID-19.

Modern Huntsman is honored to work alongside a brand that vows to have our six, wherever the journey leads.

MYSTERY RANCH

There is more than one way to climb a mountain.

First Lite circumvented what had already been done and designed for what was to come, recognizing the potential of Merino wool to alter the experience of hunters who endure hours of high exertion as well as long bouts of stillness in a single hunt.

Working from dawn till dusk, they became the first to produce Merino wool in a camouflage pattern, taking the U.S. hunting community by storm in 2007.

As leaders in foresight; both in technical apparel and their hands-on approach to environmental responsibility, First Lite is committed to carrying their cornerstones of conservation, culture and inclusion to the top regardless of the weight. They've allowed their path to be dictated by the needs of their environment, and their customers instead of peripheral competition.

Spearheading private corporate conservation practices, opening their doors to the public for hunter's education courses, and establishing mentorship programs in their community — First Lite has taken the initiative on furthering the traditions we hold dear.

Whether sitting in a Midwestern tree stand with company or stalking a quarry in the solitude of the mountain West, First Lite provides a full suite of high-functioning, thoroughly-tested garments that you can rely on.

We're thankful to have such a remarkable brand come alongside us as they weave their unique threads of tradition into a new and endurable fabric that will outfit the hunting community for generations to come.

FIRST LITE

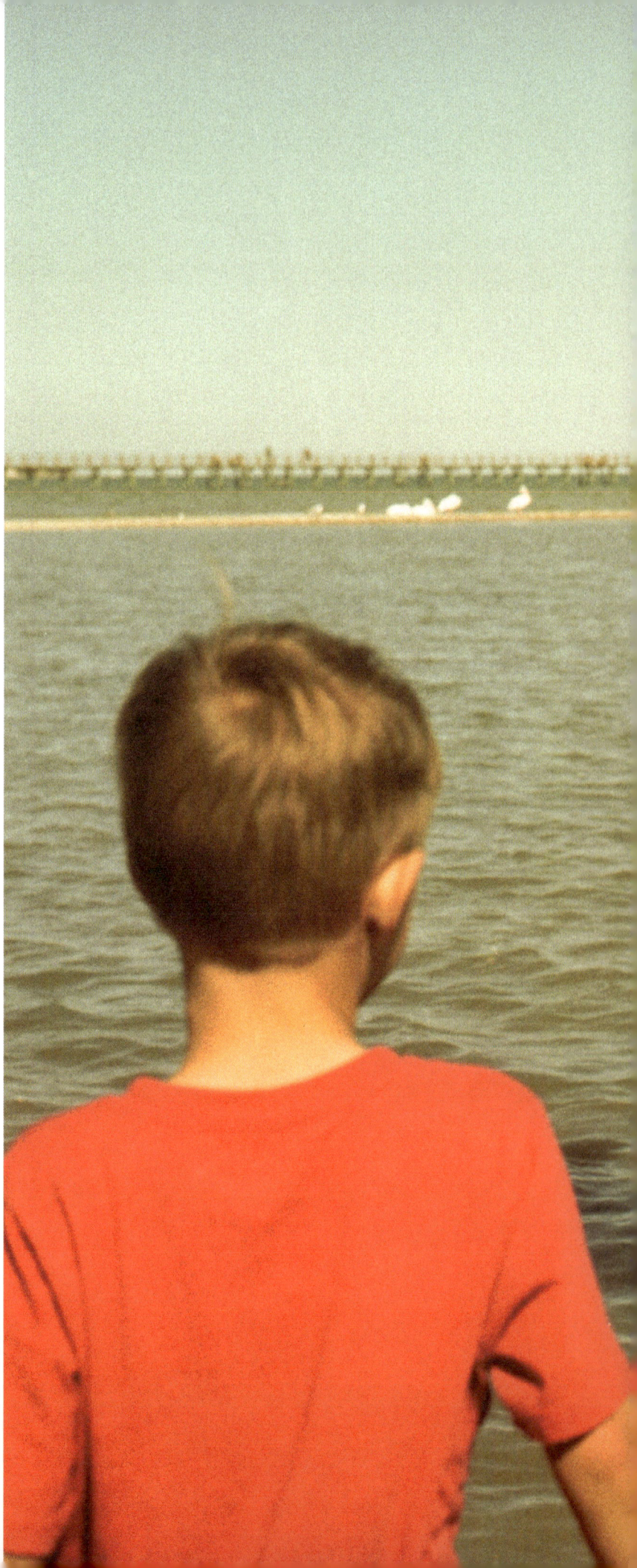

It requires resilience and trust for a company to operate across three centuries.

Tingley Rubber began in 1896. Its first product was a bicycle tire plug developed by Charles O. Tingley, who rode his bike across the East Coast to both sell his product and prove its reliability. Five generations have since led the company through world wars, global economic depression, and changing consumer demand to meet the ever expanding needs of the modern worker.

While the Tingley that operates today is a far cry from what began 124 years ago, its dedication to the customer remains the same. Fishermen, foresters and ranchers don their protective footwear and clothing knowing that they are covered by decades of innovation and the best technology available. Their confidence in these products puts fresh fish on tables, creates thriving forest ecosystems, and restores harmony through responsible land management.

Perseverance is a defining feature of this nation. It safeguards our future, knowing that we can overcome seemingly insurmountable challenges with hard work and support. As we move through 2020 and beyond, we find solace in the fact that companies like Tingley have endured and emerged stronger on the other side.

Here's to the next 100 years.

TINGLEY

— est. 1896 —

To truly discover and understand the outdoors, one must be part of it.

That understanding is different for everyone. Just as there are countless ways to experience the mountains, rivers and forests we revere, all of us have the opportunity to create our own connection to wild places. This is a founding principle for Hilleberg the Tentmaker. It pushed the company's founder, Bo Hilleberg, to develop a product to facilitate discovery — no matter the method — with the highest quality materials, craftsmanship, and purpose.

Nearly five decades of innovation have passed since Bo and his wife, Renate, manifested the idea of a double-walled tent that could be easily and quickly assembled when every moment matters. He envisioned an inner tent and fly that could be pitched together, in one crucial step, and Renate provided the sewing skills to make it a reality.

Bo and Renate raised their children in tents bearing the family name. It's why they decided that a tent should withstand winds on a remote peak and also foster traditions for those embarking on their first camping trip. That core design pillar is what makes Hilleberg the first choice for adventurers who trust their lives to their shelter in the most hostile surroundings.

The Hilleberg family's dedication to tentmaking gives us the confidence to seek the boundless possibilities of our world. We hope their story inspires you to do the same.

HILLEBERG
THE TENTMAKER

For over two hundred years, the Purdey name has defined the very essence of English gun making, creating an intersection between art and functionality.

With an unbroken lineage to the Purdey family name, the commission of a rifle or shotgun from James Purdey & Sons embodies an ambition to embrace an old-world; one of hand-forged, meticulous care, where guns are born onto this earth and not merely made. When you own a Purdey, you are, in a way, a part of their history: a fabric of gun-owners, keeping hundreds of years of knowledge and skill alive.

The James Purdey & Sons of today is far more than a gun maker. The company has set a clear marker as to the community they wish to embrace and support, with the establishment of the Purdey Awards for Game and Conservation in 1999. As the years have gone by, the Awards themselves have gained the same prestige as the guns they produce, and today, even being shortlisted for one is a coveted achievement. In this volume we will delve into the ambitious conservation project being undertaken in Northern Ireland by the 2020 winner.

By fostering an attitude and ethos of long term conservation concern, Purdey is using their heritage to help shape a community of modern thinkers, willinging embracing an active role in creating a vibrant future for our landscapes and wildlife. In this endeavor, Modern Huntsman is proud to partner with James Purdey & Sons to tell their story.

PURDEY

Gun & Rifle Makers

LONDON 1814

In an ever changing food landscape, the steadfast commitment of our regenerative farmers is shining through more than ever.

Grass-based agriculture is set apart from conventional production by approaching every choice through a zoomed out perspective. Our feature in this volume about grass-fed beef producers in the Driftless Region of Wisconsin is a tangible longview of how the regenerative mindset transcends millennia, connecting geological time with the biological. Though the Wisconsin beef farmers are not EPIC Provisions partners, their collective values show us that regenerative producers across the country are building a movement that has the power to improve the world.

Born of the ethos that we cannot outsmart the ecosystem, EPIC Provisions strives to work with nature, not against it. The interdependence between animals, humans and the environment is at the core of the regenerative model, and the EPIC Provisions mission. As our ancestors fueled their bodies with grass-fed protein, fruit and nuts, EPIC Provisions looks to these staples for their products with a holistic approach of environmental stewardship.

We are honored to have the support of EPIC Provisions as we celebrate the value of the regenerative movement and its commitment to traditional agriculture and wildlife conservation.

EPIC
PROVISIONS™

When John A. Nosler created the Nosler Partition in 1948, it changed the world. It became the benchmark by which all other premium bullets would be judged, and even today, more than seventy years later, it still is.

Forged in the belly of discontentment for anything short of perfection, John Nosler's Partition design spawned from the inadequacies of available bullets of the 1940s. This drive for innovation, focused on the ethical effectiveness of ammunition, runs through the veins of the company to this day. With a suite of new bullet and cartridge designs created in the proceeding decades, Nosler has continued to evolve, but without ever losing sight of their family values and a core business centered on the customer.

Our hunting heritage and traditions are shaped by the details of our lives, and for so many hunters around the world, Nosler is a name that provides a comfort of reliability ingrained in the fabric of their upbringing. There is a great burden of responsibility which comes with this, but now, with the third generation of Nosler at the helm, we can walk forests and climb mountains with the same confidence as those who came before us.

We're proud to be aligned with that continued history.

NOSLER®

A RESILIENT TRADITION

WORDS BY *Shane Mahoney*
PHOTOS BY *Byron & Darryl Pace*

Despite the drumbeats of doom and gloom, there are many reasons to be optimistic about hunting's future.

In a world where hunting is often misunderstood and frequently criticized, it is easy to become overwhelmed. Bombarded by a stream of sensational representations of hunting's true nature and conservation influence, we cannot help but sometimes wonder where all this is headed. So we ask ourselves how many more challenges must we face; how many more false statements must we counter? How will we ever make our critics understand? How can we deal with those who are ideologically opposed to hunting and the use of animals under any circumstances — those who will never even try to understand? Are we to be like Sisyphus, constantly pushing our arguments before us but never cresting to a plateau where a shared understanding of hunting's value is reached? Who in the hunting world does not ask themselves these questions?

It is only natural that we should worry about hunting's future. After all, it is of great importance to us personally, and we know full well its conservation value. To lose hunting would be a matter of significance to wildlife, human cultures and economies. Furthermore, focusing on our challenges is a logical response. We want to fight back, provide counterarguments, and safeguard this tradition, and we feel frustrated that others do not see the conservation and societal value of what we do. How can this be when, to us, the evidence is so overwhelming? Yes, we spend a great deal of time wondering what the future holds for hunting and wildlife. And so we should. Like conservation itself, hunting's future will be no accident; it will be secured by the actions we take, the commitments we make.

At the same time, however, we need to reflect on just how remarkable a force hunting remains in modern society. It is hardly a weakling on the verge of demise. On the contrary, it is a robust and resilient force in the lives of tens of millions worldwide. It's held close, with intense conviction and purpose, and that leads to activism and a defense of the sacred. Hunting's legacy runs deep, and its appeal and relevance radiate across a widening spectrum of society, attracting more women, urban residents, and people of

different nationalities and cultures. Its repositioning, as a healthy and environmentally friendly food procurement system, can and *will* encourage a new wave of interest in the activity. There are many reasons to be optimistic about hunting's future. Hunting is not going away.

Indeed, even for those of us who have been part of the hunting world, the scale and vibrancy of the activity worldwide is incredible. True, the screaming anti-hunting headlines and frenzied fringes of social media do sometimes capture the public's attention. However, beneath these episodic squeals of outrage rolls a quieter thunder, a deep resonance of the citizen multitudes, who on landscapes as diverse as savannas, rainforests, and glacier-fed mountain valleys pursue the hunting tradition of their forebears, passing it on to their children and grandchildren. Sharing the wild meat they capture, hunters convey to a wider gathering the ecological appropriateness of taking responsibility for animal death, an inevitable consequence of the global food web that links humanity to the consumption of wild, living resources of all kinds.

There is no escaping the great universal truth that flesh eats flesh. We will either consume it literally through our fisheries, livestock raising, and hunting, or less directly by displacing the wild others of this planet to make room for fruit and crop production. As current international trends indicate, meat consumption is rising globally. So, while some might wish to eliminate hunting, this will certainly not eliminate animal death by human hands. Perhaps, to the critics of hunting, we might say, *Choose your poison: Let animals live wild lives and die quick deaths, or live lives of confinement and domestication, and die just the same.* For me, the choice is clear. As far as humanly possible, let them live wild and die wild, participating like us in the ritual of existence. Hunting mirrors our true human ecology; often as predator and sometimes as prey. Our dentition and our physiology indicate where we came from and will dictate what we seek. Meat will be high on our list.

Hunting is no sideshow. It will not be driven to the darkened corners of irrelevance by ridiculous claims that it is frivolous and without social or conservation value. No matter how shrill the protestations, hunting will stand firm. You might hear the call to stop all hunting, but let's hear the plans to replace its conservation support and practical services to society. Tell us what will replace it. Give us the blueprint for sustained economic and political support for wildlife conservation, should hunting disappear. Please, tell us who will pay the bills. Who will pay for nuisance black bear removals, the counting of animal populations, the habitat recovery and restoration programs, the wildlife disease research, the anti-poaching and enforcement efforts, to name just a few of the issues that in North America and elsewhere are significantly, or entirely, supported by hunters' dollars? The social, economic, and conservation benefits of hunting are manifest. What is the alternative model that will provide the equivalent support over the vast jurisdictions where hunting is presently so critically important?

—

HUNTING REMAINS VIBRANT IN THE LIVES OF TENS OF MILLIONS OF CITIZENS AND THOUSANDS OF COMMUNITIES. ITS IMPACTS ON CONSERVATION AND THE ECONOMY ARE ENORMOUS AND WITHOUT PARALLEL IN NORTH AMERICAN SOCIETY. WILDLIFE CANNOT AFFORD TO LOSE IT. NEITHER CAN WE. AND WE WON'T ANYTIME SOON.

Blind faith and empty rhetoric are not enough, not when the future of wildlife is at stake. How will wildlife be cared for and managed? Why would citizens who have little, or fleeting engagement with wild animals, willingly pay for their protection and management? Who will manage the superabundant species, the threatening and dangerous carnivores, the disease agents passed between wildlife and humans?

These, of course, are practical questions. There are also more philosophical ones: Who has the right to take away the legal harvest of wildlife by individuals for their own sustenance and well-being, while industries are encouraged, and often subsidized, to harvest fishes and domestic animals by the billions for food and profit? Further, in a world altered massively by human commerce and abundance, wildlife will not be sustained without human agencies to counterbalance these potentially destructive forces. We need every community that can and is willing to support wildlife to be in the conservation game. Hunters are, indisputably, one of the most enduring and effective of these communities. Why would anyone concerned with wildlife conservation want to eliminate any pro-wildlife force?

Despite its critics, hunting is not going to disappear, and there are many reasons to believe that it will not just survive, but thrive, into the future. Nowhere is this more true than in Canada and the United States, two countries that have embedded hunting within the fabrics of their society and

within their wildlife conservation system —a shared bi-national approach often referred to as the North American Model. It is recognized as one of the most successful wildlife conservation systems on the planet, having rescued wildlife in the late 19th and 20th centuries, and brought it to incredible 21st-century abundance. Look at the deer in our gardens, the black bears in our communities, the turkeys in our driveways, and the geese on our lawns — does anyone really believe this is a beautiful accident? Who made this happen? Who invested most and why?

For over a century now, hunting has been at the heart of conservation in our countries, and in others around the world. Its social relevance and resilience have been maintained over that long stretch of time, despite the enormous changes that have occurred in our communities, societies, and natural landscapes. This is the headline we need to focus on. What has sustained hunting is the passionate commitment individual hunters have to their tradition and their willingness to give back. This is not going to change.

Hunting remains vibrant in the lives of tens of millions of citizens and thousands of communities. Its impacts on conservation and the economy are enormous and without parallel in North American society. Wildlife cannot afford to lose it. Neither can we. And we won't anytime soon. ⩗

THE PILGRIMAGE

WORDS BY *Katie Marchetti*   PHOTOS BY *Rick Hutton*

At the turn of the 20th century, the northern tier of the state of Pennsylvania was clear-cut by loggers. When the logging industry moved west, huge swaths of acreage were left devoid of industry and wild game. The state Bureau of Forestry purchased the land in an effort to reforest what had become known as the "Pennsylvania Desert."

The Commonwealth of Pennsylvania began establishing national forests, spearheading conservation, and the concept of public land use. Land was being set aside to be enjoyed by the public, and by 1913, land could even be leased. Pick a spot and apply, the legislature said. A privately-owned quarter-acre lot of public land could be yours with a 99-year lease, where you could build a camp for generations to enjoy.

In 1918, soldiers returned home to a changed world. Beneath the foreign weight of civilian life, surrounded by family and friends, in suits instead of combat boots, they found their reprieve from the Great War in the camaraderie of men at arms. When hunting season dawned, they shouldered rifles once again and stepped off the grid — a pilgrimage to cabins leased on public land, or family-owned pieces of northern Pennsylvania woods.

Hunting deer and bears in the remote forest offered a reprieve from the memories of overseas, and collars of routine back-breaking work, and families to feed in Pennsylvania's southern cities.

In their absence, clear-cut acres had flourished into an early successional habitat. A young forest with browse, food, cover, low predation, and minimal hunting pressure caused the deer herd to explode. But the depression of the 1930s swept many northern farms to state-owned public land, and World War ll would again take hunters overseas.

President Franklin D. Roosevelt stepped onto the scene with his able-bodied institution of the Civilian Conservation Corps, and state-leased camps grew in number from 30 to 3,180. Roosevelt made outdoor recreation readily accessible to the people; setting the stage for the Pennsylvania deer camp culture that is still ingrained today.

By the late 1940s, the returning heroes would retrace their steps to the cabins of their youth for two weeks each fall. Bedecked in "Pennsylvania Tuxedos" — plaids of black and white from the town of Woolrich — they made their pilgrimages north to a primitive place.

A roster hung by the cabin door, and military bunks began to line the walls. Army-issued canteens were filled, dinner plates from navy ships littered the table, and Polaroid pictures of men in blaze orange decorated the walls. The American flag sat above the fireplace, and a framed picture of the president rested on the mantle regardless of the face — the heritage of deer camp was being written on their souls.

In the field, they worked as a unit. With matching strides, they pushed deer and bear to the waiting rifleman, a 'run and gun' style of hunting seldom seen west of the Mississippi. The animals would later hang from frames in front of the cabin, the men making quick work of skinning and butchering before dark, turning animals into food for those eagerly anticipating their triumphant return back home.

They drank, smoked and talked late into the night with flickering flames dancing across their wool-clad shoulders — away from it all and more connected than before.

For Rick Hutton, this was the definition of hunting. The jostle of riding in a truck bed to the mountains ahead, held in place by the rough hands of the coal miners from which he grew. En route to the Antler Hunting Club deer camp, to find his future and history fortified under a single, primitive roof.

The Antler Hunting Club was erected at the head of Furnace Run Gap in Bald Eagle State Forest on the Union/Snyder county border in Pennsylvania in 1926. It was composed of 20 Pennsylvania Dutchmen from a two-county area in the southeast; each man paid a $1 entrance fee, and an additional $50 was put toward the construction of the cabin. Rick followed his grandfathers', uncles', and father's lead 86 years later when he was voted in as a third-generation member in 2012.

"I have been hunting there since I was a kid," says Rick. "My dad didn't let me go to camp my first year, when I was 12, because driven hunting is very tough and the guys expect everyone to keep up." Climbing incredibly steep hills covered in thick rhododendron and mountain laurel was too much for a kid, so his first whitetail was shot from beneath a tree, sitting next to his Dad.

Rick's dad deployed to Iraq that year, and so it was Uncle Ralph who made the introduction to deer camp. At 13 years old, Rick loaded his father's flintlock rifle and followed a group of strangers into the woods. Traversing the backwoods of Pennsylvania, his ears burned from the unfiltered adult conversation, head spinning from the older men's arguments about the day's deer-driving plan.

"I was nervous; it's a lot of pressure when you're a 12- or 13-year-old kid. You have to walk through the woods, stay in line with guys that you can't see most of the time who are yelling and hooting. You're shooting fast, you're reloading fast," explained Rick. "But they were a very well-oiled team, and they pushed a lot of ground very efficiently. That's the drive hunting culture."

Coordination is key in deer drives when you're racing daylight to 'push' country while maintaining narrow gaps that discourage the deer from doubling back. Men are split into two groups — drivers and posters, or chasers and watchers, terminology dependent on your camp. The posters/watchers line up, still and quiet, waiting for the driver/chasers to push the deer toward them.

When done correctly, the hours move with military precision, a deer pushed and a deer shot, each man fulfilling his mission for the day.

The armed forces have left many generational marks on the foundation of deer camp. From tools to technology, assigned tasks to working as a team, the traditions established here at home were shaped half a world away.

"Modern hunting technology was forged by the military," explains Rick. "In 1906 they came out with the 30-06 rifle cartridge for the military, which has now killed a lot of wild game in North America, and countless gun cases in America hold one today. Wool clothing and camouflage started as military technology, and boot technological advances from World War II went into improved hunting boots."

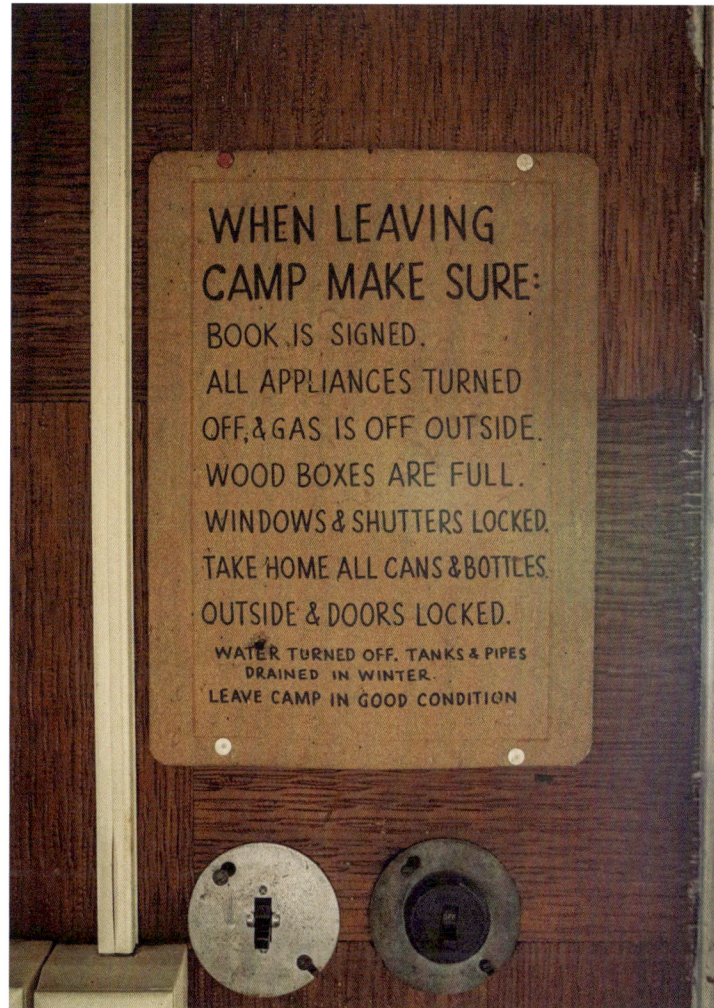

FOR RICK, A WELL-ROUNDED OUTDOORSMAN SHOULD KNOW HOW TO SET
UP A DRIVE, AS WELL AS BE ABLE TO UNDERTAKE THE SPOT AND STALK
METHODS HE UTILIZES TODAY. HE CREDITS A GREAT DEAL OF
HIS KNOWLEDGE OF HUNTING TO WHAT HE LEARNED ABOUT HABITAT
AND ANIMAL BEHAVIOR BY MOVING ANIMALS ACROSS A LANDSCAPE
IN HIS YOUTH.

According to Rick, his camp is littered with wartime memorabilia, tools given a second life when they were transported to deer camp. U.S. Military surplus army bunks and packs that once carried soldiers' rations now hold the hunter's essentials.

"Pennsylvania has great-grandsons that are now hunting in the same camps and sleeping in the same bunks that their great-grandfathers did," Rick says with enthusiasm. "Modern hunting culture was steeped by the world wars; the greatest generation coming back forged that camp tradition of camaraderie and working together for a goal. I love that; I'm very nostalgic toward that time in our history."

Hunting camp holds not only military history, but also significant family history for Rick. His grandfather Ralph, a long-time Bell Telephone Company employee and Korean War veteran, passed away at their hunting cabin on the opening day of deer season in 1988. After the morning drive, his grandfather returned to camp for lunch, where a heart attack took his life at the kitchen table.

As older generations inevitably pass on, the culture of deer driving has ebbed and flowed as well. Rick refers to the '80s and '90s as the "good old days of deer drives." Since then, social pressure, wildlife management, and habit alterations have made a serious impact on deer camp culture. Hunting in Pennsylvania today has begun to shift from drives to deer stands.

"Driving culture is really fun. It's fast-paced; you're not sitting and freezing. But you lose something found in a tree stand," he explains. "Moments bow hunting, stand hunting, listening to acorns fall through the trees, leaves rustling in the breeze as you watch nature wake up, are my favorite. You watch things unfold at a natural pace versus in a drive hunting environment where you're controlling the pace.

Rick continues, "The older I got, the more I watched television and read hunting magazines and realized they weren't writing about deer drives. I felt the burden of taking bad shots at a lot of running deer when I was younger. I didn't want to kill just any buck anymore, I wanted to try to find a nice one."

In college, while pursuing a forestry degree from Penn State, he gravitated toward bow hunting whitetails from a tree stand, returning to camp life for bear drives only, which became the common direction for camps in the North.

"Almost every one of my friends at college had a camp," says Rick. Camps varied from those that acted as a second home with running water and TV, to crude shelters with outhouses requiring fresh water to be hauled in by hand — on both public and private land all over the state. "It was interesting to hear stories and talk about camp. Everyone wanted to know how your camp was set up; it's such a part of our state history."

The United States is a crosspatch of hunting cultures, divided by the breadbasket states. Rick headed west after college, leaving deer drives behind on the eastern side of the Rocky Mountains. He fully embraced the hunting traditions of the West — spot and stalk pursuits across the open landscape of Montana. The traditions of his youth are illegal in his new home state.

For Rick, a well-rounded outdoorsman should know how to set up a drive, as well as be able to undertake the spot and stalk methods he utilizes today. He credits a great deal of his knowledge of hunting to what he learned about habitat and animal behavior by moving animals across a landscape in his youth.

Mule deer and whitetail are held in equal esteem for Rick, as are bows and rifles, drives, tree stands, and spot and stalk methods.

"I love the West," he says. "I also miss Pennsylvania deer hunting heritage and culture," he adds, remembering school being closed on the first day of rifle season in a state that in 2013 could boast 13.1 hunters per square mile. "It was crazy how many guys were in the woods hunting. I don't miss the hunting pressure of a sea of orange on opening day or it sounding like there's a war, but I do miss the camp camaraderie and that hard oak–hickory hardwood landscape. That's my heritage."

He hopes to one day pass both cherished traditions on to the next generation — the Western tradition of a wall tent camp while hunting elk in the mountains, as well as hunting whitetails in Eastern deciduous forests.

Like many men and women from Pennsylvania, Rick was shaped by the log cabins of his youth. Although traditions have changed day by day, and modern technology has reached even these remote sanctuaries, hunters still follow the familiar pilgrimages of their grandfathers into the mountains. They search for a glimpse of a whitetail bounding through the northern woods, carrying the same gun that weighed heavy in generations of calloused hands, to find each step on the well-worn path consecrated by a history of hunters in the Pennsylvania hardwoods. ⭒

LINKS OF LIVING

STORY BY *Randy Newberg*

My first deer camp was in 1970. An old logging shack warmed with a 30-gallon fuel drum converted to a wood stove; red wool clothes drooping the ropes where spare socks dried and hunters warmed between drives. My dad, whom I bragged about as the greatest deer hunter in Koochiching County, spent months planning deer camp. My favorite camp mates were Grandpa Walt and Uncle Marvin, Dad's older brother. Coming and going were assorted friends and hungry employees scraping by as timber fellers in Dad's logging business.

Only six years old, I couldn't understand it all, but it was formative. Even at my young age, I detected joviality beyond what my eyes had heretofore witnessed. The language was a bit rough for a kid, though the treats were aplenty.

Big smiles grabbed my cheeks when Mel would draw the accordion from its case and bar music filled the air. It was so hot inside we'd have to open the shack door, though I suspect mostly to clear the cigar smoke to a breathable toxicity. I remember laughing with the adults, though I was too green to understand the punch lines. Each elder made sure to compliment my hardiness, with my kindergarten mind unable to absorb the charity of these accolades.

Dad was having the time of his life. My mind was set; I would be a hunter.

A month after that ontogenic deer camp, a once-in-a-century winter decimated Minnesota's deer. The season was closed in 1971. No camp that year. I was bummed.

Before the next spring thaw, Grandpa Walt had a stroke. Grandma had her hands full. It was two long hours to the Iron Range to see them. We spent grouse opener helping winterize the dilapidated homestead Grandpa vowed to never leave; Grandma spoiled me as her sons labored. I listened as Dad and Uncle Marvin discussed if deer camp would be held in November. Eventually, Marvin opted to be the reliable hand Grandma needed for Grandpa's care.

My first deer camp would be my family's last, ended by a series of disconnected events. Life, as I came to learn, was not fair.

So much changed, so quickly. Dad spoke fondly of the family deer camp, speaking almost mystically about big bucks in the Sturgeon River country. He'd often pause, light a cigarette in his now-tremoring hand, then look down as he inhaled, as if something lost should be right there between his feet.

In his silence, I knew he was considering the reality of his now-broken life — recently divorced, fighting the bottle, adrift since his dad had died four years after that last camp. Every path he searched for explanation seemed to dead-end.

Deer hunting was the last grasp of what his life had been, or could have been. I can't trace his downward spiral to the end of that deer camp. I do know he missed it dearly. He picked up what pieces he could and filled some voids by hunting with kids and neighbors. Never again did I see the smile he held that November. It was the week I turned six; the pleasures so obvious on his face were what cemented my hunting future.

Over the next few years, struggles with booze eroded our relationship. Good times were few, the best of them were spent chasing whitetails in Minnesota's big north woods. Me being of hunting age was a milestone in his life. Sadly, the demons had grabbed him so tightly, the only semblance of a deer camp came from invites to join kind friends who sensed his loneliness. Offers to join other camps were not the same as hosting his own. His emptiness was easier to read than a track in fresh snow.

Yet, no matter what darkness hung over him, hunting was still his bright time, when his love to hunt could temporarily beat back his addictions. Each November, he was a different dad, and for sixteen days of the season, it was fun to be his son. Chasing deer raised his spirits — driving to stands, we talked of restarting a family deer camp. I hoped to see his blue eyes flash again with that hunting camp twinkle. But by Christmas, the bottle regained its control, and any chance for a new path had drifted over.

Thirty-three years after that last deer camp, I found myself in Colorado, mule deer hunting. Uncle Marvin called to tell me that Dad was in the hospital. It was deer season back home. Dad was now a non-functioning alcoholic, unable to even hunt. He passed after two months.

Going through his belongings, I found a few pictures salvaged from his house

fire, twenty years prior. The few that caught my eye were all from deer hunts — bucks, camps, smiles, a life of dreams ahead of him, a young man unaware that his difficult life would end at age 62.

My younger siblings and I sorted for the meaningful items. I asked if I could have his old buck mount, now oiled and greasy from too many years hanging in a bar. That buck came in 1976, his last real effort to build a family deer camp.

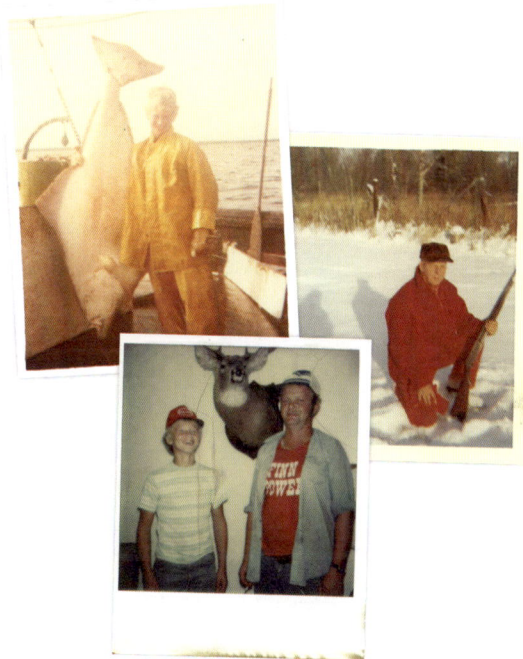

It was taken while we were hunting with his brother Marvin back home on Da' Range, not far from where his dad and uncles had first taken them hunting. It was a fine buck for the big woods, worthy of a taxidermy bill. Mostly, it became his hope for days that might be.

I've since had that buck remounted. It hangs over my desk, not the biggest among many antlers and hides adorning my room, each a reminder of special

times with special people. I find myself often looking at that buck, thinking about what might have been. What if he'd had those annual markers that get one through hard times? What if he'd had the family deer camp? Would it have given him purpose and strength to persevere, to overcome the cruel hand of fate that terminated his annual family revelry in the November woods?

I don't know that answer; I never will. When I think of his pure joy and the never-again-seen happiness that owned him in that deer camp almost 50 years ago, I'm sure losing that family tradition didn't help as he traversed a life more difficult than any man deserved, however self-inflicted.

By measuring the joy I get from annual hunts with my own son, Matthew, I can see how Dad's loss of traditions surely contributed to his struggles, his feeling of being adrift in an unfair world. Pondering the tragedy that was his life gives clarity to my blessings, my soul mostly unscarred by the blades of misfortune. I have avoided so many of the bad events of his life by my good luck, some discipline, and resistance to the temptations to which he succumbed. My eyes drift from his buck on the wall to mule deer pictures and framed limits of mallards, to Matthew's elk mounted on the adjacent wall — a bull my brother helped us haul from the deepest part of the Missouri River Breaks — all links in a chain that locks me and my son to a shared life of annual camps in the mountains, dreaming of what might be, but mostly living for what is.

WAITING FOR THE MIGRATION

Six weeks in harsh harmony with the walruses and people of the Chukchi Coast

I've always thought that flying cannot be the same experience as traveling. Traveling is an immersion in an unfamiliar world, and the experience of its unveiling. If you fly 8,000 kilometers by plane to get to the end of the world, beyond the limit of what is known to you, both socially and geographically, then it is not you who arrives. It is only a part of yourself — your scout, an avatar. It takes time for your body to make physiological sense of your arrival, and more time for your mind to become fully aware of life as it unfolds. You slowly wake into the place of the earth where you've been projected. Harmony is only possible at this price, these days spent changing into a part of the new world.

STORY BY *Jean-François Lagrot*

I traveled for weeks toward the coast of the Chukchi Sea. Slowly, held back by the elements, by the wind, I followed increasingly uncertain connections eastward. I flew on six planes to get to these reaches, trailing farther away from human habitation with every stage. The entire trip from France lasted 14 days. I spent most of that waiting on weather and measuring in my head how this land near the Bering Strait was both the end of the world and a showcase of its origins. In Khabarovsk, where I made a 24-hour stopover, life still resembled what I knew in Europe, despite the presence of the exotic Amur River and an all-powerful, all-mysterious China on the other bank. The true shock took place during the next stage, as I ferried across the river to Anadyr, the provincial capital of the Easternmost Russian Okrug of Chukotka. The water of the Anadyr River is as dark as the sky that overhangs it, the current is powerful, and the swirls have metallic reflections. The fast-running clouds over the town frayed on the edges of building blocks. Their looming silhouettes drew a chaotic line on the horizon. I had the feeling of entering a tenuous space, crushed between a leaden sky and a barely humanized nature. I entered a world I did not yet know.

AUGUST 2017: Maksim Chakilev is waiting for me at the airstrip in Anadyr. He's a biologist, aged 30, calm and cheerful — but he barely speaks English. For my part, I only know a few words of Russian. Together, however, we are going to spend more than a month monitoring the migration of walruses in a small bay along Cape Serdtse-Kamen — the coast to the distant northwest of the Bering Strait. Here, herds of walruses come to call before crossing the Strait — a vital crossing that promises a winter in milder latitudes.

A twin-prop Antonov 26 carries us to Lavrentiya, a village of a thousand ethnic Chukchi souls, where we sit and wait for one of the two Mi-8 helicopters that tour the Chukchi Coast to take off. Wind gusts ground us for a week.

Enurmino, Nachkan, Uellen … Villages of a few hundred fishermen each streak along a hostile coast, either beaten by rainstorms or trapped by an onslaught of ice, depending on the season. They are accessible only by sled in winter, and by foot or helicopter in summer. By the time we can no longer believe it, one gray morning finally sees the legendary Mi-8 torn from the ground in an intense mechanical effort.

The machine is suffering. It lifts, barely, from the cracked tarmac, and we are finally free. We fly over rippling brown sandscapes and ocher wetlands, myriad streams and bogs divided into constellations and scattered islands of rock. It's a desolate world apparently devoid of animal life. Maksim and I sit, silent in the helicopter's rusted interior. In front of us, a Chukchi family, huddled together on the wooden benches, dozes despite the hellish noise of the rotor. The shaking slowly lulls our bodies into a strange apnea.

I do not know what awaits me, but I already like this roughness, this nudity of the landscape, this monotonous tundra. Maksim knows the bay we're heading for well. Since 2011, he's spent many summer months out on Serdtse-Kamen with some tens of thousands of walruses, a family of brown bears, and the occasional polar bear lost in the Arctic summer.

The coast appears as a wire out of the gray light. Coal-colored waves advance toward the shore, sharpening into definition as they approach the beach, wanting to rip at banks of short vegetation battered by the wind. We lower next to two rows of wooden houses aligned along an artery of sand. The powerful heaving of the blades pins yellow grass to the tundra ground. A few years ago, another Mi-8 crashed at this very spot, amputating the village of many hunters and their families.

The village of Enurmino brings together a community of around 300 Chukchi. The wooden houses built during the Soviet era have been the only human improvements to the landscape. Some of them lean dangerously. Some ethnic Russians live on the outskirts of the village, as if kept at a distance from land that is not quite their own. They are in charge of the power station that supplies the village. They also provide security, an undefined sort of policing that seems to be a reminder that this is still Russian land.

A 30-year-old man named Stas is the head of the hunting community, and therefore the village chief. It is he who must lead us to the bay where we will stay, some 14 kilometers farther east. In the meantime, he leads me to the container where the young hunters of the village stay. We smoke, drink coffee and tea without interruption, and chew on pieces of whale skin dipped in soy sauce. It's firm but tasty, and it passes the time. We also cut thin slices of smoked whale tongue. Although I do not speak Russian or

Chukchi, I understand from their facial expressions that the conversation of the young men revolves entirely around fishing and hunting. There's a poster of the Cape's salmon species on the wall, and they slowly argue over which type was spotted in a stream some days before. All have weathered cheeks, tanned by the wind and the cold. I can see that it's this outer world, the world of animals, that defines them, through and through.

The wind blows daily through the sandy streets. Every morning, the men go to the hunters' house. The faces are coppery, large crevices define their features, and in their slanted and piercing eyes is reflected a large bay open on an unpredictable ocean, which, at any moment, can be unleashed with force. They're innately privy to this, and when the day of their hunt approaches, a crowd forms on the shoreline. All, with or without binoculars, scan the ocean. Far away on the horizon, fixing my gaze with attention, I spot a few plumes of flowing water that sparkle in a ray of whitish light.

Morj are small groups of walruses that cross offshore toward Cape Serdtse Kamen, keeping close to the coast. They signal that the migration to the Bering Strait has started. That morning, a spark runs through all the men's laughing eyes. For each of them, hunting is a reason to live. But the sea is too rough for them to be able to launch their skiffs and head out on the water. They know too well the suddenness of storms that surprise this coast. They seem to wrestle with their instinct to go hunting as soon as possible, to accumulate as much meat as possible, to face the winter. We are at the beginning of September, and in two months the ice will appear, sounding the death knell for the short Arctic summer and the beginning of a forced inactivity which will not end until spring. They absolutely must take advantage of these two months to fill their quotas. Some 1,500 walruses can be hunted in the Chukotka quota, which must be distributed among all the coastal villages, with five whales given to the only village of Enurmino.

Other men soon join them to watch from the dune. They've come back from a hunting trip in the tundra. Having left at 3 a.m., not long before arctic daybreak, they shot the first of the Canadian geese to have flown over the village this year. In days, there will be clouds of geese flying over the coast, heading south. The birds are no less a part of the food supply that will help the people survive the winter. Here, we are hunting to subsist. We are hunting, in the truest way, to ensure the survival of the group.

The women of the village spend days this season gathering berries — a precious source of vitamin C, from the tundra. They bring back baskets full, but still rarely enter into the houses of hunters. Certain tasks, however, are entrusted entirely upon them, particularly in the aftermath of a walrus hunt: they clean the tusks after they've been removed from the skulls, and boil the skulls to reduce the odor and refuse. The tusks are then thoroughly scraped and rid of flaps of flesh and bone, and are stored in a secure place before being sent to the administration for sale through a legal supply chain.

Each man is indeed paid by the Chukotka regional government, as a hunter providing resources for the village, according to the amount of ivory he brings back.

Being allowed to accompany men on a hunting trip on the high seas is a guarantee of confidence. Stas makes me understand that he fears that my photos will backfire on them later. His lucidity surprises me. He knows that the walrus hunt can trigger outrage on social networks around the world, that the images will be stronger than the words that justify a subsistence hunt essential to the survival of the Chukchi. I promise not to betray their intentions and to do my best to convey this message. But what impresses me the most is this fair perception of these distant issues, his knowledge of controversies, of the criticisms of a detached and hyper-moralizing world, of the possible ravages of technology, and beyond this knowledge, his own deep desire to protect an ancestral way of life. But I also know that though Stas made the deliberate choice to resist the consumer society and a more urban way of life, for many Chukchi, the temptation is great. Geographic isolation is then the last bulwark against acculturation and the loss of traditions.

> THE WIND BLOWS DAILY THROUGH THE SANDY STREETS. EVERY MORNING, THE MEN GO TO THE HUNTERS' HOUSE. THE FACES ARE COPPERY, LARGE CREVICES DEFINE THEIR FEATURES, AND IN THEIR SLANTED AND PIERCING EYES IS REFLECTED A LARGE BAY OPEN ON AN UNPREDICTABLE OCEAN, WHICH, AT ANY MOMENT, CAN BE UNLEASHED WITH FORCE.

The sea is flat, motionless. An endless mirror. There is not the slightest breath of wind as our four skiffs are distributed in the bay, moving away in opposite directions. These are the conditions we've needed. I have the privilege of being at the side of Stas, the most valiant hunter. Less than a mile from the coast, we spot a group of adults. They expel frail plumes of water at regular intervals, always moving close to the surface. In less than two minutes, Stas has reached the group. Equipped with a harpoon, the young hunter installed at the bow of the boat takes a last drag on his cigarette as if to gain strength; now he's ready. Anticipating the appearance of a large male walrus on the surface, he readies his spear and, at its next jet, pierces the back of the animal with a powerful blow. The brownish mass immediately plunges, braked by the two buoys connected to the harpoon. Soon forced to rise to the surface to resume breathing, the walrus is struck again at its spine, fatally this time.

When the hunt is done, the tension released, Stas tells me the story of a hunter from Nachkan, some sixty kilometers away, who was killed by a whale he had harpooned. Diving to escape him, the whale's monolithic tail struck him on the head, instantly breaking his spine. He died in that moment. I understand that here, one does not feel a condescending compassion for animal life — neither whales nor walruses nor seals — because everyone, animal and man, seeks only to

survive. And survival is a fight that can also be lost. There is no malice in this hunt, no desire to wrest life. Instead, there is only the desire of living and bringing life to one's own people. The death of this walrus is a gift. Hunters know its value. In the end there is a respect which needs neither words nor demonstrations. It is enough to have risked lives to receive it.

The boat has difficulty returning to the beach, imbalanced on one side by this inert mass of more than a ton. Riding under the straining power of the motor, it seems clear to me that calm weather is essential to undertake a hunting party: any wave could capsize the skiff. We have made the most of it, though. At the end of the day, eight adult walruses rest on the sand, their short fins folded along their bodies, their tusks each measuring almost a meter, their whiskers in brush. These animals seem to have come out of some fantastic bestiary. Out of the water, they look unreal to me. I linger to stare over them, curious and admiring.

A heap of bleached whale vertebrae and a few rusty containers away from the dwellings mark the altar where the hunters will cut up their catch. It will take hours of cutting in the slow-freezing cold. All the men from the village rush to participate in the event. They pare back the skins and take the meat apart. Their gestures are sure and precise. They're acting from and through a distant heritage — it can be felt.

EVERY PART OF THE WALRUS HAS ITS
PURPOSE. ORGAN MEATS ARE SET ASIDE FOR
RAPID CONSUMPTION. RID OF THE BODY AND
CUT INTO QUARTERS, THE SKIN IS FOLDED
BACK ON ITSELF THEN SEWN INTO SPHERICAL
BUNDLES, TRAPPING THE MEAT, WHICH WILL
FIRST FERMENT, THEN FREEZE IN WINTER.

Provocative, a hunter offers me a piece of raw brain. I taste it. It's melting, it's sweet. A powerful aphrodisiac, I'm told. Every part of the walrus has its purpose. Organ meats are set aside for rapid consumption. Rid of the body and cut into quarters, the skin is folded back on itself then sewn into spherical bundles, trapping the meat, which will first ferment, then freeze in winter. These are the *kimgüts*, bags of meat that are buried and later retrieved in the depths of the cold season. Today they are transported to the village by tractor and distributed. By the skinning grounds, on the outskirts of what now looks like a battlefield, dogs run and bark in all directions. A warm light passes. The cold is biting. Steam spirals from the sole thermos of tea. The hunters smoke. They are serene, happy with their day. I walk among them, hoping my presence does not disrupt their natural way of conduct. But they are kind to me, and proud to be what they are.

The next morning, the sea starts to churn. We must use the last few hours of relative calm to reach our final destination. We rush the boat out into the open water. Stas is concentrating. The Chukchi Sea leaves no respite. It changes in a snap without prediction. Men fear it every time they go out. No doubt they prefer it frozen, trapping them in winter, at least stable. The cliffs above us nest a colony of screeching puffins. Beyond Cape Serdtse Kamen, hunters can no longer chase walruses. That area is now protected. Maksim and I will venture there merely to observe and gather data on the migration. Our new home is a strip of sand with a lonely wooden *isbouchka* hut and the skeleton of a stranded barge.

After dropping Maksim and me onto the land, the boat leaves without delay. Stas will be back in a month. Maksim makes a silent thumbs-up parting gesture to the disappearing boat. He seems happy to find his hermitage. As far as the eye can see, the cliffs point east toward the Bering Strait. Sea birds swirl over the rock. We are now alone in the world, whatever happens, for a month. We drag our bag of potatoes, our canned goods and our generator to the *isbouchka*, what was once a hunter's refuge. It contains two wooden benches, a table, and a stove. Our new life begins.

Quickly, a ritual takes hold. Every day we must trek to fresh water. To reach it, we walk carefully between the remains of decaying walruses, all victims of trampling by their kin in the last migration. The coal heap, at least, is just a few steps from the *isbouchka*. It was the cargo of the barge that ran aground 10 years ago. We make use of this coincidence, digging through the black decay to find pieces that will best power the stove. Throughout every day, our thoughts hang in anticipation of the wintry conditions that approach.

A path runs along the beach then climbs among the rocks to the overlook of the bay. I look down to flocks of birds below that follow a gray whale, roaming the shallow water. The spectacle is fascinating. I feel like I have entered some alternate, virginal, unscarred world. One morning, we count up to 23 whales in the bay, feasting on krill. Over the month we watch walruses, whales and orcas in pursuit of younger walruses. On the ground, a family of brown bears comes every day at dusk to play on the other side of the lagoon. On the first evening they appear, Maksim fires a flare to announce our presence. He tells me that two years ago, he was sleeping in the cabin when a polar bear, attracted by the smell of cans, tried to get inside by leaning on the boards of the front door until it gave way. Panic-stricken, Maksim was able to chase him out, shouting like a beast himself. But I feel that this trauma is still present.

Some days the wind is relentless; on these, I lie still, reading in the *isbouchka*. Maksim writes his daily reports into a logbook. Then, one day, we hear a knock on the door.

A stranger appears, traveling on the tundra nearly 150 kilometers, on foot, from the village of Lorino. His dog is his sole company. Having left nine days before, he had stopped only for a day to shelter from the rain under a rockpile. He followed the coast to keep his bearings. Aged about 50, Sergeï carries a wise and gentle look, as keenly intuitive as he is intelligent. In the rays of light that pierce through the single window of our cabin, his angular, tanned and asymmetrical face is a story in itself. We could read the life of a Chukchi hunter — his battles at sea, his epics in the blizzards, his wounds, his courage and his fears. Hungry, he devours everything we offer him: canned reindeer and salmon in broth. It's normal that we give him everything we have. He's not bothered — this is simply how men should be. But he is also not satiated. He doesn't hesitate to go raise the fish net that we placed across the nearest stream. That day, luckily, two salmon weighing more than two kilos each are captive there, including a female full of eggs, which he prepares with salt. He speaks little, but I learn much from his presence alone.

Sergeï spends two days with us, the time he needs to regain strength before leaving for Nachkan, still a distant 80 kilometers away. I see no tiredness, anxiety, or frustration in

I FEEL LIKE I HAVE ENTERED SOME ALTERNATE, VIRGINAL, UNSCARRED WORLD. ONE MORNING, WE COUNT UP TO 23 WHALES IN THE BAY, FEASTING ON KRILL. OVER THE MONTH WE WATCH WALRUSES, WHALES AND ORCAS IN PURSUIT OF YOUNGER WALRUSES. ON THE GROUND, A FAMILY OF BROWN BEARS COMES EVERY DAY AT DUSK TO PLAY ON THE OTHER SIDE OF THE LAGOON.

his eyes. He does not complain about a delay, nor the distance yet to travel, and he does not seem weighted nor concerned. He seems happy, to me.

Each morning, we walk in the direction of the distant Cape, stopping from time to time to count the heads of the seething mass of walruses, which, day after day, piles deeper out into the bay. At the beginning of September their number increases slowly. But soon they begin to take possession of the rocks, climbing over each other until the smallest accessible plot at the foot of the cliffs is occupied. Their cry, something like the bellowing of the cow or the grunt of the hippopotamus, resounds along the walls while their acrid smell reaches us in asphyxiating puffs. At the slightest wind storm, though, they flow back to the sea where they feel more secure. In the days that follow a wind surge, the whole swarm mysteriously disappears. We wait, each time, to see their numbers surge again.

In the evening, around the stove, Maksim and I take the time to share our stories and our lives by interposed dictionary. We are friends, for in the present our aspirations are the same, our sorrows and our joys identical. Almost every day, a salmon caught in the morning complements our meals. We go to gather berries. The days go by peacefully, without surprise. Increasingly numerous and raucous groups of walruses are now invading the bay. Soon there are several thousand. I descend into the cliffs and spend hours observing them, fascinated by the morphological differences that exist from one individual to another, both in terms of body size, color and contours of the skin. Their uniquely whiskered faces make them recognizable personalities at first glance. They're not the anonymous clones that I'd imagined from a distance. Their close proximity, the folds of their flanks with reflections sometimes bronze in color, sometimes copper, all combine to make their colony a monumental work of art, a painting in pastel shades posed in a decor reminiscent of old engravings. They gather, all lit by dramatic, glinting light.

Soon, winter makes its first tracks. The humidity becomes more penetrating. A film of frost covers the sand in the early morning, and groups of increasingly large walruses play with the rollers that run up the beach. It's like they're waiting for a mysterious signal to invade.

On September 26, 2017, the day before my departure, I wake up slowly, and a deafening chatter reaches me through the boards. In the tundra burned by the wind and the cold, large white flakes cover the gentle slopes that rise toward the summits. But it isn't snowing. Thousands of geese have stopped in this bay they thought was deserted. The show is of great poetry. Each of them, wings folded, looks like a delicate flower blooming on the tundra. The wind has died down after the storm of the past few days. Following to enjoy the spectacle, Maksim, leaning on the door frame, beckons me to look on the other side, to the end of the beach. After sweeping the strip of sand from one end to the other, my eyes widen... A colony of walruses has taken possession of the entire shoreline, so camouflaged in its magenta-brown tones that it is difficult to distinguish at first glance. Although there are more than a thousand, Maksim also did not spot them at first. The day before my departure, like a playful wink, the walruses arrive in full, the absolution of their massed voyage to this bay. Maksim then curiously consults his notebook. The previous year, the walruses had hoisted themselves onto the sand on September 26.

The first hours spent in this bay come to mind as I climb alone on the tundra. When I arrived, this environment from the cliffs to the lagoon seemed incredibly hostile. Today, I regretfully leave this simple and powerful moor. I only passed through. I like to think that tomorrow the wind will blow again, the cold will become more pungent and walruses will always pile up higher on the sand.

When I reach the pass, I turn to search the immutable landscape. Nothing seems to be able to disturb the fullness that reigns from one end of the bay to the other. Maksim's silhouette stands out on the sand. The walrus colony has once again collected in its inseparable, unchallengeable mass. I never imagined that my gaze on these animals of another age would be so transformed by this experience. I never would have thought that the fate of this animal, and that of the Chukchi and of this bare, rough and magnificent land, could all be so beautifully entangled. As I am to depart on this last day, I feel in myself a pain of detachment from the great network I'd slowly come to be a part of. ⚐

THE SEA
is HISTORY

Tingley

PRESENTED BY *Tingley*   STORY BY *Tito West*

The Texas coast is a lesson in contrasts, a glaring representation of the state's great diversity. There is an incredible beauty to this desolate stretch of land, marked by salty marshes and low-lying barrier islands, and for anyone who has spent time here, or was raised here, it becomes a place unlike any other. If you are away for too long, you miss the damp, heavy air, thick with salt that sticks to your skin, and the smell of the hyper-saline bays and estuaries between the barrier islands and the mainland.

Lower Laguna Madre

You miss the shrimp boats tied to the pilings and the pale green color of their nets and tackle in the summer sun. You miss the sight of spoonbills and the flocks of green-winged teal, the whooping cranes and the sound of honking overhead as Canadian geese head north in the fall. You miss the thin, distant horizons that seem to rise out of the sea when returning from an offshore fishing trip on the Gulf Stream. You miss it all, and I know this because I spent the early part of my life here, and then I left. I left for a long time, and while I would find myself in some distant country, maybe on a long, endless track after buffalo in the dense sand of the Okavango, or up in the north country on an equally endless pack trip to some distant mountain, my mind would wander and I would feel the warmth of the south Texas sun on my skin and dream of the day that I would be back among the shrimp boats and the coastal dunes of my beloved shoreline.

The Gulf Coast has attracted many to its waters. It began with the Spaniards and Cortés, and later Pineda, and the legendary shipwrecks of the conquistadors in search of gold, eternal life and new worlds. But they were not the first ones here. The Karankawa had inhabited the coastline long before any king decreed a voyage of exploration under the banner of his nation's flag. They learned how to live in this rugged land and how to protect their skin from the relentless onslaught of mosquitoes that are perhaps the region's greatest claim to fame. Centuries later came artists like Winslow Homer

and after him — perhaps because of him — Hemingway, and eventually others, less well-known but equally devoted to the region. Artists such as John P. Cowan, Al Barnes and Dan Wingren, all beholden to the spell that the Gulf Coast casts upon those with susceptible imaginations and longings for another time, devoted their oeuvre to this place.

Another artist to have fallen under the spell of the gulf is JT Van Zandt. Though not an artist in the traditional sense, JT (John Townes) is nonetheless without question an artist, a man who has discovered, through a connection to the natural world and through the craft of fly fishing, a deep understanding of life and the legacy we pass on to future generations. He is the eldest son of the late singer/songwriter Townes Van Zandt. However, it would be a mistake to assume that his life is relegated to the shadow cast by that legendary giant. JT has become his own sort of legend, particularly in the world of fly fishing, but what I find myself drawn to is his philosophy on life. His clients are not unaccustomed to thought-provoking and engaging conversations when poling the flats or during a lull in the fishing on a scorching and windless summer day. I experienced this for myself a few months ago when I spent a day on the water with JT. I had come to discuss the idea of *traditions* with him, to talk about his journey and his love for the Texas coast, and to look for redfish.

Fulton Harbor

We met at Goose Island State Park on an unusually calm February morning in what can only be described as an idyllic Gulf Coast scene. Pelicans floated in formation near the dock, and a trailer overfilled with crab traps sat next to the water's edge. As I sat waiting for JT to arrive, my mind wandered back 25 years to when I was just a boy. I was in my grandfather's Lincoln town car, and we drove along the coast to the park where I now sat. He had brought me here to see the old, gigantic oak tree that the park is famous for, known simply and fittingly as "The Big Tree" — a thousand-year-old monument to the storied past of this coastline. The tree was here when the Spanish galleons wrecked at the confluence of currents off South Padre Island known as "Devil's Elbow" in the mid-16th century. Spain, Mexico, the Republic of Texas and the United States have all laid claim to the coast during its lifetime. It has survived hurricanes, industrial development and climate change, and it will likely be here when we no longer are.

JT arrived and launched the skiff into the water. We idled along slowly and talked about the coast and how it was changing and the influx of fisherman and the explosion of fishing tournaments. After a few minutes, JT finished the breakfast taco he was eating and grabbed a pair of headphones from under the console and said, "Right, OK, we better get started." We made our way north along the shoreline between the Aransas National Wildlife Refuge to the west and Matagorda Island to the east, each of us lost in a world of our own thoughts, lulled by the drone of the engine. The calm water was like a mirror that we floated above as it carried us past duck blinds, kayakers, and out-of-state oyster fleets that had come to the south Texas waters after depleting their local populations.

JT steered toward a small opening in one of the countless islands, leading us on a course of hairpin curves and switchbacks, eventually opening out onto a large lake. It was obvious that he knew this place well, but to me it was just one of thousands of similar lakes hidden along the coastline that the average angler would likely never encounter. The water was still a bit cool for the redfish we were seeking, but JT assured me that, given the unusually warm temperatures, we'd probably see some start to move as the water warmed throughout the morning. We anchored the boat along the shoreline near the mouth of the lake and walked a huge circle around the muddy flat, pulling our Tingley boots out of the muck with each step. Or at least I did. JT seemed to cruise

effortlessly while I struggled to keep up. We could see that the fish were hesitant to move this early, and so we decided that our best bet would be to get back in the skiff and pole along the grassy shore, covering as much ground as possible. Just as he predicted, the fish began to move late in the morning when the water temperature had warmed a few degrees, and we could see the tails break the surface as the fish combed the bottom in search of food. I'd made a few casts, paying more attention to my conversation with JT than to the fish I was supposedly trying to land, when the surface of the water erupted. It took me a second to realize what was happening. JT was telling me to get my rod tip up and start bringing in line. Before I knew it, we had the fish alongside the skiff.

These days, the redfish is king among recreational anglers who make weekend visits to the south Texas waters, but there was a time when another game fish laid claim to that title. In the early part of the 20th century, the town of Port Aransas was known as the tarpon capital of the world. In fact, at one time, its name was Tarpon, Texas. The small town, located at the northern end of Mustang Island, attracted sportsmen from all over the world. The tarpon, however, have largely disappeared from Texas waters, a result of several factors, but mainly attributed to pesticide runoff from increased agriculture as well as the buildup of dams across the state; raising the salinity in the estuaries and affecting the crab and shrimp populations the tarpon rely upon. The dredging of shipping channels and a major influx of oil and gas production along the coast have also played a major role in their disappearance. And, although they have started making a considerable comeback in the last ten or fifteen years, their presence remains far below the numbers of the "tarpon era." The history and decline of the Tarpon offers a very valuable lesson for the consequences of disrespecting the ecosystem.

When I brought up the concept of traditions and culture as it applies to recreational fishing along the gulf coast, JT sat silent. I wondered for a second if he had heard my question or was distracted in his search for redfish. Suddenly, as if struck over the head with the wisdom he was searching for, JT responded, "Traditions are great, until they're not. And culture is just what you get when a group of people never leave a place. I love traditions, but there comes a time when they have to change simply because there's a better or a smarter or a more responsible way of doing things. I mean, what would it say about us if we continued with the old way of doing things even though we know it's not sustainable?

Can we really do that just because that's how our parents or the people who came before us used to do it? No way, man. That's ridiculous. Things have to change. The nail board has to go away," he said, referring to the ubiquitous plank at every Gulf Coast dock where anglers show off their trophies. "We've got to stop bringing plastic onto the water with us. It's simple honestly, but we've developed some terrible habits over the years and they're hard to break. And it doesn't happen on a huge scale, all at once. It happens little by little, by teaching one person how to do things better, and then they pass those lessons on to someone else, and on and on it goes. That's how traditions got started in the first place, so it's really no different."

These are the lessons JT works to impart on the clients who fish with him. And he lives by his principles: no ziplock bags, no plastic water bottles, no paper towels, and no pressuring the fish by burning up the flats at high speeds. He respects the environment — not out of some misplaced notion of sustainability, but because it has given him everything. As a young boy growing up in Texas, JT found solace and comfort in the nature he explored along the coast. His mother worked full-time while his dad was on the road playing gigs across the country. But he inherited a love for the natural world and the coastal waters he now calls home. His father loved boats and stories about the sea, and he wrote some of the best songs in American literature about these things, but he never truly experienced them for himself. He was too busy, in JT's words, "... living the life of a rambler."

JT's guiding principles are vital if we aim to make generational changes that will positively impact the future of this place. The more pressing threat to the coast here, however, is the looming Harbor Island Terminal proposed by the Port of Corpus Christi Authority (POCCA). Plans are currently underway, despite ardent protests from the city of Port Aransas and the Port Aransas Conservancy, as well as noted conservationists and members of the small island community, to install two VLCC (Very Large Crude Carrier) berths on Harbor Island, directly adjacent to the town of Port Aransas. The installation would require dredging the shipping channel to a depth of at least 60 feet, displacing over 6.5 Million Cubic Yards of material. That amount of sediment, suddenly released into suspension in the water, would have a drastic impact on marine life. And, despite encouragement from the oil industry to install the terminal offshore as is common in most places around the world for this sort of thing, the Port of Corpus Christi Authority continues to push

Near the King Ranch Shoreline

He Teaches His Boys About the Sea & works
to Give Them the Tools They Will Need
As They Grow Older.

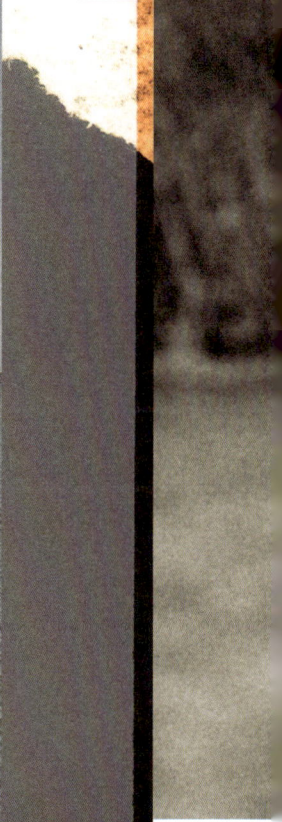

for the Harbor Island site, all the while arguing that their plans are in direct compliance with Texas regulations and the Clean Waters Act and that all conservation measures have been considered. They also claim that the resulting economic stimulus offers a significant benefit to the region. The Port Aransas Conservatory, however, has its doubts. JT is currently in conversation with several key figures in the debate, and he's working to use his platform as the host of the Drifting Podcast to inform the wider public about the issue.

We discussed all of this as we sat on JT's porch, looking out at the barges cruising up and down the shipping channel of Aransas Bay. His young boys, Townes and Isaac, ran circles around the table, begging their dad to carry their kayak to the water's edge just in front of the house. Looking at his eldest son, Townes, one can't help but think of the man for whom he's named and the cyclical nature of life and the legacy we leave to those who come after us. I wondered for a second if Townes understood the full weight of the name he was given, the legacy that he was born into. JT talked about how our fathers set the path for us, whether we choose to follow it or not, and he's right. But, we all walk our own path in life, and all you can do is try to be the person your children need you to be. JT does not fall short here. He teaches his boys about the sea and works to give them the tools they will need as they grow older. And most importantly, he teaches them *why* we do things, not just how to do them. Finally, succumbing to the desperate pleading of the boys, JT brought the kayak from the side of the house and launched it into the water. Townes and Isaac donned life jackets and hopped in the boat, heading off to explore the small rock islands near the pier. Looking on, I couldn't help but think that this was exactly how children should be raised.

Every generation worries that theirs will be the one that screws it up for good, that they will drop the ball, but it's people like JT that inspire hope. It's moments like catching a redfish on a fly in a narrow grass channel in February in south Texas that make me realize not all is lost — far from it. And if you wake early in the morning and walk along the broad expanse of beach and you look out across the Gulf, at the horizon, you are looking out toward Cuba and beyond that, to Africa. You realize how much has remained unchanged. Like the Big Tree at Goose Island State Park, the sea is still the same as it was centuries ago, when nothing was here, and the waves are the same waves that brought the explorers to the new world. Our life came out of the sea. It's what connects us all, and the history of the world is wrapped up in it. As Walcott so eloquently put it: "The Sea *is* History". But in the end, we are the authors of our own story. And the traditions we pass on are nothing more than what we make them. It's up to us to decide what those traditions are. ⚓

"The Island Rises from the Sea,
Sinks, Rises. Holds."
Peter Matthiessen, Far Tortuga

NOMAD'S LAND

Smoke rises in twisted cords from a row of tepees on a snowy knoll. At the clatter of our approaching snowmobiles, several women wound in thick furs emerge into the last indigo smolder of the Arctic evening. When we stop and alight, they whisper to one another in a language I've never heard. Children flitter in the shadows and point to us as if we're ghosts.

WORDS BY *Aaron Gulley*   PHOTOS BY *Jen Judge*

The Nenets, a tribe of nomadic reindeer herders who migrate seasonally across the Siberian tundra, have been living in this icy wilderness of northwest Russia for at least a millennium. Yet I'm here with only the second group of Westerners to ever visit this band of six families. Officially known as Brigade 20 — a relic of Soviet-era collectivization — this group travels some 600 miles down the Yamal Peninsula and back each year in the constant pursuit of forage for its animals. We've caught up with them near their southernmost range, but before the spring melt they must traverse the frozen waters of the Gulf of Ob, a 30-mile-wide ice sheet that separates their winter and summer grounds. Our goal is to make the crossing with them.

Siberia in winter might seem as appealing as, say, Death Valley in summer or Antarctica, well, anytime. Places of such climatic and geographic extremes are usually the realm of explorers, scientists, exiled dissidents, and native peoples who are shrewd and hardy enough to inhabit them. But the emptiness of the Siberian tundra, remote and removed from the comforts and distractions of modern life, is exactly what drew me. In the same way that I walk into the woods during

hunting season to press pause on the constancy of our always-on world, I hope that winter in Siberia, one of the planet's wildest and most sparsely populated expanses, will provide a backcountry escape writ large.

"This sort of experience is about stripping things back to the essentials," says Secret Compass founder Tom Bodkin, whose British travel company has organized this 10-day expedition. Siberia, like Secret Compass's other off-grid destinations, is an immersion into a simpler existence. "Have you got shelter? How and when are you going to eat? Where will you sleep?"

I wrestled with these elemental questions throughout day one. Because of packing, we didn't leave town for Brigade 20's camp until 4 p.m. With darkness closing in and temperatures sliding below 0°F, all my backcountry instincts screamed to me that it was reckless to set out across 75 miles of frozen tundra. "In winter, it's always cold and dark," said Sasha, the moon-faced Nenets who was transporting us. "If we waited for light and warmth, we'd be three months behind the reindeer." So we loaded up in snowmobile-drawn sledges — refrigerator-sized plywood boxes on wooden runners — and smashed into open country. That was when all the precariousness of the

situation hit me; I had no idea where we were going and no gear or provisions of my own. It was the antithesis of my mantra back home of absolute self-reliance, but here I was, a guest in an alien land. Without the Nenets, I'd likely die of exposure within hours. When the reindeer-hide teepees, which the Nenets call *chum*, appeared on the snowy knoll five hours after we'd set out, I breathed a deep exhalation of relief.

For the next 10 days, I'll stave off the cold wearing my host family's hand-sewn furs, eat what they eat — mostly uncooked reindeer and fish — and try to not get in the way. At night, we'll lie shoulder-to-shoulder under shared furs like packed sardines. In the language of the Nenets, yamal translates as "edge of the world," and from the moment we climb out of the sledges, that's how it feels, as if I've tumbled over a precipice of time and credulity.

Like most Nenets, whose worldwide population is estimated around 45,000 people, Brigade 20 is a family unit, in this case consisting of four brothers including Sasha, an uncle, a cousin, and all their clattering kin and chaos — 20 people in all living in five *chum*. Along with my wife, photographer Jen Judge, and our translator, Evgeniy or Zhenya (pronounced jen-yah), I'm assigned

to *chum* five, the home of the cousin, Alexey Khudi; his wife, Rosa Yaptik; and their three-year-old daughter, Marianna. The couple's three older children attend boarding school in Yar-Sale, the booming natural-gas town at the base of the Yamal Peninsula from which we traveled.

Rosa draws back the reindeer-hide door flap of the *chum* and disappears inside. Then she pops back out. She repeats this once, twice, three times, methodically pulling the flap over her shoulder as she pivots. Our first lesson in Nenet life is how to enter the tent without letting in the cold. But what's really clear is that, out here, I'm as wide-eyed and helpless as an infant. From figuring out how to take care of hygiene issues discreetly while wearing 25 pounds of fur, to puzzling through arcane social rules — such as where you can and can't put your feet inside the tent — everything is a bewilderment.

After we blunder through the front door, the frigid darkness gives way to ocher lamplight and a wood-fired stove. The *chum*, a fortress of fur as cozy as a kid's fort but strong enough to withstand the hammer of Arctic winds, is a measure of wealth and stability on the tundra, and it will be the center of our world in Siberia. Built on a frame of 32 pine poles, the structure is sheathed in double layers of reindeer pelts stitched together with tendon thread. Inside, wooden planks support the kitchen goods, meltwater pot, and woodstove. Sitting and sleeping space is on the east and west, with willow-like switches topped by hand-woven grass mats and more reindeer furs. Rosa gestures for us to sit on the west side, then goes back to her chores, preparing a meal for when Alexey arrives and stitching a new pair of reindeer-hide

slippers, or *kysii*. It feels standoffish, though we'll come to understand that the Nenets are taciturn people. We will spend a lot of our visit sitting in the *chum*, staring at one another. "Why have you come here?" Rosa will ask me more than once during the trip. "Don't you have work to do at home?"

This is a reasonable question. Life on the tundra is ceaseless work, and to shirk the most basic tasks for even a few hours, such as tending to the fire, could mean ruin. Alexey and Rosa make it clear they want us to help with chores. They don't need our help, they just don't know what else to do with us. Rosa shows me how to use what looks like a whaling harpoon to chip aquamarine ice slabs from a nearby pond and luge them on a small sled home for meltwater. Snow must be shoveled daily in drifts around the *chum* to buttress its walls and keep out wind. And Alexey leaves me piles of deadwood to split. I'm terrible at it, like the golfer who scrunches his eyes and swings too hard. Rosa shakes her head and shows me over and over how to aim the ax. I can't get it right, but with daytime temperatures often well below zero and nowhere to go but the *chum*, I'm grateful for something to do outside that keeps me warm. Even if I chop wood poorly, I start to appreciate the meditative quality of the work. It's the antithesis of my frenetic life back home.

As the days go by, teatime is the only thing more frequent than chores. Nenets rarely eat full meals, instead sitting five or more times a day for small portions of whitefish — usually muksun or cisco — served in frozen hunks that you dice from the bone. If they are near water, they catch the fish; when they are inland, they trade meat and furs with travelers. Occasionally

there's reindeer, also served frozen or raw, as well as thick slices of crusty, processed bread, which you slather with butter and sprinkle with sugar. Then comes *chai*, black tea with sugar or sweetened condensed milk. Rosa shows us how to pour it from the demitasse into the saucer to cool, then slurp.

During these break times, we start to get to know our family. Overall, Nenets are about as gregarious as deadwood, and interactions between Rosa and Alexey are spare to none, though I occasionally catch them looking warmly at one another. The couple is also stern with three-year-old Marianna, who blunders around as clumsily as a baby seal in her puff of furs. It's said that when Nenets children are very young, mothers tie them to a stick in the snow to keep them out of trouble. When the children eventually deduce how to free themselves (well before the age of three, judging by Marianna), they are considered old enough to take care of

themselves and allowed to come and go from the chum as they please. That might sound harsh, but it teaches the independence and self-reliance that's critical for surviving the Arctic.

While our hosts are mostly aloof with me and the other Secret Compass guests, they slowly thaw. One late morning, as we're sucking up the last sips of the day's second tea, Alexey looks at me and jokes, "You better get back to chopping. At your rate, you might not finish before dark." It's as if he's freed me from my stick.

There's debate over whether to call the Nenets herders or hunter-gatherers. While it's true they direct their reindeer the way you might stack rocks to divert a river into a side channel, they mostly follow the animals' natural migration and live off of them by selling meat in towns. At night, the men herd the deer into an untracked field or meadow; come morning, they return and follow

LIFE ON THE TUNDRA IS CEASELESS WORK, AND TO SHIRK THE MOST BASIC TASKS FOR EVEN A FEW HOURS, SUCH AS TENDING TO THE FIRE, COULD MEAN RUIN. ALEXEY AND ROSA MAKE IT CLEAR THEY WANT US TO HELP WITH CHORES. THEY DON'T NEED OUR HELP, THEY JUST DON'T KNOW WHAT ELSE TO DO WITH US.

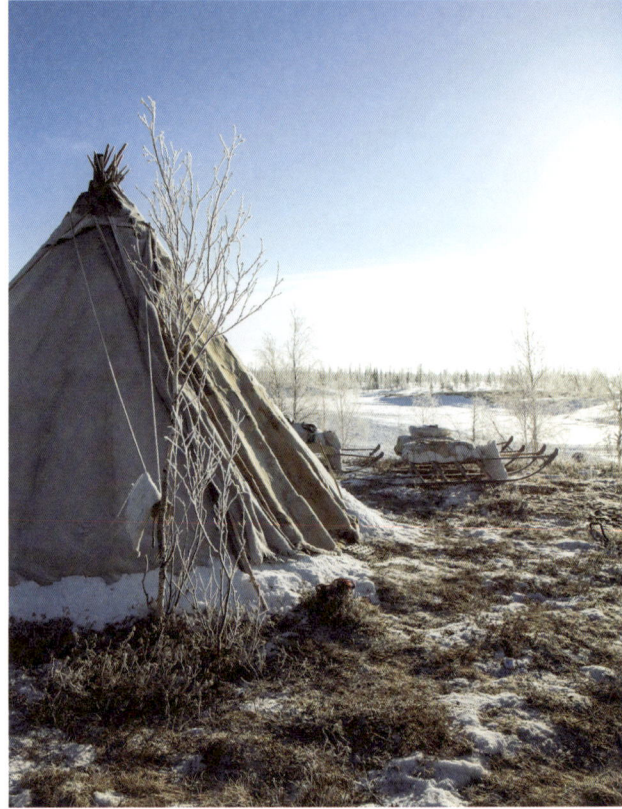

the tracks. Nomenclature aside, what's clear is that the Nenets are some of the planet's last true nomads, on the move for all but a few of the darkest, coldest months of the year.

A few days into our stay, Alexey must round up the reindeer for our first migration. He asks if Jen, Zhenya, and I want to come. When we agree, he hooks up a box sledge behind his snowmobile for us to ride in. The slate sky sputters snow and the wind chill is fierce, yet we're snug in our voluminous Nenets furs: knee-length, hooded pullovers for men called *malitsa* and longer, lace-front versions for women called *yagushka*. Alexey says that in the old days, before snowmobiles made it easy to travel long distances between the camp and the herds, the men would sleep out on the wintry tundra with nothing but these furs for protection.

After half an hour, we come upon a herd of animals so large that it stretches to the horizon. It's our first time seeing reindeer, which are smaller than mule deer and clumsy with broad antlers. They're comical creatures, rooting in the snow with their snouts for lichen and lurching like Labrador puppies with too-big feet when they run. I ask how many there are, and Alexey says 2,500. Maybe 3,500. This ambiguity is common here. Set out on a four-mile trip, and 30 minutes later, at a rest break, five miles remain. Now, when I press Alexey, he says, after a pause, "I don't think about silly details." The vagueness frustrates my analytical side, but life here focuses on the immediate, the concrete. The deer must be tended, the tents collapsed and moved, the camp raised again.

Surrounded by the herd, Alexey shows us his *tyzyan*, literally "reindeer catcher," a deerskin leather rope he wove and uses to lasso animals. He stands on the seat of his snowmobile and cries out, "Tel yat!" After a few

minutes, three or four reindeer emerge from the scrum. These are his pets, animals he and Rosa hand-reared in their tent after a nasty freeze a few years back. They come to his voice, and he feeds them bread. Next, he strides out into the herd and lassos a couple of herd bulls, then ties the animals to the sledge. When we set out again, a few reindeer follow the herd bulls, then a few more, until the entire drove is moving with us. We're staging the animals closer to camp to facilitate our morning departure. At dawn, a blizzard has engulfed the camp. Clots of wet snow blast sideways, blotting out the *chum* to our west, just 20 yards away. There will be no migrating today; even reindeer-herding nomads take snow days. That doesn't mean it's a day off. When the snowfall ebbs in the afternoon, Alexey takes his snowmobile out and returns several hours later, pulling a tree he felled. It took so long, he explains, because he had to find just

I'M STAGGERED BY THE NENETS'
PROWESS. TWO DAYS AGO, I
WATCHED ALEXEY FIX THE ENGINE
ON HIS SNOWMOBILE. YESTERDAY,
HE WAS TENDING THE ANIMALS.
TODAY, HE'S A CARPENTER.

the right tree. With his chainsaw, he planes the tree trunk into a 12-foot-long plank that's narrower than a two-by-four, with an upturned swoop at one end. He pulls out woodworking tools, which he keeps in a burnished, deer-hide satchel, and uses them to prize off a broken runner from one of his sledges, bore square-cut holes in the new piece, and whittle the freshly made part to a perfect fit. When he's done, he drags the sledge around by a rope to make sure it slides straight.

I'm staggered by the Nenets' prowess. Two days ago, I watched Alexey fix the engine on his snowmobile. Yesterday, he was tending the animals. Today, he's a carpenter. Living in remote wilderness necessitates such resourcefulness, but it's a rarity in today's hyper-specialized, technology-driven world to find people with so much broad-based, practical knowledge and skill. Something will have gone out of us as a people if we ever let our ability to sustain ourselves off the land disappear. It's sobering to consider how much of this has already been lost. Once again, I'm humbled to be here and grateful that these Nenets are keeping me alive.

Brigade 20 has stayed put for the first three days of our visit, which I gather is to give us time to acclimate. But on day four, we break camp. The first experience of the move is startling and exciting, like a carnival, but it's also as complex as a military maneuver. Imagine packing your family's home onto 13 refrigerator-size plywood sledges. Each item has an order in

which it's packed and a precise spot where it's stowed, down to the way the wash pail fits inside the legs of Rosa's stool. The sections of our *chum*'s walls, four in all, weigh 75 to 100 pounds each and must be folded carefully to prevent icing. Zhenya, Jen and I help Alexey with the task; normally, he and Rosa manage fine on their own. Even with a predawn start, the packing isn't finished until midmorning. Afterward, a few herders drive the working bulls — which are kept separate from the main herd — into a makeshift pen. Each sledge requires around four reindeer to pull it, and by the time the animals are selected and harnessed, another two hours have passed.

We travel six miles through snowy open country broken by skeletal trees. Four hours after setting out, the brigade reconstructs the camp in a virtual rewind of the morning's packing, and the silvery cape of dusk

has already settled before we've erected the chum. Inside, I sag from fatigue. I am weary and looking forward to bedtime; I'm sleeping better here on my back sandwiched between Zhenya and Jen than on my expensive bed back home. But the process of moving has been so slow and convoluted that it's difficult not to be overcome by a sense of futility. I can't imagine having to repeat the laborious process three more times before the end of our trip, yet the Nenets pack and unpack their lives almost every day. When I ask Alexey how he feels about this, he tells me he's neither happy nor sad — it's just the way life is. "I sometimes think about doing other things, but what would I do? If we moved to the town, it would be difficult without the tundra."

It's easy to romanticize the Nenets' life, the simplicity of wilderness and the incredible knowledge and ability it takes to subsist in such a trying

place. Yet life in Arctic Siberia is sheer, exhausting toil. "This is the best time of year," Alexey says over tea one afternoon. He's talking about these transitional days from winter, when temperatures can still reach -40°F and below but at least there's more than a few hours of daily light. "In spring, the animals don't stay together as much. In summer, it's hard to move without the snow. In fall, there's mud and lakes to cross. In winter, everything almost stops. Life here goes from difficult to more difficult." He tells me he'd like to move to Yar-Sale and find an easier life, but he has no skills that would allow it.

For all the hardships of their nomadic lifestyle, the Nenets are better educated and connected than I would have thought. Russian law says that every citizen must attend school, so starting at age six, the children are sent to the towns. Few make it through high school, however, and instead return to

help their families with work. But they come back with good Russian skills, modern tools such as snowmobiles and chainsaws, and increasingly, computers and cell phones. There is a baffling incongruity to watching people who can turn reindeer bone into tack and trees into tools simultaneously watch DVDs on their computers.

I came here hoping to escape the churn and demands of modern life at home. Meanwhile, the Nenets daydream of city life as an existence with less hardship. The human experience is one of striving and yearning. We can't run away from modernity; the knowledge and technology of life today is inescapable and, despite the pitfalls, precious. But the ability to exist and subsist on your own in nature — the old ways — is invaluable. I'm not running away from the future. I'm chasing what it means to be human, albeit in a different time.

One night, Alexey and Rosa load up a special treat for us: a BBC documentary about the Nenets. They coo with pride at scenes of another brigade erecting their chums and loading their caravans, and they tsk and laugh when one of the men repeatedly misses capturing an animal with his lasso. I can't help but think that watching the Nenets watch themselves signals the end of an era.

Though the crossing of the Gulf of Ob is to be the trip's crescendo, the most jarring moment comes days earlier, when we witness the slaughter of a reindeer. Most of the animals killed each year are sold to a meat-processing plant in Yar-Sale. But the brigade takes a share for meat and hides. When I ask Alexey how many reindeer his family consumes each year, he says, "What we need." It's a simple rule to live by.

In the mid-morning, after tea, a few of us are chopping wood and fixing sleds

IT'S EASY TO ROMANTICIZE THE NENETS' LIFE, THE SIMPLICITY OF WILDERNESS AND THE INCREDIBLE KNOWLEDGE AND ABILITY IT TAKES TO SUBSIST IN SUCH A TRYING PLACE. YET LIFE IN ARCTIC SIBERIA IS SHEER, EXHAUSTING TOIL.

THE BUTCHERY IS HARD TO WATCH, BUT IN THE CONTEXT OF A DIET BEREFT OF NUTRIENTS, IT MAKES SENSE. "YOU FEEL THE LIFE RUSHING INTO YOU WHEN YOU EAT THE REINDEER," ROSA SAYS, OFFERING ME A PIECE OF DRIPPING MEAT.

outside the chums when two men from the brigade, Pasha and Vassily, drive the working bulls into camp. As the rest of the men encircle the animals with snowmobiles, the two herders split the charge so that a stream of reindeer passes between them. They raise their lassos and cast them around the neck of the same animal from opposite sides. Nenets kill reindeer by strangulation, which preserves the pelt and prevents blood from spilling. The animal spasms and gasps for almost 10 minutes.

When the reindeer finally goes limp, the men clean it, then slash the jugular from within so blood pools into the body cavity. Vassily sprinkles salt into the viscous garnet soup, then dips a chipped ceramic coffee mug and drinks. The brigade circles like carrion, passing around the mug of blood and knifing gobbets of flesh into their mouths. The butchery is hard to watch, but in the context of a diet bereft of nutrients, it makes sense. "You feel the life rushing into you when you eat the reindeer," Rosa says, offering me a piece of dripping meat. Gnawing on raw venison in the biting cold of a Siberian winter will never top my culinary bucket list. But in a day when globalization is turning the planet as homogenous as suburban America, it's refreshing to have to confront and experience a place on its own terms.

If travel is meant to challenge and transport, life among the Nenets is the essence of what I chase when I go

away. The Siberian tundra is one of the most stark and stunning landscapes still left on the planet; it will also kill you with its bleak desolation. Its people are some of the most self-sufficient and skilled outdoorsmen anywhere, able to live off the land in the most inhospitable of settings, and yet they yearn for the modern conveniences of power tools and connectivity that will simultaneously alleviate their toil and dull their knowledge and skills. The simplicity of existence here feels calming and restorative, yet if it was the only option, the continual grind every day, it would probably be as numbing as office work. Life with the Nenets, just like the chaos of my busy, modern existence back home, is full of contradictions.

On the morning we're to traverse the frozen gulf, everyone exhales in relief when dawn rises windless, sharp, and bright. The 30-mile crossing is three times the distance Nenets usually cover in a day, and on the ice there's no forage and no escape. Six years ago, a blizzard struck during the migration, and the strafing winds and thick, gauzy snow pinned Alexey, Vassily, and a few others for 48 hours with nothing but their *malitsas* for cover. Almost a quarter of the herd perished from exposure and starvation. There will be no such calamity today.

Brigade 20 slides down the riverbank and onto the Gulf of Ob like a scene from the Book of Exodus. A column of

fur-clad nomads, overloaded sledges, and steaming reindeer stretches over a mile toward the horizon. The ferocious emptiness of the open ice is calming. It's a frozen desert, with fossil-like shapes cut by the wind into drifts and dunes that stretch out and merge seamlessly into the vast sky. On the back of a sledge driven by a 19-year-old herder named Jarik, I glide toward the shelter of the far-off shore at a pace I could almost walk. The only sounds are the hiss of the wooden runners through the snow and the click of the reindeer hooves like rain slapping a tin roof. For hours, we sit in silence and my mind moves as methodically as the sledge from one uninterrupted thought to another. There's no churn of silly details. On the tundra, every moment and day feels like one long, smooth exhalation. That won't last forever; life here is changing. But, at least for now, I can breathe.

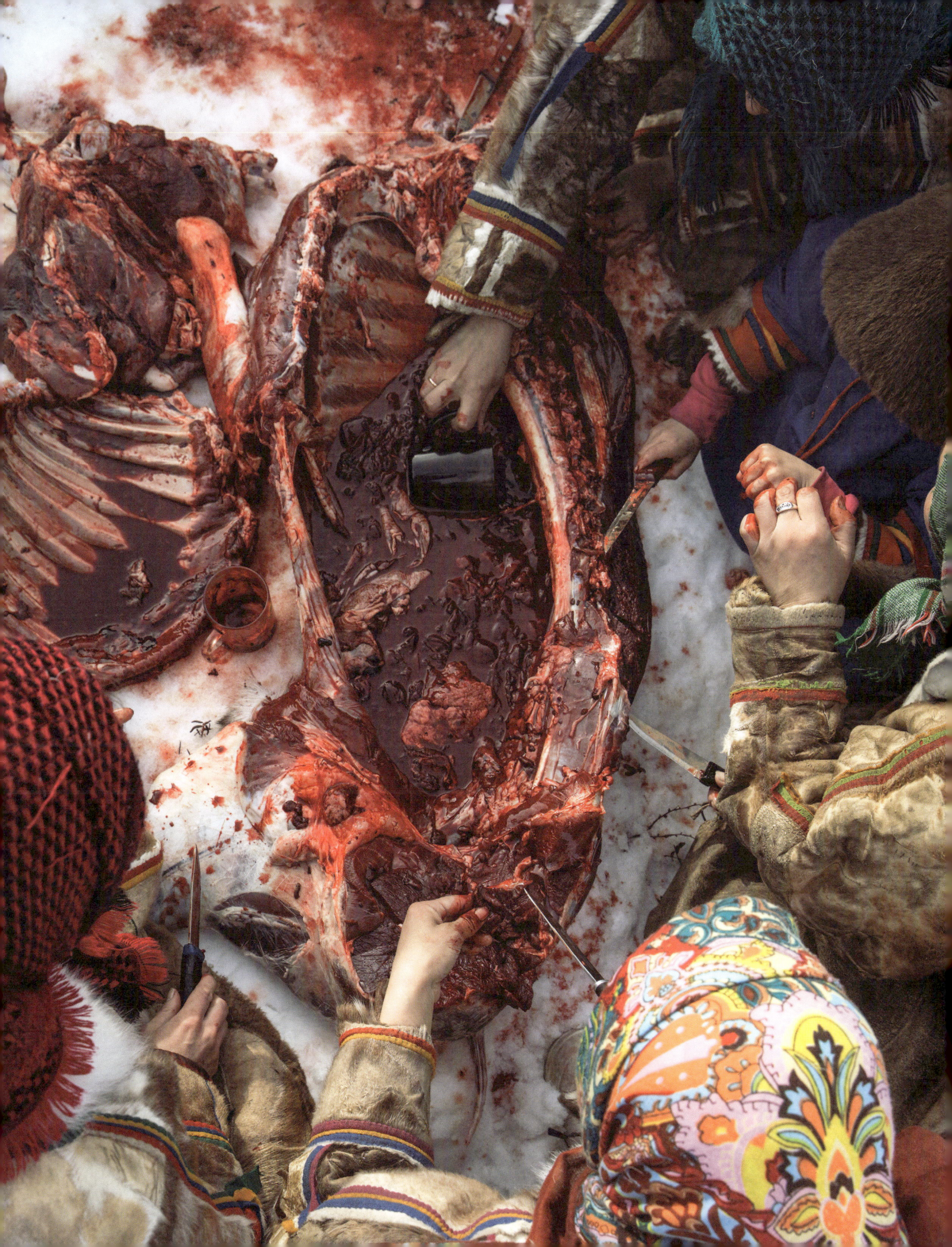

THE MAKER

THE MASTER

& *THE ARCHER*

PRESENTED BY *Mystery Ranch*

WORDS BY *Ryan Holm & Jack Evans*
PHOTOS BY *Elliott Ross*

THE MAKER

The traditional stick bow is a curious object. It is immensely powerful — as a weapon, it can kill, and as an artistic tool it can expose the strengths and failings of the artist. But all of that power lies outside the bow itself. One of the oldest, simplest technologies opens up a world for the projection of skill and the shooter's development. As the maker, the master and the archer of one bow tell us, the object is transportive in itself. More than anything, the bow serves these three men as a vehicle into frontiers of their own lives.

B uddy Gould has been forming and crafting bows for the past eight years. He describes this as his "dream job," the consummation of decades of archery practice and woodworking craftsmanship combined. On his life's rough road, Buddy has always found increasing solace and purpose in his art form. Its connection to the hunt, to moments of intensity and wild contact beyond the bowyer's shop, makes his craft all the more important.

Now, as the proprietor and maker of Poison Dart Bows, as well as the inheritor of Rampart Bows (from a deceased bowyer), Buddy feels like he's arrived at his finest place and practice. As his friend Tom Clum, Sr. says, "Buddy's got the brain power to have done anything he wanted to in life, and he took this great brain of his and this dynamite craftsmanship to the art of bow making, where he could be creative. He came up with a design of his own that turned out to be one of the finest shooting longbows in the country."

The longbow he crafted for hunter Ryan Holm, a student of Tom's, was taken to the mountains in Montana by these three men last elk season. It lay at the core of their continued cultivation of archery as a path — one of oldest practices known to hunters.

BUILDING BOWS AND TRADITIONAL ARCHERY GIVES ME A REAL SENSE OF CONNECTION WITH THE NATURAL WORLD. I UTILIZE WOOD THAT CAME FROM TREES THAT LIVED THEIR LIVES IN THE FORESTS WHERE PEOPLE CARRYING TRADITIONAL BOWS MADE FROM SIMILAR WOODS HUNTED. THESE ARE TREES THAT THEIR QUARRY MAY HAVE LIVED IN OR SOUGHT SHELTER UNDER, AND NOW THESE WOODS ARE LIVING AGAIN IN THE BOWS I BUILD, AS TOOLS CARRIED BY HUNTERS SEEKING WILD GAME.

Buddy Gould, Bowyer
@poisondartbows

THE MASTER

At some point in the 1980s, Tom Clum, Sr. decided he wanted to up his traditional bowhunting game. There was technical instruction available in the books and DVDs published by all manner of "expert" bowhunters. There were classes all over the country for the non-hunting archer, the target shooter. There was nothing in between — no synthesized method for the bowhunter to learn from, and in his search for mentorship, Tom slowly realized the path that lay before him.

He followed the routes of Olympic archery coaches, gradually gaining his own certifications — and confidence — as a coach. In classrooms and on target ranges, he studied the physical intricacies of the perfect bow shot, all the while wondering how to take the form and position into the field. How do you let an arrow fly as cleanly as it might in the mind's eye out in the bush? How do you locate grace and precision just footsteps from a watching, breathing elk?

As he found his answers to the questions, he always wondered: how can this be shared?

Coaching became Tom's lifestyle. He found that he never tired of paying attention to the details in every student's every shot. In coaching them, he deepened his practice through expression and developed both scientific and interpersonal understandings of the form. As his pupils attest, he is a consummate master of the most important instant of the bowhunt — the shot — and the world of variables that affect it.

Tom's passion lies in a single, endlessly pursued moment: the release. In the second that the arrow takes flight, the emotions, discomforts, capabilities and hopes of the archer have been exposed. This moment can be made again, endlessly, without ever losing any of its beauty. Tom, through himself and his students, will always be perfecting it.

—

THE EMOTIONAL STATE, MENTAL STATE AND THE PERSONALITY TYPE — IT ALL GOES INTO IT. TRULY, THAT BOW IS A PART OF YOU, AN EXTENSION OF YOU. AND THAT'S THE HARD PART, TOO. YOU'RE CONNECTING TO THE TARGET THROUGH YOUR EYES AND YOUR BODY AND YOUR HANDS.

Tom Clum, Sr., Archery Coach
@ tom_clum_sr

THE ARCHER

{ Let 'em fly }

PHOTOS BY *Chris Douglas*

Buddy Gould built the bow, and Tom Clum, Sr. was the coach. In the archer, they had a kindred spirit. Ryan Holm was just as enthralled by the revelations of the shot release. A lifelong athlete — climber, baseball pitcher, hunter — and Marketing Director of Mystery Ranch, Ryan found many of his fascinations synthesized in archery. As the culmination of a long and dedicated preparatory period, Ryan pursued his first traditional bow hunt for an elk.

THE MEETING

The traditional bow is a prophetic weapon — unveiling imbalances in the body and spirit that I didn't know existed. The innate, natural malleability of my first wooden bow challenged me to let go of control, let the desire for measurable perfection slip away from my thought flow, and in so many ways *released* me. I had to give myself permission to move through the process into a higher self. The physical structure I've built over the years has many flaws — changing my practice to traditional archery allowed me to test sinews in another direction.

The bowyer fabricates the bow, and the bow shapes the archer. The bow is an *affecting* tool — it etches its mark on all who use it. Buddy Gould understands this. In our first conversation, asking him to make me one of his bows, he was able to see me for who I was — and wasn't. Buddy asked about and intuited my weaknesses and sanded an image of me through the wood. My first time holding the bow he made felt different from others — like I was looking in a mirror, but not recognizing myself. The bow was poking at my ego, making me doubt that I could shoot it accurately. I wondered, then took up its challenge. It was a pleasure to befriend Buddy. To begin to hunt with him, a true privilege.

I was introduced to Buddy by Tom Clum, Sr., a man completely rooted in the traditional archery brotherhood,

ARCHERY SHOWED ME THE IMBALANCES IN MY LIFE, AND I CHOSE TO ADDRESS THEM. THE TRUTHS BENEATH THE CONTRADICTIONS ARE MY ALLY, AND HONESTY ABOUT WHO I AM IS THE BEST MEDICINE FOR MAKING THE CHANGE."

Ryan Holm, Archer

living in a bow shop, devoted to the discipline. On Tom's life's path, he's traveled country miles, facing failures and gathering endless lessons. Now in his old age, he exemplifies the truth that if you make enough mistakes, you eventually start getting things right. Tom *shares* this process, though, breaking people down to build them back up, teaching with the heart, and embodying the knowledge of his community with every gesture or word of advice. The master understands the draw force line — everything aligned — with every part of his being, sharpening those around him with every release he guides. Tom took it upon himself to positively form me into a lethal archer.

We all have steps in our lives as hunters, and I already had met the standard requirements of hunter's safety, learning a few tips from friends, and sighting in my rifle at 200 yards. I was drawn to bowhunting by a simple suggestion. An old friend of mine who knows me well said, "Since you love the process, an arrow flying at an elk from a bow will enthrall you beyond imagination." I've never been one to take the beaten path, and this had an allure, so I moved in the opposite direction of technological innovation and the distinct advantage of a rifle. I picked up the stick bow, not my first bow, but a more arduous step outside the modern process. I was seeking an endless challenge, for myself, away from complacency. I saw the value in a practice that would always evolve.

It wasn't until this way chose me that I fully understood why: to layer another current of instinct into my character. From the start, archery revealed substantial weaknesses in many areas of my life. Prepared or not, I would see who I'd come out as on the other side.

THE MIND

Discussing the weapon with Buddy was the surface. We did not meet in person, but over the phone he immediately felt close. He had a shrewd laugh and I felt like I could hear his smile. I asked him for "a simple design, only wood, nothing fancy." He said: "A longbow."

My mind sank into the next layer, the physical training. Physicality plays into the practice of archery because you are learning how to activate specific muscle fibers in different holding positions — beginning, middle, break — for an undefined amount of time. Muscle memory is an excellent teacher, letting your body adopt the positions as second nature and building you into an archer in all the slow moments before the release of the arrow. Over ten months of concerted training, I was able to gain exactly the muscular strength required for the backcountry.

It was from this point of preparedness that Tom's coaching began to break me down. When we met, it took him a few minutes to criticize my shooting sequence, revealing me to be an amateur.

"Pure talent," Tom says. "I've watched a lot of pitchers throw a lot of different ways. Unconventional throwers and quarterbacks can get away with rare form. A lot of the way you shoot is kind of like that, honestly."

The "pure talent" statement hit me in the heart like a dagger. It was true. Most everyone would take this as a compliment — ego inflation — but a talent only gets you so far. Consistent practice is what embeds your talents into your ability, and I had so much practicing to do.

"Also, you don't have giant mobility. You haven't been using your back for much, for archery or anything else," Tom added.

In the development of any skill, balancing each separate block for improvement is essential. I met with my physical therapist to understand how to enhance my back strength. But drilling into my bow technique, the central ingredient to advance, was the hardest, steepest challenge of all.

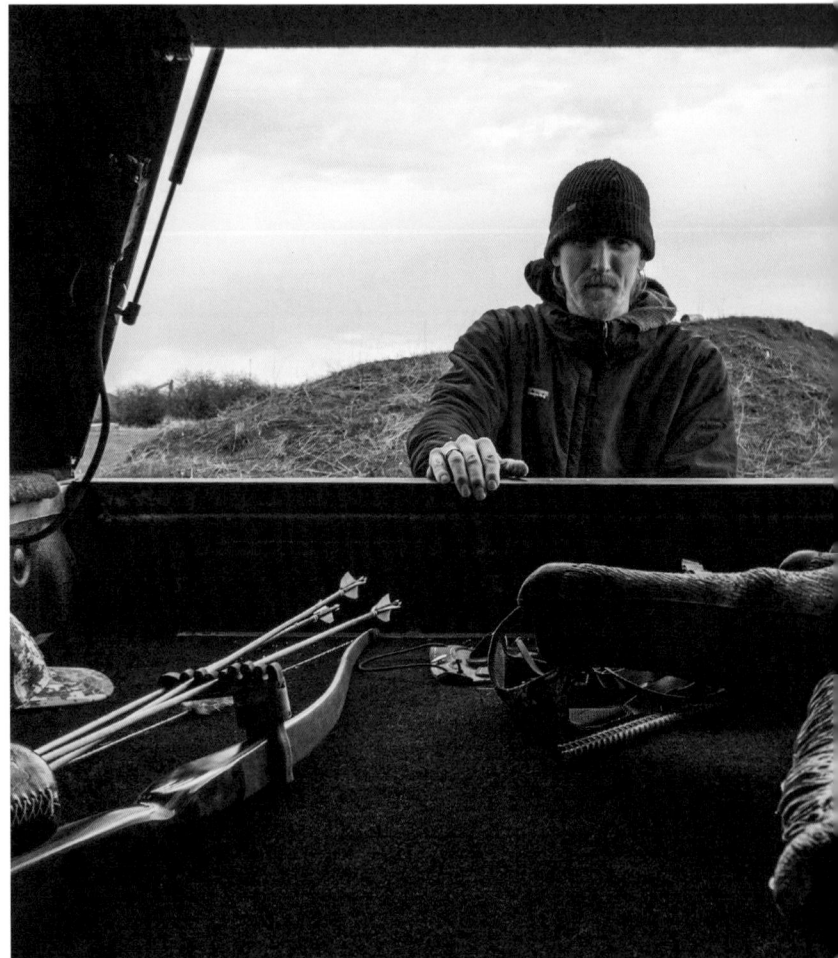

The process became meditative, revising through experience: Hook the string using three flexed fingers while drawing together the pinky and thumb, aligning the elbow with the force line of the arrow, creating an outwardly bent wrist. Relax your bow grip with your left hand with two fingers resting. The bow arm is straight, fully engaged by twisting the forearm inward (maintain this position without collapse). The pre-draw has the arrow tip pointing down and away from the target. Engage your lat muscle as you start the process with the draw arm and keep the scapula engaged. Rotate the shoulders to align with the force line, hollow your fingertips, and center your mid-section by engaging abductors. As you begin to draw, raise your bow above shoulder height, allowing you to sink your shoulder into the socket while fully engaging the scapula, down and back — draw to load. Up with the elbow to set the anchor. Focus on the aim, then soften the view of the target, watch it, see the path, then "catch the ball" behind your back while you subconsciously release.

PHOTO BY *Ben Herndon*

PHOTO BY *Ben Herndon*

We rehearsed body positioning, mimicking with a rubber band and string, in theoretical conversations all the while over the outdoor flame while it rained. Finally, anxiously, I started flinging arrows...

"That arrow is like a laser beam. It's flying really, really good," said Tom.

Eventually I reached a point where my preparation was done, leaving everything ahead to the subconscious. My practice moved into instinctive second nature. I visualized the hunt, appreciating the fragments of my learned efforts, and got ready to go into the field. I laid my gear out in the garage, checking that it was all operational, charged, fixable, backed-up, waterproof, sharp, warm, bright, safe, connected, searchable, and nearby.

The pure mysteries, the unknown unknowns, are the ones that stretch me, expose vulnerability, and strike a charge in my soul to venture me back to having a beginner's mindset. I've mourned the deaths of friends that were surrounded by an echo chamber of their own talents while rock climbing, the mountains reminding them of their fleeting time. These deaths are deeply wounding and remind me to pursue each challenge with eyes wide open. The hunt, the animals, don't care about your relative talent or accolades, so I believe in a constant return to the beginner state — approaching with humility.

"Let 'em Fly"

Traditions don't all start the same way, nor should they, and who can really connect to the certainties of the old guard and all the books your friends suggest, all the homage you're supposed to pay? The Buddha's quoted as saying: "Doubt everything. Find your own light." I began my journey with my own kind of researching — asking questions, testing my hypotheses, failing, and trying again. The Law of Attraction, that the things you need to teach you will find you on your path, is one of the concepts that has engulfed my consciousness for many years and continues to bring positive direction in my life. It's shaped my thoughtflow with flashes of visions. I have long believed in these powers that aren't wholly understood in science today. I trust these forces in channeling my emotions to manifest what I want to experience.

The body cannot go where the mind hasn't gone before. In rock climbing, I've needed a practice of visualization to be able to find focus in whatever high-risk situation may come. There is a mind shift when you are in the crux of a climbing move; feelings resonate at a deep, internal level that failure at this juncture is not an option. There, you can feel every part of your body, down to the slightest foothold. You are here and nowhere else, so practicing this mental state before attempting it physically can save your life. I found myself in the same flow state at full draw with the bow, ready to execute the release with an animal in my line of sight. Both are high-stress situations, and being cognizant of your emotions will allow you to decondition an unwanted response.

I visually rehearsed the scenario over and over before my hunt. The white-bodied bull elk is in his domain, the wind in my face, and we are alone together in the dirt. We're meeting on the mountainside, while he bellows the songs of his ancestors, shaking the cords in his throat, getting ready to dance with any fierce adversary. The playing field is fair and the stakes are high — I move in with quiet footsteps. Meditative practice allows me to come back to my breath, be present, feel my heart, my lungs, my legs, my bow, and the sticks poking into my wool socks. I've been here before and he has too, since time immemorial.

THE HUNT

I've always gone into pursuits of the heart to feel alive. It's the only place where I know where I truly belong. It can be an uncertain place, full of rage, but I cannot deny how it makes for an adventure into the mystery. Weaving through deep, dark forests, in mind and body, I can feel the definitions of my soul. There I confront my fears, strip ambitions to dust, and seek the worthy adversary who knows these timbers. The mountains have their secrets — elk have their ancestral routes, waterholes, safety spots, threats and exit strategies, all beyond my imagination.

The rain fell heavily on day one of the hunt. Time was still, the day long, and kinship was formed over arrows hitting a target as Tom coached me. We kept to the crackling fire, shelter, coffee, until it was time for a late afternoon snooze to allow my mind to digest all the details imparted from Tom.

The early fog was thick on the second morning. All was silent, as if the forest slept, soaking the rainfall into its roots. The faint trails made for tricky navigation in the dark, following GPS waypoints to guide us. We found an open meadow at the top and decided to let the Leica glass walk from there. The day was slow, hearing bugles down long canyons, from under a thick forest floor. We had encountered many recently visited bogs with fresh signs on the mountainside benches. The wind was consistent, and the ruggedness abundant. The bulls were clearly not in a rut on this day, but a few weeks back we had seen several bulls with cows in this area. We knew that patience would reveal.

Moving to a new, well-known corridor was our next move. I've rarely been attached to one area, as any hunting district holds elk, and each mountain has a slightly different and interesting atmosphere. My friend and videographer Ben Herndon moved out in front of the group, and by evening we left the others at camp to see if we could get a glimpse of what might be out there for the morning. It was a silent night — no elk, and only tired legs at the end of day two.

The early, early mornings are the best time to track down bugling bulls and get a read on where they've been at first light. I've heard more bugles between three and four in the morning than at any other time during the hunting season. It's the ritual they use to communicate before pre-dawn, discussing their day, and how they will work together to navigate our pressure. One of my favorite games to play with my father was chess, and that taught me more about patience and strategy than any game in a field. Understand your opponent, calculate their movements, and revisit your plan with every move, considering several sequences in advance.

The third morning arrives with a brisk chill, and our intentions of getting to the top of a mountain, starting at 3 a.m., set the stage for an intense hike. I can hear the elk bugling in the distance from the top, and I note their signaling as a reference as we march across a lower field, thick with sage. We make it through the entangled brush when, out of nowhere, there comes a rumbling sound of heavy struts in my direction. In the pitch black, my instinct kicks into gear — dropping my bow, reaching back for the bear spray and up to my 1911 in my binocular harness. I shout a loud "HEY," and the animal diverts to my right. Though I never glimpse the animal, I feel blessed that it made the decision to flee rather than fight.

We arrive at a grazing fence, move through it without a squeak, and start side-hilling down into the aspen grove wetlands littered with boulders. A bull sounds a deep bugle from below, maybe a few hundred yards from where we stand. Bingo. Calling back to it, I intertwine bull calls with cow mews. As the bull gets charged up, the rest of the group joins in as they come up behind us. We start the procession of calls directed at this same bull. He comes closer with caution, unaware of how this challenger, the rival bull we imitate, has approached. Unsure of the situation, the bull stops communicating and walks away. We hold for a moment, then continue upward, traversing below the ridgeline with the wind in our faces. We find grassy-timbered, thoroughly rubbed trees — clearly a bachelor pad for bulls. We stop for a water break, remove a layer of clothing, listen, and replenish. The heat arrives with the thermal change of wind direction, allowing for downhill navigation in our circle. We hear the bull bugle, like a chuckling, not far from where we left him. We move down to get a visual and he sounds again — he's even closer. I unlace my boots, Ben throws them over my pack by their knotted laces, and we stalk our way down the pine needle floor. I whisper to Ben to give me space of about 50 yards. The bull bugles again, lifting up his head, and the sun rays glimmer off his antlers. I shift gears into a fast, quiet jaunt toward the bull. Approaching, I come around a pine tree, and there he is. He stares me down at less than 80 yards.

The place is a small ravine, thick with tree cover, the wind in my face. I step back into cover, and let out the raspiest, angriest bugle in my vocal cords. The bull starts walking right at me, and at a slow, steady pace — time freezes. I can hear his distinct footsteps in stride. Entering a Zen mode where every movement makes sense, I set up my bow the way I'd practiced hundreds of times. The situation couldn't have been written any better for my first traditional shot at a bull elk — visualizing the moment, as he comes around the tree, placing the Valkyrie Jagger broadhead in the vitals right behind the crease in the front shoulder. I set the hook, secure the handle with the bow hand, set the draw force line, tension in the back, and draw back and down into the scapula. I bring the elbow up, focus aim, soften eyes. I have not forgotten the sound of his steps as he approached.

Here we go — Let'em fly. ↰↲

This adventure will be continued in a feature-length film to be released in 2021 by Mystery Ranch.

BUFFALO COUNTRY

For all the freedoms that the Nez Perce and the buffalo miss in modernity, one remaining religious hunt still nurtures their sacred contact.

WORDS BY *Jack Evans*   PHOTOS BY *Chris Douglas*

For a week, 180 bison have been spreading out over the snowy grounds of the Gardiner Basin within Yellowstone National Park. A dozen Native Americans stand in the parking lot of a trailhead, on the other side of the wooden "Park Boundary" sign, waiting for any of the herd to walk into a square quarter-mile, government-prescribed shooting zone where tribal people are allowed to continue their ancient subsistence hunting ritual. If the buffalo don't enter that zone, then there is no chance to hunt.

So the people ask, as they've always asked, for the buffalo to make their choice.

A Nez Perce prophet once foresaw the replacement of the bison on the land by a "white buffalo." Nakia Williamson, Program Director of the Nez Perce Cultural Resource Center, paints him here. It wasn't long before introduced cattle grazed the plains where the great bison herds had roamed.

Glenn Hall Jr., a member of the Blackfeet Nation, quarters a buffalo that gave up its life on one morning of the winter hunt.

To the Natives, this land is Buffalo Country — where their people have come for the entirety of their history in convergence with the migration. The buffalo herds would leave the garden of Yellowstone in the deep winter and migrate north into the Paradise Valley. For 16,000 years, they would meet the people called Nimiipuu there — those we know as *Nez Perce*. These people rushed them off cliffs until they had bows and ambushed them in passing until they had horses. Then they rode through the migrations, killing what they needed to survive.

So there are many bones in that ground called Paradise. Bones of buffalo who gave their lives for the people to prosper, and bones of men and women in their funeral dress. To all beings, it is hallowed ground, where a vital exchange takes place and the most important kind of relationship is cultivated: one of mutual sacrifice.

The Nez Perce see the buffalo as an older and wiser species than us, and its agency — its *choice* to give its body up to humans — is part of a sacred covenant. The hunt, to the Nez Perce, is more than a feast. It is a dialogue, a communion.

The Nez Perce enacted this throughout their entire history. They lived in relationship with lands spanning 19 million acres — from the mouth of the Columbia to the Dakotas. They were a people of the Pacific salmon and the Plains bison alike, and that is to say they *relied* on these animals' offerings. From buffalo they sought food, clothing and shelter. But in their heads, hearts, stories and songs, the Nez Perce were searching for the right and true laws of life that all the elder beings around them embodied. Through the hunt, they cultivated reciprocity, connection and faith.

Both the buffalo and the Native Americans were nearly wiped out over the past two centuries by white settlement.

Now there are houses, fences, highways, and that one prohibitive signpost that keeps the hunters and the buffalo in the narrow confines where they're told to roam. The natural right to return to Buffalo Country is reserved in many of the 19th-century treaties that the U.S. government signed with Northwestern tribes. These are the same treaties that were famously abused and ignored, codifying rights that are legally recognized and yet must still be fought for. It was only in 2005 that the Nez Perce Tribe won a sort of re-recognition to carry on their hunt. The concessions that were settled on were a plot out to the west of Yellowstone and the parking lot area at the trailhead called Beattie Gulch. They can shoot the buffalo that enter that area only when the herd makes its way north, leaving the harsh winter of the Park to test ancient memories of a migration that once stretched into Paradise Valley and far, far beyond.

The old, free way of life may have been destroyed, but the communication between the buffalo and the people is not lost. I saw it enacted by fourteen Native hunters with cheap plastic rifles, shooting an animal they see as a savior on a Sunday morning, while the highway noise whirled into Beattie Gulch from the Valley of Paradise and bystanders filmed on the sidelines.

For a week before that, they were all just waiting in the parking lot. Families from the Nez Perce tribe had driven from Idaho and coastal Washington, overnight, when they'd heard that the bison were appearing on the border of the park. Blackfeet tribe members came down from near Canada. Four Yakama men, all blood-related, had shown up even earlier and had their old trucks circled in a kind of campout. Each was far from their "home," but they all felt this valley in southern Montana to be deeply familiar.

I arrived one February morning in the frozen dark. As the sun crept forward, a dozen trucks pulled up and gathered, idling, everyone sipping coffee in the front seats. Beattie Gulch lies in the Gardiner Basin, a sharp-sided canyon cut by the Yellowstone River. It's a bottleneck between the park lands and the Paradise Valley. The mountains close on either side are formed curling like giant, looming waves. In the dawn, it's vast and jagged and gorgeous. By midmorning, though, everyone was out of their vehicles and could see that the buffalo had not moved at all overnight, and that it would be another long day of waiting. There was absolutely nothing any hunter could do.

Many of them were men in dirtied hoodies, the fathers with waist-length black braids and weathered faces. The younger generation drove newer trucks, and from conversation I figured out that nearly everyone in each tribal group was blood-related. There were a few families with their children bundled in the back, chatting about tribal basketball leagues and reservation gossip. The main topic of conversation, though, was the rules.

The rules are the confines around the opportunity of many Native Americans. There are the reservation boundaries, the hunting zones, the seasons, the treaty rights on paper and their actual, fraught implementation. Then there are the less definable rules of poverty, discrimination and prejudice — all of which make up what is and isn't possible for a people that, in their worldview and memory, are as endlessly free and equal as the buffalo should be.

"Take a look at Yellowstone National Park," a Nez Perce man named Nakia Williamson explained. "People view that as a wild, fully functioning ecosystem, but it's not, because tribal people have always been a part of that landscape and we currently aren't. We are as much a part of that landscape as buffalo, as grizzly bears, as elk."

So we stayed, pacing and gazing out of the tiny hunting zone and the buffalo stayed in the park. This was not the cinematic Great Plains pursuit that I had envisioned. It was more like a barbecue in a prison.

"That one just kinda looked our way," said one of the Yakama guys, every few hours. There were always eyes on the animals.

The tension between us and them stayed tight. "I reckon tomorrow they'll come this way."

"Maybe you should burn some sage," another offered.

"Different tribe, man."

We stood around for three days, and essentially nothing changed. We stared at the buffalo half a mile away, talking over their every circular maneuver and never questioning that they might be thinking of plunging *en masse* into the shooting zone the next minute, though this was never going to happen. The passive-but-determined standing-around was of the distinctly masculine sort that huntsmen all over the world excel at. The men chatted constantly through the slow, sunny afternoons, making rapid-fire jokes about each other and the absurdities of life on their reservations.

"You ever heard of those White Claws? My woman loves 'em. We're serving them in our casino now, but in Huckleberry flavor *so it's indigenous!*" They always laughed in a chorus. Few of the other jokes are printable. None of them had the feel of tired, recycled campfire bullshitting. It was a steady, hilarious stream of banter in a brotherly attitude. I asked one group how long they'd been waiting out there.

"Eight days."

When I asked why, they all talked about how much it would mean for them to bring a year's worth of meat back home. It occurred to me that you didn't need to get eight days off work for this if you didn't have a job.

Looking at some of their battered trucks, thinking of the time they'd invested, I felt a sense of privilege to be sharing this strange, slow hunt with people who genuinely relied on the Earth's original food system. They would eat as we were always meant to, from the land.

One Nez Perce man told me, "In a way, it's not so much of a hunt as a *harvest*. I *wish* we could be riding all over the Great Plains, and I wish the buffalo were free too. But this is what we've got, and at least we can take this meat home like we used to. It's a step in the right direction."

Still, the buffalo did not come over the shooting line. They were making a move for it on the second day, until one infamous and much-discussed resident of Beattie Gulch took her dog for a walk in front of them and turned them around. She lives near the hunting grounds in a cabin of glass and orange logs, and I was told she had a reputation of interfering with the hunt when she could.

There's been a wealth of criticism angled at the treaty hunts. Locals who moved to Buffalo Country in the past few years say that the hunts endanger their homes. There are

US Representative Isaac Stevens, 1855 Treaty of Walla Walla

ranch owners who don't want buffalo moving north at all — threatening their grazing land and carrying cattle diseases. Then there are white Westerners who weigh in to decry any rights unique to Natives.

It's easy to take shots at the treaty hunts because they don't have the look of ethical hunting as Americans tend to think of it. The buffalo only leave the Park in the winter, when the females are carrying calves, so they're sometimes killed. And when the shooting does start, it occurs like a firing squad. Anti-hunt activists sometimes film it. But then, few of these outsiders ever approach or ask questions of the Natives. "We never used to hunt in the winter because we knew they were carrying," a Nez Perce man named Thomas 'Tatlo' Gregory later told me. "Now we're kind of forced into this little box, waiting on them to come out of the Park."

"We did not create these boundaries," Andre Picard Jr. said. "The government created that situation, and they need to take responsibility. And if people are going to film it, I think they also need to let the world know that we've got a right to be here. It's a sacred tradition, and they're taking pictures of it to use against us. It's very serious."

Bill Picard, of the Nez Perce Tribal Council, elaborated: "They seem to think that we're over there taking their stuff. But it's really not their stuff. It's not our stuff. It's its own. It's of the land."

It was actually this same vicious, annual criticism from non-Natives that first alerted me to the hunt. When I asked a Nez Perce Fish & Wildlife employee if they'd ever had any *good* press, he said no. Indeed, when I arrived on the first morning with camera and notebook, there were a few Natives who refused to shake my hand. That was how I began to understand. The history of the treaty is a wound.

Per the Constitution, treaties between sovereign nations "are the supreme law of the land." In the minutes of the 1855 Treaty of Walla-Walla, which codified U.S.-Nez Perce relations for all time to come, the government negotiator Isaac Stevens is quoted as telling Chief Looking Glass: "... He can kill game and can go to Buffalo when he pleases ... on any of the lands not occupied by settlers."

And to the entire assembly of tribes and U.S. representatives: "We do not want you to agree not to get roots and berries, and not to go off to the Buffalo. We want you to have your roots and to get your berries, and to kill your game. We want you, if you wish, to mount your horses and go to the buffalo plains, and we want more. We want you to have peace there." What immediately followed was the cultural denigration of Native America and the intentional extermination of the great bison herds — genocidal efforts that complemented each other. At the beginning of the 1800s, there were an estimated

60 million buffalo on the wild landscape. By 1900, there were less than two dozen.

It is a testament to conservation efforts that this population recovered. Yellowstone National Park nurtured the species' survivors, and by 1989, they had recovered to a number of 3,000. There was no longer enough grazing and haven in the Park for them to survive the winters, and they began to seek their old migration routes north. But it wasn't long at all before they hit a wall. In 1995, the State of Montana, on Yellowstone's north border, sued the National Park for allowing bison to roam outside of it. The settlement created a "tolerance zone" — a line past which buffalo could not roam.

The Department of Livestock cited the threat of the ungulate disease *brucella abortus*, or brucellosis, passing from free-range bison to livestock if their calving and grazing areas were to overlap. That has never occurred between free-range bison and any private cattle herd, but if it did, it could downgrade the State of Montana's brucellosis-free market status. Martin Zaluski, the Montana Department of Livestock's State Veterinarian, explained: "Previous brucellosis transmissions from wild elk cost the industry millions of dollars in marketing costs, quarantining, and limited sale opportunities until we dealt with that problem. This does affect ranching families. We've had a robust risk mitigation program in place for decades, so there's not been a case transmitted from free-range buffalo to cattle."

Advocates of the buffalos' expansion are quick to point out that brucellosis can and does spread from wild elk to cattle. The difference between bison and elk is that elk don't take over grazing lands fit for ranching. One such advocate is Stephany Seay, a coordinator for the volunteer watchdog group Buffalo Field Campaign. "The real story is the grass and who gets to eat it. It's a control issue. It's a centuries-old range war. On the surface they say it's about brucellosis. Bullshit." She's not alone in her opinion. While we wait in Beattie Gulch, the talk returns and returns to a sense of greed within the ranching industry. The hunters gesture north, toward the vast, open grazing in the Paradise Valley.

The industry's interest in limiting buffalo-cattle contact, at odds with the widespread Native interest in herd expansion and combined with the innate complexities of public wildlife management, led to the formation of a conflict-settlement council, the Interagency Bison Management Plan. "The IBMP's been successful in equally angering everyone involved," says Tim Reid, Yellowstone's Bison Management Coordinator. "It's met its goals of maintaining the herd and preventing brucellosis transmission … But bison are different from other wildlife. They have huge social and economic impacts on the landscape, so the issue of tolerance zones is a reality."

The immediate reason for Beattie Gulch's tightly restricted hunting area is a lack of huntable public land (or "open and unclaimed land," in the language of the 1855 Treaty). On a broader timescale, however, the tolerance zones are what keep the herd curtailed. Naturally, the Yellowstone herd is growing at a rate of 10-17% a year. The IBMP has agreed to restrict that growth by authorizing the killing of hundreds each year. This winter, roughly 800 bison were taken out of the ecosystem.

Treaty hunts contribute to that — Natives will have taken some 250-300 home from the hunting grounds this season. The bulk of the cull, though, occurs through a maze of metal gates, chutes and ramps — a trap — called the Stephen's Creek Facility.

The Facility is a corral where bison are herded, tested for brucellosis, then either quarantined, let loose, or shipped to various Indian Reservations for slaughter. Although sited in and operated by Yellowstone National Park, the facility is off-limits to public visitation. The park's website is clear: "We understand that many people are uncomfortable with the practice of capture and slaughter. We are too, but there are few options at this time."

Yellowstone's official language around the trap refers to its necessity to the multiparty interests within the IBMP. Still, Reid and other Park representatives are adamant that the brucellosis threat is real and pressing and worth keeping tolerance zones firm against. "If it was possible to drop our tools and walk away from the bison and watch them repatriate the Great Plains on the hoof, we would be at the front of the line to do that. But unfortunately, that's not the reality. The idea of what a free-ranging, living, breathing continuation of the great indigenous herds really looks like in a New West landscape is being learned right now, so their management is important work. Right now, we support expanded tolerance zones that are forged out of the IBMP." Such an expansion is unlikely to happen in that forum.

"That'll be a difficult proposal," Zaluski says. "It's come up in the past, but only briefly because of the goals agreed to by all parties to prevent a transmission."

Brooklyn Baptiste, who sat on the Nez Perce Tribal Council for ten years, describes the environment of the IBMP forum:

"I never thought that we, as a tribe, were taken seriously in any long-term decisions. I spent many hours in front of the [Nez Perce] public defending decisions made by the IBMP in Montana. That was not easy. We have a deep connection to the bison in that place that predates Columbus. But try and tell that to the ranching, the hunting and recreational forums there…"

With a hypothetical brucellosis outbreak considered unacceptable by the Department of Livestock, the impasse is created.

The Bozeman Daily Chronicle, in a 2015 article entitled: "Poll: Most Montanans Don't Hate Bison," reported that 80% of residents surveyed supported the creation of a state buffalo herd, managed *as wildlife* — like elk, like deer, like bears. Still, the herd is kept to an annual average of roughly 4,200 animals — not its biological carrying capacity, but rather the limits of "tolerance," and another invisible line is drawn. The boundary is marked at Yankee Jim Canyon, just before entry to Paradise Valley. "Expansion beyond Yankee Jim Canyon will be at odds with the goal of the IBMP, which is to prevent a transmission of brucellosis from bison to cattle," Zaluski says. "Because beyond that line, there's a high number of ranches with a high number of cattle."

As Nickeles Two Moons, a young Nez Perce Fish and Wildlife employee puts it: "That line's like one of the dams they put in front of the salmon."

Neil Thagard, the Director of Nez Perce Fish and Wildlife, agrees. "Bison are ecological engineers — we just need to let them get out on that landscape and be able to do their work rather than confining them." Neil is not Native — he's from Asheville, North Carolina. Years ago, he left a career with Western-style conservation groups to work within the ecological vision that the Nez Perce have cultivated over millennia.

"There's a cohesion between the proper expansion of the buffalo herds and the Nez Perce ideals. Their knowledge of the land runs so deep; they understand it. You look at the way that they've always conducted themselves as part of the land, as caretakers of the land, and you realize ... they *are* science. But we've treated the buffalo just as we've done the Indian people. We put them on a reservation called Yellowstone National Park. We've attempted to confine them because of certain special interests: livestock, landowners, competition for grass, fears of brucellosis being transferred from bison to cows — that has not happened in a free-range setting. And the trap facility ... it's disgusting."

Today's situation in Yellowstone — for buffalo and Native Americans alike — is defined by its social, legal and political entanglements. The Native concern, however, tends to look beyond these. Nakia Williamson, the Director of the tribe's Cultural Resource Center, explains, "The Nez Perce, even with the longstanding relationships we've had with our land, endeavor to perpetuate more sensitivity. We have core values about how we express that, through hunting and prayer and contact, but the main consideration is: Are there still going to be Nez Perce hunting buffalo 10,000 years from now? That's

something that we hope for. To maintain that as sensitively as possible."

In another conversation, I ask Josiah Blackeagle Pinkham, an ethnographer for the Cultural Resource center, how that dedication to future generations can be maintained. "By *doing it*," he replies. "People overlook the idea that hunting is an act of prayer to us. Because we're going out and we're humbling ourselves to these animals, and saying, 'Give us something, help us, we need this.' Bison have always been a keystone species of our support network. They say: we will give our bodies up to you, and you can choose to return us that respect. Nez Perce culture is the result of those spiritual relationships. When a person strikes up a spiritual relationship with a being or phenomena, they know what it will require — a sacrifice for a sacrifice. And so you make that to bring the good of the other back to your culture or your family. It's crucial for us to understand that we're dependent upon something, and it's quite complex. The cultural expression of hunting is something that radiates from a core value of gratitude. Killing is not the center of it."

A Nez Perce hunter and tribal Fish and Wildlife employee, Andre Picard Jr. is a man with a generous aura. He is young, but already a father, and already with the waist-length black braid. He explains what it's like to return to Buffalo Country. "For us, it's like everything has a law," he says. "That chair's law is to wait there for someone to come and sit in it so they can look out at the day."

We look at the chair. I try to imagine it following its cosmic calling. It seems plausible.

"I think part of the buffalo's law is to be one of those holy teachers that show us how to take care of ourselves," Andre says. "They're these great consumers that ultimately give up their lives for *us* to consume. The hunt is our ancient agreement. If we *don't* go and hunt the buffalo and be part of that relationship, then we're ... I guess you would say that we're sinning. We're breaking our law as a human that *we will hunt you and allow you to teach us and lead us.*"

The reverence for animal life that hunters of all ideologies can understand usually carries with it a *care* for ecological harmony. Nez Perce culture, based around this, has created the same concern on a multi-millennial, deep community scale. "The Nez Perce are trying to perpetuate a sensitive relationship with the land," Josiah, the ethnographer, explains. "And no matter who you are — your ethnic background, political background, whatever — you depend on that. Indigenous populations carry that responsibility."

Neil Thagard, from tribal Fish and Wildlife, agrees. "I think all hunting communities can start to appreciate seeing a holistic, fully functioning ecosystem. It should be important to all of us." It was a considerable victory that, after 150 years of abuse of the treaty, the Nez Perce did manage to re-establish their right to hunt.

As Council Member Bill Picard explains, "You have to understand that the treaties didn't *give* us anything. We have been eating from the land for thousands of years. That's our natural relationship with it. The Treaty of 1855 only *reserved* the rights we already had."

"For hundreds of years, these lines were drawn and we weren't able to return to our hunt," says Rebecca Miles. She was the first chairwoman of the Tribe, serving from 2004-2009. "The Indian Wars are still being fought," she explains, "but now it's in the courtrooms. In 2005, we were prepared to struggle and really fight for our right to go back to Buffalo Country, but it just so happened we were walking into a friendly administration."

One hundred and fifty years after the right to hunt in peace was promised to Rebecca's ancestor, Chief Looking Glass, Montana Governor Brian Schweitzer surprised the Tribe members by personally welcoming them back to their hunting grounds. "What our battle is now is this negative perception."

Anti-hunting, anti-bison and anti-Native rights sentiments have all angled against the treaty hunts since then, and the pressure is felt by those on the ground in Beattie Gulch. Still, despite the angry attention, the hunters are never apologetic about the practice they know to be necessary.

As Josiah says, "To maintain that spiritual relationship, you've got to have people and you've got to have bison, and some way to connect them. Since they're an important food source, somebody's going to be killing them, and that's a necessary part of that relationship. But how you view that killing is what's crucial."

The great ancient ritual of the open plains hunt is not possible today, with limitations laid all around the buffalo, the people and the land itself. The scene of hunters standing in the parking lot, waiting on the buffalo to cross the highway, pushes questions: What kind of *values* created this? What kind of greater relationship with the buffalo do we, as Americans, want to create for the future?

The Natives are aware of the intractability of their situation at Beattie Gulch, but there is gratitude enough for the ability to make contact again. In the re-establishment of the hunt, a new kind of ritual is being created. One Sunday morning, the hunters receive what they have come asking for: 15 buffalo have roamed over the shooting line.

As the sun approaches from behind the jagged canyon walls, the snowfield starts to glow up blue. There are dark

YOU HAVE TO UNDERSTAND THAT THE TREATIES DIDN'T GIVE US ANYTHING. WE HAVE BEEN EATING FROM THE LAND FOR THOUSANDS OF YEARS. THAT'S OUR NATURAL RELATIONSHIP WITH IT. THE TREATY OF 1855 ONLY RESERVED THE RIGHTS WE ALREADY HAD.

Council Member Bill Picard

Hunters of many tribes converge on Beattie Gulch — all are quick to point out the diversity of their experiences, and that Native Americans "are not just one kind of people."

forms waiting out there. Among the hunters, there's urgent strategizing and pent-up rush. Those with rifles crawl up to the crest of a hill. When the light is up, the shooting starts, and it goes like it usually does, with some whoops, some laughter, some cursing and some shouts of, "That one's mine!"

They bring the buffalo down, and at once every tension of the past days dissipates. The families take their sleds and tools into the field where the bodies lie, and they beam with expressions of approval, of success. The great beasts are rolled over in all directions, silent, grounded. They seem gathered in the number and group of a family themselves. To me, they look serene. Everyone runs their hands into the deep brown furs around their giant faces, all admiring. The sun rises fully and the snow glitters. The mood in the air among us, enveloping the new day, is beautiful. It's a corporeal joy, and the gratitude is palpable. We all share it, shaking hands, slapping backs, inhaling sunlight, and wrestling the massive buffalo bodies into position to skin them, together. Those families that stuck to their own trucks, to their own tribes over the cold dawns are now all smiling together, laughing, helping. Wives and daughters I haven't seen before are out on the skinning grounds, and I notice that I've never quite been a part of such a *celebration*.

I've hunted all my life, but I've never been a part of a *community hunt*. It strikes me: for the countless years that humans have hunted, it's nearly always been done as a group. There is powerful individual revelation in the act of hunting alone, as I know it, but harvesting together brings an incredible and genuine multiplication of the reward — of the hardship overcome and of the gift. It fills the air among us.

I mention this to Lee Whiteplume, the Nez Perce's Conservation Enforcement Supervisor, a stern and intelligent man who's been here for every hunt since 2007. He stands by his truck overseeing the day, and he picks up where my thoughts leave off. "When white Westerners go to hunt, they have to say *I* am going to get *my* tag to hunt *my* elk for *my* family. You never heard us say that." It's true. "*We* go to get *our* buffalo to feed *our* families. I think a lot is lost when you just see hunting as between one animal — 'your animal' — and yourself."

This culture has amazed me not because it's magical, but because it's simply and deeply communitarian. At every level, the tradition teaches that the purpose of the individual is to enhance the good of the group. The great beauty lies in a heartfelt expansion of "the group" to include the more-than-human world of beings. In this, I've begun to realize that the knowledge lost to Western society is not in how to manage wildlife, it's in how to care for each other.

While some sudden passers-by stop to take photos from the road, I help a father and son from the Blackfeet tribe plunge into the carcass of the old cow they shot, paring back the hide. They're happy to tell me what they've gone through, how every year they drive down from Browning, Montana, nine hours away. I ask a few questions about the issues they've faced with the hunt, the restrictions, and they dutifully run through them, but between breaths as we work away at the hide. Really, we're all overjoyed, and no one is complaining in the moment.

I give the son, Glenn Jr., a lift back to the Super 8 in the town of Gardiner to get the rest of his gear while Glenn Sr. stays sawing at the meat and bones. Driving back, Glenn Jr. tells me about sprinkling tobacco when he approached the old buffalo, in a kind of quiet way no one might have noticed. "Everybody does different stuff, praying. People used to keep and eat the liver, like in the old ways. Me, I put the heart and liver away from the gutpile. Just to honor them, you know?"

"Yeah, I do. It was really quite a sight," I mention. "Amazing that they finally came over the line."

"Yeah, but you know ..." he replies, "those buffalo are smarter than us. They live out here. They could have stayed put behind that line, behind the Park. But they chose to give themselves to us. They came out." And for a second it stuns me, the way he's rightly described what I just witnessed.

I look out over the sparkling day and listen to the laughter and the happy groaning and the work of axes and knives, by fathers and sons. There are just over a dozen hunters of all ages and genders out there. We look like a herd too.

For the Natives, there is a parity between their herd and the buffalos'. It is not a case of one man hunting one of many buffalos. It is a relationship of the many and the many, of one community and another. The Natives stand together, staring across the plain at the herds of bison, talking about them, speaking to them and wondering. The buffalo stare back, as if they know that this will always go on. This relationship of communities of different life forms, kin, will meet for millennia to come, with the result that on some right days, when chosen, they come forward — and fourteen Natives kill fifteen buffalo.

"SOMEHOW OUR LIVES AS TRIBAL PEOPLE ARE SUPPOSED TO BE SUSPENDED IN THIS IDEALIZED TIME, THE 1800'S OR WHATEVER, BUT BETWEEN THEN AND NOW... WHAT HAS HAPPENED TO THE LANDSCAPE? LOOK AT IT.

THERE'S THIS IDEA THAT WE'RE SUPPOSED TO BE OUT ON THE OPEN PLAIN LIKE IN SOME CHARLIE RUSSELL PAINTING—YEAH, I WOULD LIKE TO DO THAT! ...AND NOT HAVE TO NAVIGATE THE HOUSES AND ROADS THAT ARE BUILT IN THE MIGRATION AREA. THE FENCES, THE PEOPLE, THE DAMS—THOSE ARE TREMENDOUS IMPACTS AND CHANGES TO THE LAND THAT *WE HAVE BEEN FORCED TO DEAL WITH*. THE OTHER PEOPLE OF THIS NATION DON'T CONSIDER THAT WHEN THE LAND CHANGES, WE CHANGE, BECAUSE OUR WAY OF LIFE IS TIED TO THIS LAND."

Nakia Williamson, Nez Perce Cultural Resource Center

How the mountains changed my life.

PRESENTED BY *Hilleberg the Tentmaker*   WORDS BY *Filip Örnerkrans*   PHOTOS BY *Hans Berggren*

Some uncertain noise wakes me up. The first few seconds are always a bit blurry and confusing when you awake in the middle of the night. Startled, I soon realize it's the wind pressing at the tent fabric. I am in the middle of Jämtland county, a vast public wilderness in midwest Sweden.

My backyard. The Hilliberg tent is sturdy, being of Swedish make, and I know it can handle the winds. I have chosen the spot carefully with consideration for the direction of gales, which are strengthening. Although I'm wearing earplugs, the sudden bursts and rushes won't let me go back to sleep. I start reflecting on the fact that I am actually lying here, tucked down in my cozy sleeping bag far from any roads, people or everyday matters. I'm doing a five-day trip in the mountains in pursuit of capercaillie, black grouse, valley grouse and ptarmigan. I have been hunting this area for more than 20 years and I have come to deeply love these adventures. Some areas can be hunted on a day trip, but it feels different, better, waking up *in* the hunting area. The night allows me to acclimate to the rhythm of the place and get my mind right for hunting.

It's hard to say what drives us to become hunters, and as I try to recall my early years to find my starting point, I see my grandfather's face and know that he would have loved to hear of these adventures. The glow in his eyes is something I will never forget. I think there is a special connection between generations of hunters — a bond formed by knowledge, understanding and mutual memories that's not found in other pursuits. So, how did it all start?

HUNTERS FORMING HUNTERS

I didn't always know what my grandfather Nils' cunning introduction to the world of hunting, fishing and exploration would come to mean to me. From the age of five, I remember watching him cleaning his rifles, waxing his fly lines, and telling exotic hunting stories of the past. He spoke in such a passionate way, and it was impossible to not be invigorated with the images. Nils was born in 1898, and by the late '70s, he was suffering from Parkinson's disease and was no longer able to hunt on his own, even though his mind was clear. In his great wisdom, he found a way to plant that glowing seed in my mind. He told stories of great bull

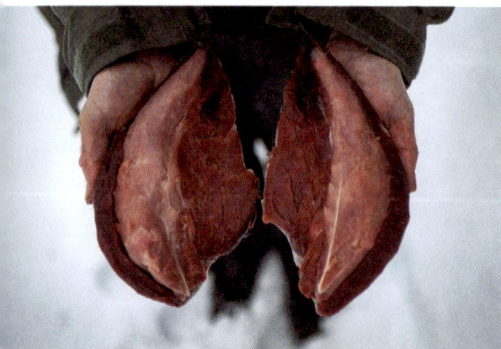

moose and the fox that got away; of the 40-pound pike that he had to shoot with his 12-gauge shotgun before it was possible to lift it into the boat; and of the vibrant encounters with the great, silvery salmon of the famous River Mörrum. He lit the spark of the hunter within me, and for that I will be forever grateful.

At the age of 12, I already had a strong fascination with firearms and ballistics. Making black powder and building my first shootable gun was something I never thought would end up in my curriculum vitae, but it brought about my relationship with Donald. He was a sharp old man who built key-harps, violins and, most importantly to me, gunstocks. His workshop lay on the route I biked to school, and after months of seeing my gloomy face peer through the window of his workshop, he invited me into his room of magic. The mighty feeling of entering what seemed a mystical church from the medieval ages was something I will never forget.

Then and there, I understood my calling. Making decisions based on deep desires, beyond financial goals, and acknowledging passion and prehistoric urges was the most important lesson of my early years, imparted by these mentors. With my hunting and gunmaking fascinations combining, the distinction between work and freedom was forever blurred. The final drop was poured into the pan of life, and my days have been filled with joys, dreams, hardships and friendships ever since.

HOW HUNTING AND THE MOUNTAIN YEARS HAVE CHANGED MY PERCEPTIONS

I must confess that hunting had little to do with carrying on traditions, respect or humility when I was young. It was all about getting to that moment when I could pull the trigger. The thoughtless eagerness of youth was bliss in many ways, but it definitely wasn't the way to achieve a successful hunt. Only

gradually did I realize that harvesting the game was just a small part of the whole. We always took care of the meat and skins of the animals, and preparing the meals soon became an important part of the "why."

I grew up in the southern part of Sweden, where hunting wasn't exactly a grand adventure. It was mainly stalking ducks and geese, calling for roe deer during the rut, driven hunts for hare, fox and roe, and the yearly moose hunt sitting in a stand. It was never that far from a road.

I vividly remember thinking there had to be more to it than that. My best friend and I spent nearly all of our time in the forest looking for whatever game we could harvest and cook. We built huts in the woods and took long hikes to unknown territories, always carrying our air guns, bows or slingshots. I wanted the hunt to be so much more than waiting for an animal to come by the stand I sat in. I wanted to be an active part of the process and for success not to be some fluke, but something worked for.

THE SENSES ACQUIRED

In exploration, I came to understand that there is more to the stories of the past than simple tales. The words of my grandfather began to ring differently in continued retrospection — they all had a kind of hidden message. As I grew as a hunter, I was looking at nature in a different way. It had to do with how I processed the information from my senses.

SIGHT: I read the foot, paw or hoof prints in the areas I hunt and remember the paths they take for following years. I pay attention to weather and winds, to signs of mating and antler scraping. I watch, always, for the feeding and bedding areas — the signs of the animals' homes.

SMELL: Discerning the scents of the animal landscape is not a quick nor easy

skill to learn, and many overlook it. I remember telling a fellow hunter that it smelled of capercaillie during a stalk with my pointers. He laughed. It didn't take long before the dogs were pointing and a grand rooster took to its wings. I didn't smell the bird itself, but the fragrances from the right herbs, trees, and humidity, when all put together, told me there was a bird right under our noses.

SOUND: It takes a good ear to listen and mimic the sounds of the animals, and I fear the day my hearing isn't with me anymore. That learned knowledge, to me, seems like a necessity to be a part of and interact with the creatures I'm hunting. Calling has always been an integral part of many of my pursuits in Sweden. But that intentional listening is not only important to be a better animal. Plenty of lessons are picked up from hearing other hunters. Taking your time to learn from the mistakes and success stories of others is a fountain of knowledge. Getting to follow someone

with a deeper connection, themselves, to the area and the game is a beautiful thing.

LEARNING THE FOREST TOGETHER

I remember a time I was stalking behind my dear Sami friend Habbe during a moose hunt. I was teaching him how to call moose, but more important, as it turned out, was what he taught me. As we strolled along, I saw him break twigs off of fir trees that we passed. At first I didn't want to ask, but after a while I couldn't resist. The answer came swiftly: "I don't know when I might have to stalk through here next time, but I will surely make less noise then than I do now." It was a revelation to me at the time. The Sami people are reindeer herders and live by the rules of the forest and the mountains. He and his ancestors before him always needed to plan ahead, and ahead doesn't necessarily mean for the next months. It could mean helping oneself years down the path. "It takes three years

to create a trail," Habbe said. "After a while, the animals start using it. They then help me finish the trail I started making. This helps us both."

I have realized that knowing the behavior of the animals has made a huge difference in how I go about my hunting. I often mimic the sounds of several animals interacting when calling moose, for example. This makes hunting in new areas a fact-finding mission before anything else. Finding and understanding the do's and don'ts has broadened the hunt to something much more vast and complex than what I experienced as a young boy. Bringing these sensations and subtle keys together is probably the closest thing possible to attaining an elusive sixth sense.

FINDING MY PLACE ON EARTH

My personal inspiration and insights gathered from all the above led me to new hunting grounds. When it was time to launch my gun shop in the late '90s, I thought deeply about what was essential to me. I realized that starting down in the urban South would place me 850 kilometers from where I wanted to wake up each morning.

A year later, I opened the doors to my first workshop on an estate about 25 kilometers northeast of Sweden's largest skiing resort, Åre. One thing led to another, and in combination with my craft as a gunmaker, I started working as a hunting guide and shooting instructor. One could say that guns and hunting became my life, and to top it off I have led it in one of the most awesome places in northern Europe — an expanse filled with public lands for hunting and creeks full of trout.

I was by no means the first to set foot in this area seeking adventure and a free lifestyle; many prominent people have traveled far distances to quench their thirst over the centuries. Even Sir Winston Churchill spent time in the area, along with a long line of English noble sportsmen of the era. But there is one big difference: they all had to leave, while I got to stay.

FINDING THE ELUSIVE CAPERCAILLIE

The fascination with the creatures of this land led me to get pointing dogs and to start calling moose. Autumn was filled with days among the glowing birches as the landscape shifted colors and finally let the leaves blow free. Darkness and winter would come, covering the landscape in deep snow. I had heard and read much about the winter hunting for capercaillie and grouse. I had even tried and failed at it, but was persistent in learning. I started following experienced mountain hunters and poring over maps. I had to find the places where pines grew on the edges of marshlands, or high country that gave me glassing advantages.

About 20 years ago, I found an area that has kept calling me back. It has

everything: old gnarly pine trees, vast marshes, and plenty of capercaillie.

THE HUNTING

My skis push forward through the snow, my binoculars wait at my chest — we're scouting every tree. Conditions are not in our favor as the winds are harsh and the snow is sharp. We've only seen a few black grouse, but I am happy to be back in my favorite area, with friend and photographer Hans Berggren.

We've camped in the open marsh, and ski out to search a few of the

capercaillies' feeding spots. They have their favorite trees: pines with higher sugar levels that they keep in their memory. We know where to look. But day goes by and no birds are found. The late winter's been strange. Temperatures as high as +7 degrees Celsius, with rain and hard winds, melting the snow to the ground where the birds can feed right off it. I can't help but wonder how this form of hunting will be affected during the decades to come. What will our winters look like in the future? I am saddened by the prospect that my

future grandchildren might not be able to enjoy this endeavour, but I won't let the despair linger.

Nevertheless we push on, tiring from many kilometers of skiing, shoulders fatigued by heavy packs. Somewhere in the back of my head, a grinding thought is brought to life. The final hour of the day has so many times been the moment of success. As light fades, we decide to make a final push with what energy we have left. Out of nowhere, two male capercaillies appear over the treeline. They see us through

our camouflage and turn. Here, the experience from years prior kicks in. I know they will not fly far, and as we creep through a grove, we spot them in the treetops a few hundred meters ahead. There is no time to lose. They are agile, but I have to give it a shot. I find a pine tree to use as cover, and close the distance as much as I dare. I range 264 meters from where they sit. I lie down against my pack and carefully take aim. My pulse rushes. I gauge the side wind, aim just on the edge of the bird, and take a final breath. In the crack of the rifle, I lose sight of it. But

it felt like a good shot. Hans sees the capercaillie tip over as silence returns to the marsh.

It's hard to describe my feelings as I move toward the place where it lies. There is no more fatigue. The memory from the hours prior plays like a film in my mind, and once again I feel thankful for the knowledge passed on to me and the insights I've gathered myself. Put together, they led to success. Darkness settles quickly, and on our return to camp it is completely dark. After a quick meal and a sturdy whiskey, paired with some smoked moose heart, we collapse. Since nights are long here in January, we have nearly eleven hours until it is time to wake up again. We decide to have a feast the following morning to celebrate, and sleep comes easy.

MOUNTAINS ARE CALLING

We gorge on a stew of the lean meat with lentils, chilis and red rice, and pack our gear in the sleds to go farther into the mountains. The sleds follow us easily over perfect snow, and a few hours later we arrive at the last birches on the foot of Mount Santa. Preparing dinner in the dark, we hear grouse chuckling nearby.

I unzip the tent fly to find no less than ten valley grouse just meters from where we wcrc sleeping. They sound like they're laughing as they take off. Valley grouse and ptarmigan have different cackles, so even in the early morning they are easy to recognize. All the way up the mountain slopes, we hear the shouts of both species out of sight. I hunt with a small-caliber rifle in .22LR, which is accurate, but sensitive to the winds. Unfortunately, there is no lack of wind, which shifts fast in direction and intensity.

We fight it, climbing higher and higher, above the valley of Lundörrspasset. It forms a deep pass between the higher mountains, the *Fjäll*. Such passes can be treacherous, as the winds compress into them and rush to incredible speeds.

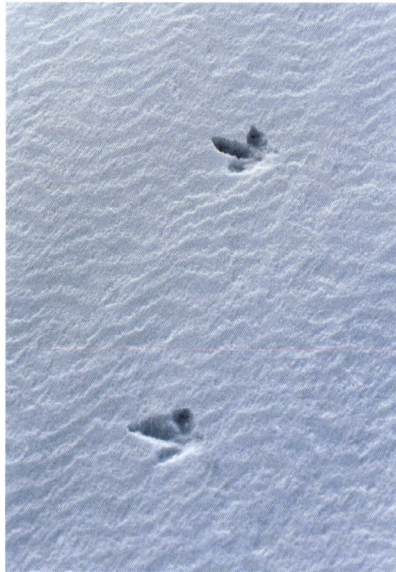

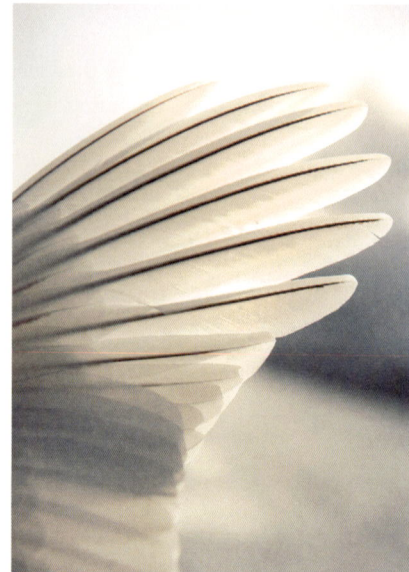

IT'S CLEAR TO ME THAT MY DEVELOPMENT AS A PERSON, CRAFTSMAN AND HUNTER IS ALL DELICATELY WOVEN TOGETHER. ALL ARE THE FRUIT OF TIME AND EFFORT — LISTENING, TRYING AND LEARNING. THE DEDICATION TO FOLLOWING MY PATH, THE TRUST I'VE PUT IN MY SENSES, AND REFLECTION OVER THE DIFFERENCES IN LIFE — WHILE KEEPING AN OPENNESS TO NEWNESS — HAVE FORMED THE LAYERS OF MY KNOWLEDGE.

This hangs in our minds when we pitch our tents. Reindeer, too, are feeding here, and we travel to stay clear of them. Disturbance might push them to another area, making it hard for the herders who look after them. The wolves give those people enough trouble.

But there's always an abundance of grouse where the reindeer have fed. They scrape through the snow to eat at their favorite lichens, which opens up the bare ground for the grouse to find food, in another perfect cooperation of nature's species.

Suddenly, I spot a couple of round, white balls on a ridge a hundred meters away. We stalk carefully and keep low. I don't use winter camouflage when grouse hunting. I have this idea that they get nervous when they can hear but not spot a stalker, so they maintain a safe distance. They use camouflage themselves where other animals don't. That is their advantage. What they do not know is the reach of the .22LR, and I manage to get the first bird of the day.

While holding this beautiful creature in my hands, I can't help but feel whole and a part of the brilliantly complex ecosystem, tuned into my own senses to be the best animal I've developed to be. I take responsibility for the meat I eat, and in doing so, I get to be a part of the past and the future. I get to be the person I want to be and live the life I want to live.

It's clear to me that my development as a person, craftsman and hunter is all delicately woven together. All are the fruit of time and effort — listening, trying and learning. The dedication to following my path, the trust I've put in my senses, and reflection over the differences in life — while keeping an openness to newness — have formed the layers of my knowledge. Combined with self-reliance, stubbornness and sacrifice, it's shown me an alternative way of measuring success and reaching contentment. It's why I will remain a hunter for the rest of my days. 🦢

ONE

MORNING

STORY BY *Jeff Moore*

Every waterfowler has a lifelong story. This is mine and only mine. My intent was to celebrate my sport with what I did, what I remembered, what I felt. My hope is that it elevates to a more profound statement in the end.

One morning,
I followed my father down a bar ditch
between the rice fields near Hockley, Texas
and sat still. Too young for a gun.
Too poor for decoys. Just hoping
a specklebelly, snow or blue would fly over
low enough so my father could shoot
his Remington Sportsman 48.

One morning,
I bought a Faulk's duck call for $4.95
at the neighborhood Ace Hardware
and blew it on the walk home.

One morning,
I shot my first duck — a hen shoveler,
decoying into a small lake
near Sealy, Texas.

One morning,
I entered a duck-calling contest,
did not squeal and came in second.

One morning,
the law said I could not shoot a canvasback.

One morning,
the law said I could shoot two.

One morning,
 I painted a duck stamp.

One morning,
 I waded in the decoys and watched
in slow motion as my Chick Major's duck
call insert dropped in the water.

One morning,
I hunted snow geese in dense fog on a rice
field called "Yankee Stadium," next to
an old man wearing a P.E.T.A hat.
(People. Eating. Tasty. Animals.)

One morning,
I hunted on a national wildlife refuge.

One morning,
I thanked a veteran with a hunt.

One morning,
I mastered the northwest wind.

One morning,
I watched an 11-year-old Labrador
with two ball-less hips chase down
a crippled mallard in pure muck.

One morning,
I waded in Arkansas' flooded timber.

One morning,
I canoed on the Delta Marsh.

One morning,
I passed a school of dolphins
on the way to the blind.

One morning,
I witnessed the golden age of waterfowling
for just an instant as a flock of 3,000 birds
decoyed to our North Dakota field.

One morning,
I broke the golden rule of waterfowling:
Never climb a barbed-wire fence
in your waders.

One morning,
I grabbed the guns
as our overloaded 14-foot jon boat sank.

One morning,
I felt the masterworks of the Ward Brothers
and Charles Walker in my hands.

One morning,
I helped pay to save the roof of Charlie
Perdew's old river rock home
in Henry, Illinois.

One morning,
I returned to my childhood hunting lease
in Hockley, Texas and found a gas station
where I once shot snows, blues,
and pintails.

One morning,
I bought a 100-year-old duck club —
with a storied history of grand hunts with
Illinois governors and illegal baiting with
barges of corn.

One morning,
I photographed an eider decoy
that someone bought at Sotheby's
for $767,000.

One morning,
I couldn't hunt without my roboduck.

One morning,
I took my daughter hunting
and watched her fall asleep in the blind.

One morning,
I hunted with six of my best friends.

One morning,
I hunted alone.

One morning,
I realized I can't be a waterfowler
for just one morning. ⚑

INDELIBLE SOUNDS OF WILD SKIES

{ The Artistry of Josh Raggio }

STORY BY *John Dunaway*

Your dad has been there. There's a good chance your grandfather has too. They took their places in the silence of a cold winter's morning, waiting impatiently for the first chance to split the air with a few methodical notes from their duck call. You might have heard the same notes coming from the garage, or muffled behind a closed truck door in the driveway, sparking your curiosity as to just how that sound was coming to life. All of those mesmerizing sounds linked together to pull you in just like an early morning flight of ducks.

You were hooked without even knowing it, following a tradition in waterfowling that has eluded many, and encouraged most, but always left a waterfowler in awe when perfected. The notes come from your lungs, but the song of a duck caller comes from the heart. It is how blocks of wood turned at the hands of skilled craftsmen become working pieces of art, echoing duck calls through the woods for the next generation. That is what keeps tradition alive.

Following a tradition is not the same as imitating the past. You must feel it in your heart enough to carry the torch, while seeing a path of your own to move forward. This is what makes Josh Raggio follow in the footsteps of fading craftsmen, turning duck calls by hand, because "if they could do it back then, why can't I do it that way now?" The simple truth is that we all can, but the vision into its value and the desire to pursue the effort is rare. In Raymond, Mississippi, that tenacity sends tiny wood shavings flying off Josh's lathe at 3300 rpm in a personal quest to stand proudly among the call makers that came before him. His turning of blocks is just the beginning of a process that will encompass many stages before the finished call arrives in the hands of the owner. Not one step can be compromised, or the end product will suffer. That is unacceptable to Josh. Drawers of throwaways in his filing cabinet are proof that one flaw in the crafting process

will mark the end of a call's life before it ever sings. A look inside Josh's workshop helps explain these meticulous decisions.

I left Texas before the sun rose, sipping coffee from my thermos with the radio serenading me eastward, to Mississippi. There was a story to tell — one that felt incomplete from a phone conversation. Josh welcomed me into his home to truly embrace it.

Adorning the walls of the front room, as a shrine to waterfowl history, are several cabinets housing a collection of duck calls from many of the greats dating as far back as the 1920s. To the untrained eye, they may appear simple, but a look at the vast variations in shape and aesthetics shows the record of individual ingenuity. Considering the limited tooling available to the old masters, their craftsmanship is truly impressive. They built from the ideas of their predecessors, but innovated with their personal touches. "Each generation has pushed the envelope on sound and artistry," Josh says. Among the vast collection are some of Josh's own calls, placed not out of vanity, but to serve as a reminder to the personal evolution in his process. He has the ability to hone in on a trade that flows through his waterfowling ancestry. Early calls were works to be improved, but now a characteristic shape and tone has come to signify a Raggio call. He opts not to engrave

the exterior, nor to place a sticker as a signature, saying that "tradition would be watered down by a precise engraving on a perfectly imperfect piece of craftsmanship."

His own calling ability is validated by the plaques hanging on his shop walls from Mississippi State Calling Championships, but the real made treasures reside on the shelves. Each call has an intimate story, a unique voice when it comes to attention. A leather journal, in which his father, Ronnie, recorded every single day of duck season, conveys just how strong the ties to the Mississippi Flyway run in this family. Serving as director of the Mississippi State and Regional Duck Calling Contest, Ronnie is no stranger to calling either. He always kept a call in his pocket, blowing those notes around the house daily, in and out of season. For Ronnie, calling promoted a bond among friends long before Josh was around. By the time Josh was ready to join in, waterfowling was hardly welcoming to children, but that didn't stop them. The young boy had to adorn excessive layers of adult clothing to stay warm, also serving as insulation between the frigid waters and the chilling skin of canvas waders. I can envision the resemblance to Ralphie's brother in *A Christmas Story*. With limited mobility, teeth chattering, Josh got his first taste of why his dad blew that call every day. The fire within could warm even the coldest water.

Josh's story hits home, reminding me of my own first hunt. It was so cold then that the laces of my wading boots froze in place, but when it was time to leave, that fire within kept me warm enough to want to stay. Or perhaps the hypothermia just did not allow my lips to move. It's those early memories, though, that keep all of us chasing the wild waterfowling life. Now, in hearing the call crack through silence, an appreciation from that pursuit grows.

Today, we have boundless opportunities for suiting into the best materials during our pursuits. Decoys come in every shape and size imaginable — so uncanny, you can see hunters sometimes shoot them off the water. A call can arrive in nearly any material or color, but Josh likes to pursue the roots. Wool layers covered in waxed canvas are his staples as he touts a small bag of hand-carved decoys into the backwaters. He was inspired by an old neighbor who did it all this same way — carving his own decoys, turning his own calls and training his own dog. There was little fuss to his process, just an appreciation for each item and the time he had to chase ducks. It's not the path for everyone, but in 2009, it sparked an idea in Josh: "I'm going to make my own call one day." It was not to happen overnight, but you can see that from the evolution of those 15 original calls residing in the front room.

There are immaculately clean tool stations lining the outer walls of Josh's shop. Each has a role in the finishing of the

ADORNING THE WALLS OF THE FRONT ROOM, AS A SHRINE TO WATERFOWL HISTORY, ARE SEVERAL CABINETS HOUSING A COLLECTION OF DUCK CALLS FROM MANY OF THE GREATS DATING AS FAR BACK AS THE 1920S. TO THE UNTRAINED EYE, THEY MAY APPEAR SIMPLE, BUT A LOOK AT THE VAST VARIATIONS IN SHAPE AND AESTHETICS SHOWS THE RECORD OF INDIVIDUAL INGENUITY. CONSIDERING THE LIMITED TOOLING AVAILABLE TO THE OLD MASTERS, THEIR CRAFTSMANSHIP IS TRULY IMPRESSIVE.

product. The vital, coveted lathe, named Jolene, glows in the room under two spotlights as if she is a museum piece of her own. Under a mural of Raymond, Mississippi, Josh stands firmly under those lights to bring his calls to life. The table before that lathe shows the stages of his current projects, from wood blanks to unique, artful calls, turned to customers' requests.

Some have gold bands, while others are engraved ornately with silver. Some glimmer with oil-shine off the smooth Cocobolo wood, while others are intricately stippled by hand. Regardless of these details, each of them wears the signature Raggio shape on the exterior and houses the tone board, which echoes sound. It's Josh's intention to be known by that shape. Just as the trained eye can look into the front room and pick out the famed callers from the cabinets, Josh wants you to spot these calls on a lanyard without hesitation. That shape signifies quality, a testament to the countless hours spent in solitude flinging wood from a block into art.

These calls are not for everyone. They are not readily available on a shelf, nor do they ship overnight. You must patiently join the waiting list to receive your instrument, often waiting as many as eight months. At best, two calls per day will reach completion in the shop by Josh's own hands. It's truly a one-man operation, one which cannot be rushed.

It's a meticulous process, right down to the shimming of millimeters on the reed that makes the music. When the last fulfilling note leaves the end of that duck call, Josh will engrave his name on the tone board, package it up with care, and send it into the world so that traditions can be formed by its owner.

To pursue waterfowl is a dream for many. It pumps the blood through our veins every day in hopes of that next season, forever feeling distant and never seeming to hold long enough once it does arrive. In those long days away from the blind, our memories serve as a beacon to the golden days ahead. The craft and the world of tradition around it keep us keen until the frigid mornings return. These sounds filled Josh's ears through childhood. When they echo now out of a Raggio call, you know the notes came from your lungs, but the origin of the music comes from the heart. If it weren't for duck calls, Ronnie and Josh might not get to spend each day together. For now, they can continue to share those traditions of waterfowling as the next generation plays outside in the mud, becoming hooked in it all without even knowing it.

MUSINGS FROM HANK SHAW, A CHEF

WORDS BY *Jens Heig*   PHOTO BY *Northwoods Collective*

When I told Hank Shaw how we typically prepare our woodcock in the fall, he unapologetically told me it was a crime, dishonor and disservice. In many ways, he was right.

The offense in question was our removal of the tiny bird's skin. He wasn't malicious in his criticism, but rather genuine. To Hank, the character of wild birds can only truly shine when the feathers are plucked, leaving that important layer to lock in flavor when roasting and to crisp when laid in a hot, oiled pan.

My family has been eating skinless timberdoodles for decades. Each small bite is a blessing. I revere them, and often daydream of their flight over a backdrop of young aspen and the musings of Aldo Leopold. Hank has helped me recognize my responsibility to uphold that love with an extra step from field to plate. While our preparation isn't necessarily wrong, he exposed the need for us — as hunters — to put our food traditions on trial, to call tattered, handwritten recipes into question, and reform our preconceived notions of wild game cooking.

Our conversation was lengthy and wandering, much like our preferred pursuit of ruffed grouse and woodcock, and will be featured in full on the Modern Huntsman website. In the meantime, enjoy this excerpt and one of Hank's favorite recipes for seared duck and rye spätzle.

JENS HEIG: Many people have different superstitions about the best way to prepare classic game foods. Is there power in those traditional recipes? Are there misconceptions? Do they need to change? Should they?

HANK SHAW: Yes to all of that, but there's a lot of unpacking to do with what you were just saying. Is there power in these old traditions? Absolutely, because food has to think good as well as taste good.

A classic case of that is the popper. When I started doing wild game, I used to look down on the popper, and what I'm talking about is a jalapeno, a piece of meat, bacon, often with cream cheese that's wrapped in a roulade and grilled. A decade ago, I went to a dove hunt in Brownsville, Texas. When you're in dove country, the popper on Labor Day is as important to that holiday as turkey is to Thanksgiving. It's a talisman. It's a representation to mark the rhythm of the year. It's not a terribly sophisticated recipe, but nor does it need to be, because it means more than just sustenance. That's an example of a very classic dish that can be tinkered with, but it deserves to live.

There are other dishes that I think should not deserve to live. A classic case would be a wonderful bird like a fat mallard or pintail, skinning it, and cooking the hell out of it. That is the reason why many people think they hate eating duck. It, along with goose, may be the most abused game in the United States. At least with something like venison, typically a family will have some way to make it, eat it, and they'll be okay.

It's why the first single-subject cookbook I wrote was *Duck, Duck, Goose*, because there's much that needs to be explained and demystified when it comes to waterfowl that is not widely held knowledge. The problem is that people think ducks are birds, but in the kitchen, ducks are not birds. In the kitchen, ducks are beef. You treat a breast like a steak and you treat the legs and wings like brisket, slow and low. If you get that, you've cracked the code.

Be sure to page through one of Hank's celebrated cookbooks or discover a new recipe on his website, Hunter Angler Gardener Cook.

Honest-food.net | @huntgathercook

Full interview, on modernhuntsman.com

DUCK WITH TURNIPS & RYE SPÄTZLE

RECIPE BY *Hank Shaw*   SERVES: *4*   TIME: *Prep: 45 mins | Cook: 45 min | Total: 1 hr 30 min*

SPÄTZLE

2 cups rye flour

1 egg

1/2 to 3/4 cup milk

1 teaspoon salt

Vegetable oil for coating

Spätzle maker

DUCK & TURNIPS

1 pound baby turnips or radishes, with greens

2 tablespoons squash seed oil or other high-quality oil

1 tablespoon salt

1/2 cup red wine

1/2 cup duck glace de viande or demi-glace, or 1 cup beef stock boiled down by half

1 whole large duck or small goose breast (both halves, about 1 1/2 pounds)

1 tablespoon duck fat or butter

Salt and black pepper

Splash of malt vinegar

INSTRUCTIONS

1. Remove duck breasts from the fridge, salt well, and let them come to room temperature.

2. Start with the spätzle. Mix all the ingredients together in a large bowl, except for the vegetable oil. Batter should be sticky and flow like thick lava. Set aside, and bring a large pot of heavily salted water to a boil.

3. Load your spätzle maker and prepare a large bowl of ice water. Fill the pot of boiling water with the dumplings. Once floating, cook for 2 minutes. Remove with a slotted spoon and blanch. When cooked, remove from the ice water to a tea towel and let the dumplings dry for a few minutes. Place on a baking sheet and toss with the vegetable oil to prevent them from sticking.

4. Preheat oven to 425°F. Remove the greens from the turnips and set aside. Toss the turnips in the squash seed oil, salt well, and roast on an uncovered baking sheet for 35 minutes, or until lightly browned.

5. Meanwhile, put the red wine in a small pot and boil for 2 minutes. Add the glace de viande and keep boiling the mixture. Taste every few minutes to avoid a bitter taste from overcooking. After 5 to 10 minutes, remove from heat.

6. Pat the duck breasts dry with a paper towel. If they are fat, start them in a cool sauté pan. If they are lean, add a tablespoon of duck fat or other oil to the pan and get it hot before adding the duck breasts.

7. If you are using goose breasts, cook at medium heat. For mallards or other typical wild ducks, use medium-high. For teal or other small ducks, use high heat.

8. Start skin side down. It should sizzle like bacon. You can press them down for 30 seconds or so; this keeps them flat. Cook undisturbed for 3 to 8 minutes, until the skin is crispy.

9. Turn the breast over and cook on the meat side from 2 to 8 minutes, depending on breast size and preference. I prefer medium-rare.

10. Before resting the breasts, tip them on their sides, fatty side down. This gives that edge, which often has a fat pocket, a chance to crisp up. Cook for a minute or so. Remove breasts from pan and rest, skin side up. Grind black pepper over them.

11. When the duck is resting, add the turnips, turnip greens and half the spätzle to the pan you cooked the duck in. Sauté over medium-high heat for 2 to 3 minutes, until the spätzle is hot and the greens are wilted.

12. To serve, give everyone some of the spätzle-turnip mixture and pour over some sauce. Slice the duck breast thickly and put it on the spätzle. Splash malt vinegar over everything. Serve immediately.

POR EL AMOR

{ For the Love }

WORDS BY *Gloria Goñi*   PHOTOS BY *Fabio Purroy*

I would go so far as to say that almost everyone has a fishing or hunting story to go along with their heritage, whether they know it or not. Mine begins in the north of Spain, or as I would call it, Europe's version of the Wild West.

My family comes from a town where, for one week out of the year, men and women run with bulls, watch them get slaughtered, and have an excuse to drink during the day. Some claim this week of the year to be art, others tradition, and others a tremendous waste of time.

Day to day, we have *la comida* followed by *la siesta*. Between the hours of two and four in the afternoon, families come home from work and school, gather at the table, and eat a large meal they prepare from scratch. Then they take a short nap and return to their school or jobs.

Every Thursday evening, people gather at bars for *juevintxo* and eat *pintxos* (tapas) while socializing with friends. On the sixth of January, we open gifts from the three kings. And on New Year's Eve, we all dress up in costumes and flood the streets. My town is set in its ways, and I wouldn't have it any other way.

Subsistence fishing is another tradition of Spain, one I am more inclined to study and participate in. Being surrounded by the Atlantic and Mediterranean oceans, the peninsula historically provided an abundance of food for its people. In northern Spain, they fish for Atlantic albacore, octopus, muscles, squid, sardines and other species found around the coast. Traditionally, fishermen used long wooden rods or handlines to fish, or they set traps for octopus on the ocean floor. Being a country of tradition, not much has changed over the years, and these methods are regularly used today. Every day, men and women still load their boats or plant themselves on wooden docks to explore the waters and fish for food.

"The sea was like a swimming pool," Fabio recalls between clicks of his camera shutter. "The ocean was flat

and the sun was rising when Fredi met us at the docks with his bike." Both artisanal and commercial boats were leaving the port. The previous day, Fabio and his father Carlos met Fredi on the breakwater as they all fished for *caballas* (mackerel) from the shore. The father and son were on a trip to Galicia from the province Navarra to escape the crowds flocking to San Fermin for the Running of the Bulls. Fabio showed interest in fishing from a boat and Fredi chimed in to say he had one, and invited them to come along the next day.

"We talked about life and work, but mostly about fishing," says Fabio. Fredi motored the small boat to the nearby cape, Cabo de Home, which lies close to the national park, Islas Cies. These islands are protected, and you need special permission to fish from them. Approaching the *bateas* (mussel farms), they took out their rods, added some weights and bait, and let their lines fall to the ocean floor where they waited for a bite. They quickly found themselves with an abundance of *fanecas* (pout), a species of small fish that live in the depths of the ocean and use the mussel farms as habitat.

After fishing the *bateas,* the three men made their way back to the rocks near Cabo de Home, where they trolled the sea floor with a hand line, a bare hook and colorful bait. Once the hook reached the bottom, they began to pull up the line as they kept trolling. They did this a few times with no results. Finally, they pulled up a prized catch, an octopus. This delicacy is one of my favorites when prepared *a la gallega* (boiled with a bit of olive oil and paprika). While the Spanish government has taken regulatory measures in recent years, *pulpo* (octopus) are becoming harder to catch due to commercial overfishing.

Lastly, the crew headed for *las rias*. These narrow areas of ocean resembling fjords are perfect for catching *caballas* (mackerel). Here, the sea funnels in and it's easier to go after a bank of fish than in the open water. They alternated between trolling with handlines and using rods, which provided a successful

bounty. Satisfied with their day, they headed back for the port, where they brought their catch to a nearby restaurant to be prepared. Afterward, Fabio and Carlos returned to their home, their daily jobs, and their modern lives. Fredi returned to work, but they all keep in touch via phone and email. This was two summers ago, but because the gear and methods haven't changed in centuries, it could have happened at any point in time — Spanish artisanal fishing is about as timeless as it gets.

As artisanal fisherman continue their tradition, larger corporations have begun to fish the same waters. These industrial crafts carry large nets or many lines. "Industrial fishing produces great imbalances in the ocean and needs permanent control. It is not, in itself, a sustainable activity," explains Javier Gonzalez Purroy, a producer of fishing and hunting documentaries.

Artisanal fishing alone cannot support the current population of Spain, and industrial fishing has harmed many species like the endangered Cantabrian anchovy. In recent years, Spain has been outsourcing their fish and acquiring species like Atlantic salmon from other country's salmon farms. As populations grow around the world, feeding people in sustainable ways becomes increasingly difficult.

"When I worked on the large fishing boats, we genuinely abused the sea. The sea will never forgive us for how we destroyed it," commented a fisherman named Arturo. This fisherman left his job on commercial crafts and returned to his roots, where he catches just enough for himself and his family.

Artisanal fishing will not make you rich, I'll tell you that now. So if they don't do it for the money, for great quantities of fish, and don't use modern gear or extravagant vessels, then why? The answer is simple. It's done this way for the love of the sea and tradition, for the feeling of wind on your face and the tug of a fish, for the joy of living — of really, truly living. 〽

ARTISANAL FISHING WILL NOT MAKE YOU RICH, I'LL TELL YOU THAT NOW. SO IF THEY DON'T DO IT FOR THE MONEY, FOR GREAT QUANTITIES OF FISH, AND DON'T USE MODERN GEAR OR EXTRAVAGANT VESSELS, THEN WHY? THE ANSWER IS SIMPLE. IT'S DONE THIS WAY FOR THE LOVE OF THE SEA AND TRADITION, FOR THE FEELING OF WIND ON YOUR FACE AND THE TUG OF A FISH, FOR THE JOY OF LIVING — OF REALLY, TRULY LIVING.

LESS THAN

A THOUSAND

{ The fortunate ones }

STORY BY *Gunnar Guðmundsson*

As I face into an eastern breeze, a fine spray of sea water causes me to squint through the droplets. I watch, transfixed at the white band across the pectoral fin of a minke whale. As we cut gentle waves in our Zodiac, the first of many northern gannets circle the boat above us, before tailing our wake. This procession follows us in increasing numbers, seemingly pleased that we ventured to their remarkable home — the isle of Skrúður.

I embarked on this adventure with my good friend, hunter and photographer Robert Cabrera, accompanied by Óðinn Logi, a seasoned puffin hunter and East Coast native. We've been circling the island, soaking in place names, legends, and hunting stories from Óðinn's youth. At a young age he became a full-time puffin hunter during the summer months, learning the ropes from his relatives. Like them, he would become a guardian of the island. The breath-taking scenery is more than we expected, and while writing down these memoirs, I struggle to give it the justice it deserves.

Diving puffins, guillemot, cormorants, and harbor seals watch our every move. Their intrigue is more of curiosity than fear, implying that the sight of humans is quotidian in their world.

Óðinn claims that since the settlement of Iceland in 872 CE, less than 1,000 people have stepped foot on the island, a claim I have no reason to second guess.

The strong currents around the narrow cove we intend to anchor in soak up every ounce of horsepower the Zodiac's motor can provide as we ride the waves, with bare, exposed rocks on both sides, beaten and weathered by centuries of rough seas.

Once secured in the calm of the inlet, we unload the equipment from the boat, ferrying the tools in a human chain over steep, slippery, and nasty rocks covered in seaweed. As we work, Óðinn continues telling us about the folklore of this place.

"The legend says that the island Skrúður is inhabited and guarded by a mythical being: The farmer of Skrúður. He acquired a distinctive taste for full-curled rams from herds of sheep roaming the island during the summer months. Historically the islands around Iceland had been used as summer sheep pasture for farmers with limited land resources, providing herds with grazing in the summer months, before being brought back to the mainland in winter months."

The landscape of the island — steep hills, narrow paths, and vertical drops — is most likely the explanation for the noticeable rate of death among these rams, rather than the farmer's penchant for eating sheep. However, it isn't only the livestock that the farmer of Skrúður seemed to have his eye on.

"Allegedly, the farmer also abducted a priest's daughter from a nearby fjord and forced her to live with him on the island. Once he had obtained his bride, they disappeared into a giant cave, which was later covered by a landslide. After that, the newlyweds were never to be seen again."

"If you don't believe this story," Óðinn continues, "You must dig the landslide up to prove me wrong".

Up the narrow path, we continue onward, overwatched by puffins within arm's reach. Just like those who came before us, we tread step-by-step into the unknown, keeping our focus firmly on the trail — one misstep could be our last.

High up, within a rock formation that looks like an avocado cut in half with the stone removed, lies our base camp. The island's 5-star hotel. Built in the '80s by Óðinn's relatives and used during the puffin season, it would surely be a welcome sight after a long day hunting on the cliffs.

We leave our gear and pack the essentials into camp before we head over to the opposite side of the island. The sun is up, and as we ascend further, I get a feel for how abundant puffins are on the island; we can't seem to take a step without falling into a puffin hole. The warm weather, green hills, extraordinary wildlife, and surroundings make me realize that the nickname "The Galapagos of the North" is a justified comparison.

Once on the other side, we are amazed by the spectacle that greets us; thousands of puffins fly by for as long as we stand watching. There seems to be no end to the flow of these majestic birds.

We follow Óðinn downhill as he reads the wind and picks our first 'high seat' for the day. He sits down and directly gets into it. Within minutes, he effortlessly catches the first three birds of the day, demonstrating his unique skill-set, honed and perfected over the years.

Harsher weather, limited biodiversity, and overall rougher conditions compared to most other places on Earth called for hardy, fierce inhabitants. After the settlement by Viking explorers in 870 CE, the settlers quickly had to learn how to survive and live off this new land. Despite resources being less plentiful than in mainland Scandinavia, they were able to rely on skills well-known to them: fishing, hunting, and gathering. Building materials were hard to find, and rocks were used instead of timber for building shelters.

Historically, Icelanders had to make the most of each season, with food resources limited throughout much of the year. They planted crops, kept livestock and harvesed nature's bounty. Every element was essential if they were to survive. Each part of Iceland offered different opportunities and resources, which people could reap the benefits of. If done with care, they would be available year after year. Guillemot colonies provided one important food source — thousands of eggs could be sustainably taken each year, along with the large numbers of birds. I know for a fact that those who harvested birds from Látrabjarg felt they weren't prepared for winter unless they could eat a bird each day. One bird for a grown man, half a bird for a woman, and the other half for a child.

We Icelanders are very proud of our ancestral heritage — a hardened people forged from severe conditions where only the strong survived. Although we can by no means compare modern-day society or modern Icelanders to our forefathers, we still hold on tight to some of their traditions. Traditions that unite us. Traditions that make us genuine Icelanders.

Everywhere you look in human history, you'll find varying cuisines or food traditions determined by the landscape and culture, evolving around resources. Some might be unappealing, some might be delicious, and some might be ethically unacceptable in modern society. What these traditional foods all have in common is that they are regional, seasonal, and usually descended from methods of storing food. The same ideology goes for the method of take. Humans have always figured out a way to feed themselves and their own. Those who did not fell off the train through natural selection.

From stones and traps to spears and snares, bows and arrows to modern-day weapon systems, all these tools were functional for their time in history, and they all made up for our lack of natural weaponry. The opposable thumb and our brains —"the crowning achievement of evolution" — made it possible for us to make and use these tools. With these, we became more efficient hunters.

Using a net to hunt puffins is a technique we Icelanders learned and adapted from our relatives in the Faroe Islands in the mid-1800s. It was more efficient and ethical than the methods used previously.

Today, netting puffins is a shadow of the past, a tradition practiced by only a few and under strict regulations. Hunting is only permitted on a small number of islands now, and only for a short period, often with a bag limit imposed. Yet, netting and eating puffins plays a significant role in the islanders' traditions. Not only are they one of the best-tasting seabirds, they also bind us to those who came before, a reciprocal link in the chain that connects us to our ancestors. By honoring their traditions and making them our own, we honor them.

As I immerse myself in the experience now upon me, it is as if my ancestors are passing the torch, and I feel the weight of this burden.

Although an experienced hunter like Óðinn makes the act of netting a puffin look relaxed and natural, I quickly find out that looks can be deceiving. In his own words, the formula goes like this: "You wait for the right amount of wind. The puffins circle the hills when the wind is blowing perfectly. Too much wind, and they won't fly. Too little wind, and they won't fly." When asked what he considers to be the perfect amount of wind, he replies, "When the puffins are flying." He goes on to explain the necessary tools of the trade to me.

"The net itself needs to have two metal or wooden spikes with a V-form attached to a three- to four-meter-long long pole. The netting is attached between the spikes. The V-form is important, because a full-circle, like regular fly-fishing nets, will scare the puffins away from the swinging net.

"You place yourself in the hills in front of boulders or cracks, so your silhouette blends in with the background. Then,

you wait for the right moment. When a flying puffin comes within reach, you kick the pole off your thigh and raise the net in front of the puffin, catching him into the V-formed part of the net.

"With a puffin in the net, you need to work quickly, and simultaneously reel the pole in as you're lowering the net in the same direction it was flying. Then you release him from the net, keeping an eye out for his beak — they tend to bite quite hard. Quickly snap his neck, and get ready for the next one. In good conditions, an experienced hunter can net over a hundred puffins in an hour."

With the bar raised high, I aim for immediate success. As a former national team hockey player specializing in redirecting pucks into the net, I am confident the hand-to-eye coordination I've developed over years of training will give me an unexpected advantage.

I take a seat, imagining I'm back in front of the net during a playoff game, as the D-man throws me a gentle wrist shot, cutting between the crowded high slot. I'm blocking the goalie, and there is nothing left to do but tap the puck into the net. The puffin lines up perfectly. I raise the net. It's a swing and a miss. Nothing else to do but to try again, and again, and again. After dozens of failed attempts, I step back. Netting puffins certainly isn't as easy as it looks. Patience is key, and after some time, I begin to get the hang of it, although I certainly wouldn't qualify as a commercial puffin hunter just yet.

The wind settles down, and the notorious east fjords fog slowly moves in. We decide to continue our journey toward the gannet colony in the north of the island. We tie our catch together and wrap them around our necks, just as the puffin hunters of old always did. Óðinn jokes about the small, parasitic sea-bird's tick, which will inevitably vacate the cooling bodies of the deceased puffins in search of warmer climes. He insists that a few bites will only toughen us up, and that having a beer or two in your system will make us immune. I read from the grin on his face, though, that I should probably leave it up to others to put his theory to test.

Once we make it over to the Northern gannet colony, our jaws drop for the third time that day. Thousands if not hundreds of thousands of individuals roam the bare rocky hillside, from hatching eggs to feathered chicks and everything in between. Although young gannet chicks are also harvested from the colony, dispatched with wooden clubs, we have enough puffins to bring home to our families, so we spent the afternoon filling memory cards rather than our freezers. Heading back to camp, we serve up a Nordic cuisine dish fit for any Michelin restaurant: grilled puffin breasts with scurvy-grass, dried fish, and butter. After all, we're staying at the only 5-star hotel on the island.

With bellies full and content, we push off from the shore. Ægir, the Norse god of the sea, roughens the waves as a reminder of how small we are. My mind wanders to those who came before us, those who survived on the island's resources, and those who never found their way back.

We sail home in awe, with Skrúður's fantastic scenery, wildlife, and history forever with us. Now we belong to the original thousand. We indeed are the fortunate few.

WITH A PUFFIN IN THE NET, YOU NEED TO WORK QUICKLY, AND SIMULTANEOUSLY REEL THE POLE IN AS YOU'RE LOWERING THE NET IN THE SAME DIRECTION IT WAS FLYING. THEN YOU RELEASE HIM FROM THE NET, KEEPING AN EYE OUT FOR HIS BEAK — THEY TEND TO BITE QUITE HARD.

THE ATLANTIC PUFFIN — A TRADITIONAL TREAT OR A TOURIST ATTRACTION?

People travel across the globe to lay eyes on these magnificent animals. They are also willing to pay a pretty penny for it. Tourism has evolved around puffins, and that supports many Icelandic families and local businesses. Others put puffins on their family's tables, the traditional way. The two do not necessarily go hand in hand, yet they both have a right to exist.

This clash of worlds makes me think of a story my grandfather told me. He had been hunting arctic foxes on top of Látrabjarg — the largest seabird cliff in Europe. Four days straight in no-man's-land, and he had run out of food. He was desperately craving nutrition as he reached Bjargtangar, the westernmost part of Europe and the roots of the Látrabjarg cliffs. With knowledge of the area being suitable habitat for puffins

to dig their holes, he knew his hunger would come to an end shortly. Crawling quietly to the edge of the cliff, he cautiously snuck up from behind a lone puffin and grabbed him firmly with his steely hands. Elated with his successful stalk, he was holding the puffin, ready to snap its neck, when he heard strange clicking sounds behind him. To his surprise, 30 Asian tourists armed with cameras had lined up to photograph the "savage" islander. These were the early days of tourism in Iceland. Caught red-handed, my grandfather petted the puffin's head before releasing him to the wind. Applauded by the cultural explorers, he walked away, confused and hungry.

Some people have never experienced pure darkness, never been cold, never woken up alone on a mountain, or fallen asleep to the sound of a river. Take these things away from a person's life experience, and to a great extent, they have lost their connection to nature.

To such folks, the idea of feasting on a puffin is understandably absurd. Walking on concrete all day long, eating mass-produced food, and traveling from place to place on predetermined paths in an urban jungle is equally absurd to me. It's debatable if there is truly a right path, and everyone should be allowed to form their own opinion. All I'll say is that our views do not outweigh facts. Personal feelings toward different animal species don't determine if a population offers a sustainable harvest. The use of a natural resource without inflicting ecological damage is, in my view, the responsible action, wherever that is possible. We have done it "my way" for millions of years. We have done it differently for the last 70 years, and where has that gotten us?

Some years back, while collecting guillemot eggs under the cliffs of Látrabjarg, we were accompanied by two scientists: wildlife biology legend Ævar Pedersen, and a Danish colleague

of his, Carsten Egevang, a researcher for the Greenland Institute of Natural Resources in Nuuk, Greenland. I asked them about the impact these traditional gathering methods had on population sustainability. Ævar laid it out in his usual calm, detailed manner. "A guillemot's lifespan under normal conditions can range from 20-35 years. The oldest Icelandic puffin known to man was 38 years old, tagged in Vestmannaeyjar. To sustain the species' population, each bird must breed, raise and repopulate two or three times during the span of his life."

Studies have shown that for each egg we pick, the same individual will lay down another one in the same spot. We can, in theory, remove three eggs from the same bird each year, and it will still manage to repopulate that season, given that all other pieces of the puzzle fall into place. Puffin eggs were eaten in the past as well, but today, purely as a preference of taste, it's mostly eggs from common guillemot, razorbills, and black-legged kittiwakes that are picked from the bird cliffs.

Like many other seabird populations, the Atlantic puffin conservation status as assigned by the IUCN is vulnerable — a population that is likely to become endangered should the current circumstances threatening survival not change. Due to climate shifts, the puffin's food resources of sand eels, herring, and sprats are suffering, and in parallel, so too is the puffin population. The Icelandic population in 2014 was estimated at two million nesting pairs, which despite these population declines, makes the Atlantic puffin the most common bird in Iceland.

I will leave it up to educated biologists working for the Icelandic Environment Agency to determine the future of puffin hunting in Iceland, just as they do with any other species. They base their evaluations on scientific research, counting, and harvest returns. Through

SOME PEOPLE HAVE NEVER EXPERIENCED PURE DARKNESS, NEVER BEEN COLD, NEVER WOKEN UP ALONE ON A MOUNTAIN, OR FALLEN ASLEEP TO THE SOUND OF A RIVER. TAKE THESE THINGS AWAY FROM A PERSON'S LIFE EXPERIENCE, AND TO A GREAT EXTENT, THEY HAVE LOST THEIR CONNECTION TO NATURE.

this data, they can quickly determine any changes from the usual trend. Hunters actively participate in gathering data for biological research, providing wings, skulls and other specimens needed to conduct studies. With evidence-based science, the environment agency and ministry issue the yearly hunting quota, season lengths, and restrictions.

Bird watchers, nature conservationists, tourism companies, hunters, and landowners all enjoy mutual benefit from the healthy population of all species. Having a game animal temporarily or permanently removed from the list of huntable species is always tragic. It should be in everyone's interest to work toward a joint goal: for these species to be hunted on the back of a population recovery.

Recent studies of other bird populations in Iceland have proven that responsible hunting barely plays a role in the equation, with the implications of weather, habitat, and food resource changes of far greater concern. A future where

hunting continues will have to account for the complex web of these effects, many of which are driven by climate change.

It might not be too late to change our current, globally destructive path. It is my genuine hope that we will alter our ways, and focus on returning to a time where we give as much as we take from the land and sea. If not for us, then for our children and their children; they will need the wild animals that also call this planet their home, more than we are able to comprehend at the present time. It is my hope to keep these traditions alive for generations to come, so that we Icelanders, as well as many other cultures around the world, can remain connected to our unique heritage as we always have. ⚜

PHOTO BY *Ray Gadd*

TRADITIONS WOVEN TO LAST

{ First Lite }

FORD
VAN FOSSAN

Conservation Manager

PHOTO BY *Captured Creative*

PRESENTED BY *First Lite*   WORDS BY *Katie Marchetti*

I lean forward on my trekking pole to seek relief from the burden on my back. The dark closes in around me, shrinking my world to a headlamp halo at my feet and the weight of a quartered mule deer divided between my pack and my partners in the late November cold. I wipe the sweat from my brow and grin into the spotlight illuminating me. "Do you want to shed another layer?" he asks. I shake my head. The wool base layer against my skin pulls the dampness of exertion away from my body, the fleece a barrier from the night air chilling the world around me.

His question conjures up memories of my youth and Dad's unremitting advice, "You never know what can happen in the Sierra Nevadas — layers could save your life." And on this midnight Montana pack-out, I'm thankful for the layers of traditions I've retained and those I've added along the way.

Traditions underlie our every journey into the woods; what we wear and carry, how we communicate, and how we conserve our resources. Some traditions we inherit. Others we forge for ourselves, testing our theories in the rugged labs of the wild, with our survival, or at the very least comfort, hanging in the balance.

Nestled in the small mountain town of Ketchum, in the Wood River Valley of central Idaho, First Lite has married new traditions with the old, reliable natural fabric of wool. Working from dawn till dusk, founders Kenton Carruth and Scott Robinson, alongside Ryan Callahan and now-President Ross Copperman, became the first to produce Merino wool in a camouflage pattern, taking the U.S. hunting community by storm in 2007.

Blazing new trails up a mountain is hard, lonely work, and steady progress requires that each foot is secure before taking the next step. First Lite circumvented what had already been done and designed for what was to come. In recent years, their company has reached the summit to find a multitude of loyal customers following their trail, heralding them as a leader in foresight; both in technical apparel and their hands-on approach to environmental responsibility.

Despite their size, First Lite was vocal where others were silent when it came to conservation; they could have written checks to get the work done, but instead worked the ground on bended knee, the sweat-stained ball caps proving their commitment far more than a signature ever would.

A debt of gratitude is owed to Ryan Callaghan — who now serves as MeatEater's Director of Conservation — for being the catalyst behind conservation for their company. As employee number one, he made bold strides to incorporate conservation into their company's DNA, a legacy which has continued with Ford Van Fossan.

As a student of conservation biology, Ford's deep passion for the subject has served the company and on-the-ground conservation well, but even he was skeptical of First Lite's approach to hot-button issues in the beginning. "There was this decision made that we were going to be a little outspoken about these issues, about public lands and conservation, and while I thought it was the right thing to do, I didn't think it would grow our business," admitted Ford. "Fortunately, I was super wrong about that. It's become a core element of our brand and I think it's something that differentiates us today."

While First Lite's outspokenness about conservation individualized them in the beginning, today they've gone above and beyond by implementing ways of giving back to the wild places they promote exploring. They employ initiatives such as "Round-Up for Conservation," which allows customers to round up their purchase by a dollar amount of their choosing to benefit a selection of conservation organizations that are doing good work in the field.

Ford decided to push the envelope even further with company-funded conservation — directly.

"I was looking around for where dollars turn into deer. That's where the rubber meets the road on this, and there so often seems to be a lack of clarity on where our money goes," said Ford, who took a deep dive into where they could physically make the biggest impact, and landed on winter range for wildlife in Idaho. In their region, deer and elk come down out of the mountains in Central Idaho and winter lower in the sagebrush desert, traveling a general north-south migration. They're eating bitterbrush and sagebrush all winter to conserve calories in the slightly warmer temps with less snow.

According to Ford, the suppression of wildfires has led to out-of-control burns when they do come through, which decimates the winter range that deer and elk survive on. The burned area is quickly pioneered by an invasive plant called cheatgrass, which slows down a succession of sagebrush and bitterbrush. "While deer will eat the cheatgrass, it's of so little nutritional value. We've found plenty of deer that died of starvation with a belly full of cheatgrass."

Efforts have been made over the last decade to raise bitterbrush seedlings and hand-replant those shrub communities in Southern Idaho. "First Lite is now directly purchasing thousands of those shrubs ourselves, and our employee base is planting them. We've taken on this direct on-the-ground work as a company, slowly rehabilitating this local area acre by acre."

Other brands are following suit, which for Ford has been thrilling to watch. "I think that trend for 'private corporate conservation' is one of the more exciting things we've seen in the industry here in the last couple of years."

For Ford, it all began in a pit blind, the reverberation of a shotgun blast, and a goose falling from the Maryland sky. Growing up on a farm in the "Old Line State," he was playing bird dog for his dad at five years of age.

"I would go out in the dove field with him, and pick up doves that he shot, because we didn't have a dog," Ford explained

with a laugh. By the age of nine, he had taken hunter's safety and joined the long-standing goose hunting tradition.

In the Van Fossan family, goose hunting is a social event. On special occasions, there can be over twenty guns divided between three blinds, looking to the skies. "It was very social, and in a way that I feel like Western hunting really isn't; it'd be hard to replicate that exact tradition here," said Ford. "I'll be going back to Maryland for Thanksgiving for as long as they're around — honestly, it's a tradition I want to keep."

Ford has added new traditions to his hunting repertoire out west, hunting every elk season opener with his friend Josh, who welcomed him when he first arrived in Ketchum. That open invitation from Josh would be a deciding factor in how Ford views the hunting industry's need for change. "While unintentional, I don't think hunting has been made accessible enough. We need to be more welcoming and inclusive," he said adamantly. "Positioning ourselves as hunters and non-hunters is setting ourselves up for failure."

In an effort to change the conversation, First Lite set up the R3 focus day: a two-prong initiative designed to encourage adult-onset hunters. Headquarters will host a hunter's safety course composed of Backcountry Hunters and Anglers "Learn to Hunt" curriculum and Hank Forester's QDMA Field to Fork course. Ford and Casey Hawkes have both become Idaho State Hunter Education instructors in a desire to continue the mentorship they received as young men.

Designing the course in a mountain town alters the trajectory of the class for many. "They don't need to know how to pack a backpack, or filter water. They need to learn how to hunt and to be spoken to as an adult, whereas most Hunter's Ed curriculums today are designed for 10-year-olds," explained Ford.

Ford and Casey aren't the only First Lite employees to step into positions of leadership — their mentorship pledge extends throughout the whole office. "We're going to incentivize our team, so that every person who mentors a new hunter next fall or next spring will be entered to win a prize," said Ford, who believes that the one-plus-one regimen will grow exponentially to encourage the tradition of hunting to flourish.

Their story has been shaped by men and women from all over the country, weaving their unique threads of tradition into a new and endurable fabric that will cloak the hunting community for generations to come.

For Minnesota transplant and Community Manager Kevin Harlander, the traditions established by Scott, Kenton, Ryan and Ross have unified the employees together in such a unique way that has spilled over to create an unprecedented loyalty among their customers as well. "Being around a group of people that are so like-minded in the pursuit of what they do is something that I don't think exists a lot in other workplaces. There's so much connectivity to the mission."

"THERE WAS THIS DECISION MADE THAT WE WERE GOING TO BE A LITTLE OUTSPOKEN ABOUT THESE ISSUES, ABOUT PUBLIC LANDS AND CONSERVATION, AND WHILE I THOUGHT IT WAS THE RIGHT THING TO DO, I DIDN'T THINK IT WOULD GROW OUR BUSINESS. FORTUNATELY, I WAS SUPER WRONG ABOUT THAT. IT HAS BECOME A CORE ELEMENT OF OUR BRAND AND I THINK IT'S SOMETHING THAT DIFFERENTIATES US TODAY."

Ford Van Fossan

The First Lite headquarters physically reflects their unique company culture, creating space for an arrow-fletching and bullet-reloading bench, a partial mechanic garage, a fully stocked bar, four game freezers, two crowded gun safes, and a gear room filled with waders, skis, packs, mountain bikes, decoys, and a small duck boat. By living the life they center their business on, they can serve their customers in unprecedented ways. If a customer calls about hunting in Alberta, odds are that someone in the First Lite office has hunted there and can talk to them, which is part of the First Lite tradition as well.

Kevin arrived with long-standing hunting traditions of his own, and found new traditions to add to his lifestyle at First Lite. "For me, this company has created a new tradition where at 5:01 p.m., that door is swinging, and everybody from customer service all the way to our president is out there getting after it in the woods," explained Kevin.

The woods of the Midwest shaped Kevin's view of the world, following his dad and grandpa's lead in search of what hunting would come to mean. "I was really fortunate to grow up being part of a family that hunted, and experiencing the traditions of hunting at our place in northern Minnesota."

Hunting for Kevin was a once-a-year event, beginning in mid-November when the Harlander family would make their way to their family deer camp; a cabin built by his dad and grandfather near the headwaters of the Mississippi River. "The pilgrimage to deer camp always signaled the start of fall for us; there's an air of preparedness and tradition of getting ready to go to deer camp."

It wasn't ever about killing deer, Kevin said, but a sense of belonging during a critical time in a young man's life. A time to learn what is important; belonging as part of a family and being self-sufficient; a carding of the mind and character being intentionally woven into something much stronger. "I learned how to do things right; how to build a fire; how to identify trees and figure out where tracks led. That time was just so pivotal to all these other skills that you need to have in your work and life."

Like many men of his generation, Kevin felt the lure of adventure and travel tugging at his young mind. At 19 years of age, he headed west and began firefighting for the state of Oregon. "The people in Oregon took me into the fold," explained Kevin, a fold which invited him to take his first steps into the woods in search of elk, adding a layer of experience to the hunting traditions he held dear.

"It turned into this obsession for me, something that I knew I was supposed to do," said Kevin, who would go on to become an elk hunting guide in eastern Oregon.

Guiding for Kevin allowed him to follow in his dad and grandfather's footsteps hundreds of miles away, passing on the tradition of hunting to others — albeit strangers. It would also add to his quiver of skills needed to understand how to communicate with those who were new to the sport. This would serve him well in his new role as community manager for First Lite.

"The tradition of the sport can only be passed on if people who are really passionate about it choose to engage with people who aren't. Our traditions need to change, in that we need to be way more inclusive with who we involve in hunting," explained Kevin, whose own life has been enriched by the passionate people who have been willing to introduce him to new places and new species. "I think as we continue to bring new people into the fold, there's going to be more traditions that evolve and change and come to light."

Life at First Lite is very cyclical; their office is ruled by the seasons. Spring turkey hunting and searching for sheds and mushrooms blooms into bear hunting, fishing, and scouting throughout the summer, with the rising anticipation of antelope archery season, bird hunting, deer, elk, moose, and sheep, and right on into spring again.

"The difference between growing up a whitetail hunter and a bird hunter and then transitioning to a Western hunter is that we get to do this stuff every day of the year," marveled Kevin, who still makes the pilgrimage back to camp with his family every year. Some traditions are worth their weight to carry throughout the decades.

———

"THE TRADITION OF THE SPORT CAN ONLY BE PASSED ON IF PEOPLE WHO ARE REALLY PASSIONATE ABOUT IT CHOOSE TO ENGAGE WITH PEOPLE WHO AREN'T. OUR TRADITIONS NEED TO CHANGE, IN THAT WE NEED TO BE WAY MORE INCLUSIVE WITH WHO WE INVOLVE IN HUNTING."

Kevin Harlander

KEVIN
HARLANDER

PHOTO BY *Max Benz*

GREGG
FARRELL

Whitetail Product Manager

From the beginning, First Lite gathered people who possessed talent and passion, but most of all character, creating a company culture that is for the people, and for each other before anything else.

"Sometimes the best person for the job doesn't hunt or doesn't fish, but they do a good job of bringing on those who have the ethos of how to be a good human; those that appreciate the natural world in a different way," said Kevin, explaining that First Lite conducts their business based on the traditions of the family. "Our relationships supersede that of a normal business. They're part of our story, and we show up for each other in unconventional ways, filling the needs we see."

Their relationships with their staff, ambassadors and partners appear seamless; individuals spinning together in tandem with very little coaching. They've all been selected because of who they are rather than what they do, and this leads to a tangible, cohesive mindset.

First Lite's whitetail product line manager, Gregg Farrell, believes that the tradition of sharing has been foundational to their team, their company, and their customers as a whole. A Monday morning in fall leads to a slow start at the First Lite office, with dogs winding between legs, hands holding coffee cups, and the retelling of the weekend hunts.

"To have a group of people with this shared level of enthusiasm for these hunting pursuits was not something I'd experienced previously. Sharing those experiences on a Monday morning, it's like every hunt you go on, you almost go on it twice — when you go on it and then when you relive it with the telling of it," added Gregg. "That's a new part of my hunting tradition since working at First Lite."

As a Midwestern school teacher, Gregg brought traditions of his own to this Idaho family; although unconventional out west, deer stand whitetail hunting has been the passion of his life.

Before Gregg could even legally hunt, he was, like many Midwesterners, sitting in a tree stand, earning the right to continue practicing the art of stillness in the shadow of his father and uncle. His mentors had taught themselves, forging their traditions with upland birds, turkeys, and then the lure of whitetail hunting.

Their family hunting camp was just down the road from where Gregg called home, and his dad often picked him up from school when the clock struck three to head to their respective deer stands, bows in hand.

Ironically, his long-held heritage of bowhunting, although foreign to Idaho, would mean he was cut from the same cloth

PHOTO BY *Andrew Miller*

PHOTO BY *Captured Creative*

as the First Lite community; they both take hunting very seriously. "You're doing it before work, you're doing it after work. For me as a kid, it was before school, after school and that's very much like when I lived in Idaho. When the season's on, everybody's coming into work in camo and leaving work in camo."

Gregg's entrance into the First Lite family came alongside jokes about eating cheese curds in trees. However, whitetail archery hunting has a worthy ambassador in Gregg. "Being so fired up about it, it has definitely changed some people's attitudes. It's totally in my blood," said Gregg who is now working in a position that he designed himself.

A self-proclaimed 'gear nerd,' Gregg used to purchase outdoor gear and then modify and improve it on his own. It's a unique vision and skill set that Ross recognized early on, adding Gregg to the payroll in hopes of what has been created today.

While First Lite was largely built around Western big game hunting, Gregg saw the opportunity to fill a need in the whitetail hunting space — pushing the needle in the right direction. "I've had access to these unbelievable technologies both in textiles and trims. All the things that we've built our very technical Western line with I've been able to utilize and build world-class whitetail gear that hasn't existed in that space before."

PHOTO BY *Captured Creative*

———

"I'VE HAD ACCESS TO THESE UNBELIEVABLE TECHNOLOGIES BOTH IN TEXTILES AND TRIMS. ALL THE THINGS THAT WE'VE BUILT OUR VERY TECHNICAL WESTERN LINE WITH I'VE BEEN ABLE TO UTILIZE AND BUILD WORLD-CLASS WHITETAIL GEAR THAT HASN'T EXISTED IN THAT SPACE BEFORE."

Gregg Farrell

As the new role developed and the product line expanded, Gregg returned home to Wisconsin, back to where it all started for him, breaking a new trail for First Lite.

First Lite's growth has matched that of the wool itself: a natural growth with a yearly harvest before it is cleaned, carded, spun, and woven; a constant breaking down, testing, and rebinding of the strongest, most resilient fibers until they've reached a worthwhile product.

They are an apparel company born not out of competition but innovation, who instead of flooding the marketplace as their popularity grew, operated under the adage that "if it ain't broke, don't fix it," and dedicated themselves to building only what was missing from the outdoorsman's kit.

"What that did was set the precedent that we don't bring a product to market unless A) it solves a problem that's out there, or B) this product isn't out there yet," explained Gregg, noting that in years with fewer product releases, each piece was a problem-solver. "We're able to do that because we weren't forced to grow at any specific rate."

First Lite won't release a product until it has been thoroughly tested, used and abused in the field and additionally sent to a third-party testing facility to ensure an unbiased review. "Our customers can't be the guinea pigs. It's not fair for us to ask somebody to spend their hard-earned money unless it's a needed, approved product."

First Lite's company culture remains largely unchanged as the office has grown from eight to nearly 30 employees in recent years. Today there are still many canine companions napping beneath desks, arrows being built, ammo being reloaded, and dirt bikes reassembled in the garage. "That's part of what's also been unique about the growth of the company. We've been able to maintain that culture — our identity," said Gregg.

President Ross Copperman began eight years ago as employee number two, and since then has helped the company navigate its growth in a way that is sustainable in the fickle marketplaces of commerce today.

In those early days, Ross, Ryan Callaghan, and the original founders of First Lite, Kenton Carruth and Scott Robinson, used Merino wool in winter sports ranging from alpine skiing

ROSS
COPPERMAN

President

to ski touring and ski mountaineering, as well as spring mountain biking and hiking.

"Scott and Kenton realized that you could go on a multi-day trip and use the same base layers with no odor," Ross explained. "As hugely passionate archery hunters, they wondered why no one used it for hunting. They did their homework and found out that it was because nobody knew how to print camouflage onto 100% Merino wool."

While the word 'wool' conjures up memories of hugging Grandpa around the waist, our cheeks roughed by the prickly fabric of his coat, or the itchiness of an old scarf wrapped around our necks destined to be abandoned despite a mother's plea, Merino wool rose in popularity because its thinner and softer fibers made it more comfortable when worn close to the skin.

Merino wool base layers regulate body heat better than most synthetic fabrics and retain comfort in a wider range of temperatures, qualities which First Lite knew would alter the experience of hunters who experience hours of high exertion as well as long bouts of stillness in a single hunt. When it's warm, the wool can absorb 30% of its weight in moisture and transport that moisture and warm air away from the skin, which also helps to control odor. When it's cold, the wool traps the warm air and keeps it close to the skin. Its absorption of light, but lack of UV reflection, keeps Merino

"INSTEAD OF PUTTING ANY CERTAIN TYPE OF HUNTING THAT MIGHT NOT BE ACCESSIBLE TO EVERYBODY ON A PEDESTAL, WE CELEBRATE THE ACT OF PARTICIPATING IN THE FOOD CHAIN."

Ross Copperman

wool from broadcasting your location, and wool in motion creates no sound.

A long-standing tradition of outdoorsmen was summiting new horizons of utilization when they began testing how the fabric would retain printing. "They started with a very simple pattern," said Ross. Today, First Lite is able to utilize nine colors in their patterns, an ongoing evolution of design. "As we developed technologies, we became better at it. To print at that level of detail and most importantly at that consistency is really difficult, but I feel like we've gotten where we want to be."

Ross couldn't have foreseen where he would be today when he was introduced to hunting by his mom in Portland, Oregon. As a 10-year-old, Ross shot a rockchuck, and when he brought it back to camp, his mom impressed upon him the weight of harvest, and cooked it over the fire for him to eat.

Ross continued to hunt, albeit more selectively, taking advantage of the fantastic waterfowling around his hometown of Portland, Oregon. From the delta of the Willamette and the Columbia Rivers, he charged ahead through freezing mornings in his six-dollar army surplus waders all through high school.

After he moved to Idaho, his hunting pursuits expanded to big game rifle and archery hunts, all of which, for Ross, were tethered by food.

PHOTO BY *Ray Gadd*

"Hunting what I enjoy eating, or what my family enjoys eating, is kind of my number-one passion at this point," said Ross, who has begun passing on the traditions of hunting to his two daughters. Over the years, upland hunting has risen in Ross' esteem because of its simplicity. "I love hunting mule deer and elk, but it's a big undertaking. At this age in my life, being able to just throw the dogs in the back of the truck; grab the shotgun and go out and spend an afternoon with them — I just really appreciate the simplicity of it."

With Ross at the helm of First Lite, their company has retained its simplicity as well. "There were only four of us when I started, so it's always been very informal, but it was a 'get-shit-done' place and still is today despite our significant growth," said Ross. "I 100% subscribe to the theory of hiring the smartest people we can and letting them figure out how to do things, and it's worked really, really well."

Despite the informal atmosphere, they are serious about empowering their people to enjoy their outdoor pursuits, wherever the mountain may lead. "Hiring the people who actually do it, live it, walk it, and believe in it — it's been a huge part of why we've been successful. Making sure that our employees can get outside and experience the mountain-town lifestyle keeps them happy and engaged, especially during hunting season."

First Lite has utilized their sphere of influence well, celebrating all types of hunting with a wider lens for the tradition as a whole according to Ross. "Instead of putting any certain type of hunting that might not be accessible to everybody on a pedestal, we celebrate the act of participating in the food chain."

Ross is thankful that other brands have begun creating their own traditions of conservation as well. "I'm really proud of the fact that I think that we have taken a de facto leadership position in mobilizing people and showing the importance of conservation to a younger generation."

From wool to wear, we are shaped by our environment. Whether sitting in a Midwestern tree stand with company or stalking a quarry in the solitude of the mountain West, there are traditions to which we hold fast and others that are shed as we age.

First Lite has left behind what doesn't serve them and their community as they've forged a new trail up the mountains of production. Committing to carrying their cornerstones of conservation, culture and inclusion to the top regardless of the weight, they've allowed their path to be dictated by the needs of their environment, and their customers instead of peripheral competition. As a young leader in a long-standing industry, First Lite has utilized the age-old traditions of hunting and refined them into a richer legacy that can withstand the rigorous and winding trails of time. ⚬

CANADA

Bison

American Sporting Traditions

MODERN HUNTSMAN

Elk

Cutthroat Trout

Pacific Ocean

Mallard

Mule Deer

Whitetail Deer

Wood Duck

MEXICO

Raggio Custom Calls

COURTESY OF LEWIS & CLARK

OLD WORLD, NEW MAPS

{ Artist Feature: New World Cartography }

WORDS BY Katie Marchetti   PHOTOS BY Paul King

A map unfurls and fingers trace the leading lines of where we're going and where we've been. Whether the year is 1784 or 2020, an aerial view of land and sea allows us to navigate environmental intricacies.

Formed in the lowcountry of South Carolina, New World Cartography resides where the past and present meet. For centuries, explorers have charted their course into unknown territory by the maps that would deliver them home again. Today, two men continue the tradition of hand-drawn maps, crafting 21st-century landscapes inspired by the antique maps of old.

For founder and designer Travis Folk, maps were an essential tool in obtaining his Ph.D. in wildlife biology and continuing his conservation work at Folk Land Management. As his fascination with maps grew, so did his desire to translate the sterile presentation of the information he was gleaning into a medium that was robust with life.

He partnered with classically trained artist Tony Waters in 2015, and they now work together in the age-old craft of producing accurate, informative maps with captivating original drawings depicting the unique flora and fauna of the topography.

Tony entertains a life-long enchantment with the history and allure of pirates and treasure maps to be found along his coastal home of Charleston, South Carolina. Each modern map conveys the same enchantment, his handiwork noted in the skill of hand-drawn lines and text, showcasing the brilliance of hand-applied coloration.

"It's somewhat like the monks and their illuminated manuscripts," said Tony. "The words are there, but the calligraphy and illustrations draw interest and attention."

Reviving the tradition and process of originally designed maps, each commissioned piece is drawn, printed and then colored by hand — adding to the distinctiveness of each piece. Coloration techniques vary from watercolors to colored pencils selected for a specific look and feel. Each map is also affixed with a unique serialized nameplate to the rear of the frame, further underscoring the individuality of each map.

"I like maps because they are such a different way to look at the world, whether it is historical or current day," explained Travis. "It amazes me that I can ride down a creek or road in the lowcountry that you can also find on a map from the 1700s."

"I hope our maps help people remember and understand particular parts of the world," said Travis. "I think maps can remind someone of a great experience in a particular part of the world or enhance their understanding of the world around them."

He and Tony were commissioned by Modern Huntsman to create a map that reflected the traditions and stories bound within these pages, as a beautifully informative addition to Volume Five: Traditions.

IG: @new_world_cartography | *To read the full interview with New World Cartography, visit our website at **ModernHuntsman.com**.*

199.112 (

A LEGACY REWARDING THE FUTURE

PRESENTED BY *James Purdey & Sons*

WORDS BY *Byron Pace*   PHOTOS BY *Byron Pace, Sarah Farnsworth, and James Purdey & Sons*

It was easy to see why some consider the landscape barren. There was little obvious life to be seen as we forged headfirst into the stinging front of snow, which had abruptly obscured our view. Even as the icy flurry subsided, harsh winds dragged over dancing shrubs in hostile acknowledgement that this wasn't an easy place to eke out an existence. Often, however, it takes time to understand the importance of what we see and experience. These rolling swathes of purple moor-grass and dwarf shrub heath, a woven mix of heathers, cotton grass, sphagnums, and a host of other flora, supported a myriad of macro-ecosystems and associated wildlife, above and below the canopy we looked down upon.

The landscape was formed under a series of niche climatic conditions that created one of the world's rarest upland habitats, but as is true of so much of our planet today, exploitation has rapidly reduced the historic range and adversely affected much of what remains. I was in Northern Ireland to learn about an ambitious, collaborative project, restoring the uplands to their previous abundance of Irish grouse, hare, raptors and waders, which today barely tip the balance between extant and extinct. For a decade, tireless work by the Irish Grouse Conservation Trust (IGCT) had begun to turn the tide of decline, and this year, The Trust was acknowledged, winning the prestigious Purdey Award for Game and Conservation.

The Purdey Awards were established in 1999 by the legendary gunmaker James Purdey & Sons when they took over the Game & Conservation Awards, previously set up by Laurent-Perrier Champagne (UK) in 1986. The Awards are an acknowledgement of the need for positive promotion in the conservation activities undertaken by shooting concerns around the United Kingdom. Their aim is to promote a wider appreciation of the benefits that properly managed shoots can have on the broader environment, biodiversity and species beyond those being pursued as quarry. Every year, the finalists reflect a wide range of outstanding achievements from a diverse array of geographic regions. Since 1999, over 250 shoots around the country have submitted for consideration, presenting conservation initiatives from grouse moors to grey partridge projects, from wildfowling clubs to wild pheasant shoots, with 75 winners sharing more than £100,000 in prize money. Entry requires considerable effort, with a detailed, comprehensive questionnaire establishing a baseline for further query and investigation by a 16-person judging panel, chaired by the Duke of Wellington. As the years have gone by, the Awards themselves have gained the same prestige as the guns produced by Purdey, and today, even being shortlisted for a Purdey Award is a coveted achievement.

There is arguably no name more synonymous with fine English gunmaking than James Purdey & Sons Ltd; indeed, I would venture to suggest that Purdey may be the most famous gunmaker in the world. It's a position earned over 200 years, through an enviable international reputation. The hallmarks of their craft are founded in the elegance of hand-laid, deep lustring linseed-finished walnut, the intricacy of engraved scrolling, and the refined depth of sumptuous blueing. The epitome of combined extravagance, wonderment and old-world craftsmanship, without question, lies in a pair of hand-made English shotguns. Sought out by kings, queens, and the highest echelons of society, the Purdey name not only carries with it an undeniable draw for those fascinated by the intersection of art and functionality, but basks in an undeniable status that few brands can command.

The first time I entered the Long Room at Audley House in London, I stood for a moment at the doorway, the expanse of this historic place stretching out before me. Seventy-six years before, General Dwight Eisenhower had sat here with the Invasion Committee to plan the D-Day landings. Behind me, I was aware of the gentle background murmur from the font shop as customers swooned over fine leather works, rich tweed garments and selected shotguns and rifles on display. With deliberate, steady steps, I absorbed the flowing history told through oil and canvas, wood and steel, reminding myself that I was achieving a boyhood dream to be welcomed into the most prestigious gunmaker in the world, to tell their story as a writer and photographer. It's sometimes easy to rush past these moments, but I wanted to take in every second.

"Men do not go to Purdey because they want to economise; they go to him and pay his price with the utmost cheerfulness because they are well aware that by doing so, they will have done for them all the art of smoothbore making can do." This summary of James Purdey as a gunmaker, printed in the 1880s in Land & Water magazine, reflects the standing and reverence with which the man was held. Just as in 1880, commissioning a gun from Purdey today is far more than a quest for function alone. It is a desire to embrace the heralded Purdey lineage of craftsmanship, which embodies the origin of fine gunmaking, and exists to this very day.

When you own a Purdey, you are, in a way, a part of this history: a fabric of gun-owners, keeping hundreds of years of knowledge and skill alive.

Arguably, the history of James Purdey & Sons really started in Scotland. Without the unrest of the Jacobite uprising, James Purdey may have not made the long journey south to London. However, this was not the Purdey who would eventually have his name above Audley House, but in fact his grandfather. Born in 1700, he would name his second son James, who, growing up in the heart of an industrially booming London, would find early employment as blacksmith in the Minories parish — an area around the Tower of London, also known for the production of firearms parts. His third son, born in 1784, would also be named James. It was this James Purdey who would go on to be one of the great English gunmakers. At the age of 12 years, he would mourn the passing of his father, and as such would apprentice as a gun-smith under his brother-in-law, Thomas Hutchinson, for seven years.

James Purdey, the Founder — as he would eventually be known — went on to hone his craft under the watchful eye of Joseph Manton, a man often referred to as the King of gunmakers. Purdey said of Manton, "But for him, we should all have been a parcel of blacksmiths," and it is without question that Manton's guiding principle of "endless attention to every detail" was carried forth into each gun stamped with the Purdey name from the first day.

WHEN YOU OWN A PURDEY, YOU ARE, IN A WAY, A PART OF THIS HISTORY: A FABRIC OF GUN-OWNERS, KEEPING HUNDREDS OF YEARS OF KNOWLEDGE AND SKILL ALIVE.

In 1814, James Purdey established his own company and began forging a path to greatness that few manufacturers would ever match. It was a time of turmoil and war in the world. In the same year the company was registered, British forces were laying siege to Washington D.C., eventually capturing and burning the White House on August 24th. Today's iconic white building was painted as such to hide the scorch marks scarring the walls. Napoleon was still a year away from defeat at the Battle of Waterloo, and The Times of London newspaper saw the first automated printing, operated by steam-powered presses. The evolution of gun design was firmly in the epoch of the flintlock, although it would be about to enter a period of transition with Forsyth's first attempts of percussion in 1807. The demand for Purdey's guns continued to grow, expanding from just 6 in the first year to 165 a year within a decade.

Although probably most well-known for his shotguns, James Purdey had a deep-seated fondness and fascination with rifles, manufacturing 1,400 muzzleloaders in the early years of his business. Demand for rifles continued to grow as the British Empire expanded through Africa and India, and as Queen Victoria's very public love of the Scottish Highlands and deer stalking encouraged an upsurge in interest. The advent of the double rifle, now firmly associated with dangerous game, evolved from a period before repeating rifle design and with origins in the Highlands. At the time, it was common practice when stalking deer to carry two rifles, offering rapid deployment of a second shot should the opportunity arise. Purdey overcame and perfected the complexities of barrel convergence when building double rifles, producing his first in 1827. They quickly became a common sight in pursuit of red deer. Later, it was found that the reliability of the design and quick second shot endeared double rifles the most to hunters of dangerous game.

James Purdey would leave an indelible mark on the history of rifle manufacturing, engraved into the very core of our vocabulary with the introduction of the *Express Rifle* in 1852. Muzzleloading rifles had long suffered from bullet stripping when attempting to gain increased velocity and accompanying downrange energy delivery. As a result, those who sought more *punch* had to be content with large bores and slow projectiles. Given velocity limitations, the only real way to increase impact energy and terminal effectiveness was to crank up the weight and drive a bigger hole through the intended quarry. Deliberating this issue, James Purdey experimented by reducing the number of rifling grooves, cutting just two wide slow twists, turning one full rotation in six feet. A purpose-made conical projectile, designed with two corresponding 'wings,' allowed for easy loading. In the advertising spiel, the rifle was said to be "like an express

Facing Page: Harold Delay, Stocker, 1964
Upper Right: A true art form: bespoke engraving.
Lower Right: A case hardened finish on a 12 bore side by side.

This Page: Blackening the action for fitting: a process which hasn't changed since the founding years.

Facing Page: The final finish: a hand laid process which takes months to complete.

Irongate Wharf, 1950

train," and hence the term Express Rifle was born. This died out with the evolution to breech-loading guns, but we still see "*Express*" used in vernacular to this day.

In 1877, the business changed its name to James Purdey & Sons to reflect both Atholl and James Purdey III joining the company. It would be impossible here to recount all the intricate details of Purdey's history. To portray the stories of dueling pistols, the development of the Wem ejector system, the construction of sniper rifles in World War I, the creation of the Highland Handle for the Royal Flying Corps, or the design lineage for Purdey's over and under could not be achieved with any justice without running to many hundreds of pages. For those intrigued by the depth of heritage, a detailed, meticulous account can be found in the book *Two Hundred Years of Excellence*, by Donald Dallas, to whom I owe a debt of thanks for the company history I have presented here.

The Purdey of today has changed and adapted, but at the company's core remains the beating heart of what James

Purdey built. Much of the world we live in now has cast aside the burden of human capital investment. Globalization has driven a web of time zone arbitrage, labor cost outsourcing, and hyper-mechanisation. We want 24-hour production cycles driving high-volume output and market capture, eliminating every sliver of what is seen as inefficiency. Any way in which a task can be achieved faster and more cost-effectively should be pursued. What is lost in this endeavour isn't tangible in the dimensions of life we can explain with physics. To hold a Purdey, brought into existence in the hands of skilled craftsmen, forged with hundreds of years of experience, defines a holistic endeavour. What it means will be different from person to person, as the emerging soul of such a gun goes beyond the mere grain of wood and curves of steel. Just as love is a human construct, one we cannot truly define beyond the neurochemical surges in dopamine and serotonin, a gun forged from the workbenches of Purdey is more than its component parts. It consumes you in wonder and awe.

Walk among the craftsmen and women today, and in many respects very little seems to have changed since those early, founding years. The rows of benches have witnessed decades of gunmaking , with the craft residing in the minds and hands of people. Weathered fingers still work oil into the swirled grains of meticulously selected Turkish walnut. Flames still lick carbon black faces to guide the fine adjustments of fitting. These old-world skills, honed for a modern era, have carried Purdey's reputation through the ages. Today, a matching pair of Purdey shotguns is the epitome of perfection when it comes to selecting a gun fit for a day's driven shooting. Is there truly any finer accompaniment to the richness of purple-clad heather, the heritage of tweed, and the agile, effortless speed of a red grouse than the fine, seductive lines and finish of a Purdey? Many would say there isn't.

James Purdey & Sons have no need to differentiate themselves when it comes to making shotguns and rifles; that standing is carved into the very history of gun evolution. However, the inception of the Purdey Awards made a clear statement of the importance of harbouring a future where our environmental impact and role in conservation as a community sits at the forefront of our minds. The 2020 Gold Purdey Award winner defines this very attitude.

Just a week after attending the award ceremony at Apsley House in London — a rather grand location, boasting the address No. 1 London and the residence of the Duke of Wellington — I made the quick hop over the Irish Sea from Scotland to meet gamekeeper Alex Rodgers and Director of the Irish Grouse Conservation Trust (IGCT) Adrian Morrow. I wanted to find out more about the Trust, their history, and the conservation work they're currently undertaking.

Being from a fellow Celtic nation, the landscape of Northern Ireland had a familiar feel for me. One striking difference from the Angus Glens of Scotland I call home was the apparent lack of investment in landscape-scale conservation. The future written here was one defined by extraction and maximized agricultural output. I had limited understanding of the historical context behind these observations, and I was eager to expand the realities of my initial impressions.

I had briefly met Alex in London just prior to him being presented with the Gold Purdey Award for Game & Conservation. Given the burden of responsibility on his shoulders, as the only full-time gamekeeper in Northern Ireland, I was surprised by how young he seemed. At just 26, he had taken up his current position three years previously, undertaking one of the most ambitious restoration and naturalization projects in the country. By his own admission, he had limited formal education, leaving school at just 15, but what I experienced over the following days was someone deeply enchanted by the science of upland management, harboring a depth of care, concern, and understanding that is rarely attributed. It was obvious that he was absorbed in

a passion to create a landscape better than the one he came to. Over the following two days, between conversations with Alex and Adrian, I began to build a picture of the environmental decline that the IGCT, along with others, was working so hard to reverse.

It has been suggested that the smoldering catalyst responsible for the degradation of a once-thriving ecosystem in Ireland was an unintended consequence of a series of historic Land Acts, breaking up large estates into much smaller, less economically viable farms. As a result, much of the traditional sporting management gradually disappeared, and in the 1960s, Northern Ireland lost its last full-time employed gamekeeper.

Around the same period, the European Common Agricultural Policy (CAP) was enacted, focused entirely on increasing food production. These subsidies were paid on a 'per head' basis, encouraging the overstocking of livestock across the Irish countryside. Cows and sheep were soon being over-wintered on the land, breaking the more sympathetic shifts from upland grazing in summer months to lower pastures over winter. A flowing rhythm practiced by generations cognizant of environmental recovery was broken. The collapse in ground-nesting bird populations quickly followed, but it wasn't until the 1990s that the system was reformed, with payments made on a land-based structure instead.

From the 1970s, almost all land management in Northern Ireland had ceased, and the dominant presence on the hills was sheep, facilitating an era of mass overgrazing. With that came the drainage of the moors, cutting deep channels known as grips through the peat to accelerate water runoff from the hills, lower the water table, and increase potential pastures. I have seen this across many parts of Scotland and England — a land-use adaptation that was actively encouraged by the government through subsidies. We are now suffering the consequences, with hydrological shifts and associated ecological impacts, downstream flooding, and the direct risk to ground-nesting birds, forced to negotiate this lattice of death traps for their offspring. Liming of heather was also widespread, shifting the pH of the soil and encouraging the growth of grass.

This period was also marred with vast swathes of poorly planned, inappropriate tree planting, not just in Northern Ireland, but across the United Kingdom. On Glenwherry, 2,500 acres of fast-growing conifers had replaced what was once upland dwarf shrub heath and peat bog. Not only did this destroy the existing, fragile and globally significant habitat, but long-term studies have now highlighted the impact of lowered groundwater levels and increased peat scouring, along with associated carbon loss resulting from the drier, exposed land inside the forests. To suggest that the

outlook was bleak is to underplay just how much work would be required to undo this damage.

The project Alex is a part of evolved from the 2003 Irish grouse survey, which estimated a total population in Northern Ireland of just 200 pairs. That same year, the Northern Ireland Environment Agency listed the Irish grouse (*lagapus lagapus hybernica*) as an endangered species. Although still contested, according to research carried out by Dr. Barry McMahon from University College Dublin, the Irish grouse is thought to have sufficient genetic variability to be classed as a separate species from the mainland red grouse (*lagapus lagapus scotia*). There is concern that further declines will continue to increase the risk of potential genetic bottlenecks.

Despite the dire outlook, no funding or help was made available to curb the deleterious effects of current land use, and this prompted the owner of The Antrim Estates, Lord Dunluce, to take action. Along with a small number of like-minded souls, the Irish Grouse Conservation Trust was established. As a charitable organization, with founding

members all in their twilight years, their ambition was noble, knowing that they would likely never reap any benefits for themselves. This was a quest to create a better future for the generations that followed.

When the project at Glenwherry Hill began in 2008, the ten-year baseline population for red grouse was just two to three pairs. Game records from the 1920s paid tribute to the ground being one of the most productive grouse moors in the country, with 100 brace days a regular occurrence. Today, the estate spans 7,000 acres, but only 1,000 acres of this is considered suitable grouse habitat. There are several designated sites within this territory, including an SPA (Special Protection Area), ASSI (Area of Special Scientific Interest), and AONM (Area of Outstanding Natural Beauty).

The first and most immediate action was to begin a structured system of predator control. This would run alongside planned habitat improvements projects, headed up by the first gamekeeper to grace the land in 50 years. Now, this sat on Alex's shoulders: implementing a monitored program focusing heavily on the control of foxes through legal, regulated snaring and shooting, as well as extensive corvid control and trapping of rats and stoats. The current body of existing research highlights the importance of predator control, not just for waders, but for all ground-nesting birds, including raptors. Partnered monitoring of hen harriers with the Northern Ireland Raptor Study Group accounted for a 95% nest failure due to predation across Northern Ireland.

The positive effects of controlling predators are being borne out in the evidence, with the IGCT providing a transparent collation of surveys and data under the collaborative Glenwherry Hill Regeneration Partnership, which includes the Agri-Food and Biosciences Institute (AFBI) and the Royal Society for the Protection of Birds (RSPB). This has allowed an adjacent 10 km2 area, currently being studied for breeding wader success, to come under the same umbrella of predator control and improved landscape management. Independent research has already shown benefits for a host of bird species, including merlin, hen harriers, golden plover, lapwing, meadow pipits, skylarks and the Irish hare. In 2017, the first curlew chicks fledged here in twenty years, with three chicks leaving their nests. One year later, four chicks successfully fledged. Given the bird's status as the species of greatest concern in the United Kingdom, the lessons from this success carry great importance. For the Irish grouse, a similar story unfolds, with the 2019 counts on Glenwherry hill coming to 90 pairs.

Predator control is, however, just one element in their ambitious, structured approach to restoring the once abundant wildlife and thriving ecosystem. Restructuring of land management principles and practices has also been crucial. The first step in this was blocking drains previously cut across the landscape, allowing the regeneration of sphagnum coverage through re-wetting of the land. Grazing pressure was also evaluated, balancing the optimal stocking density of livestock to complement heather regeneration through grass suppression, and economic farming value. This led to a shift away from flocks of texel in favor of Scottish blackface sheep. A radio-collaring project by the College of Agriculture, Food and Rural Enterprise (CAFRE) found that the dispersed nature of their grazing habits more efficiently and sympathetically complemented the landscape. According to Professor Jim McAdam of Queen's University Belfast, this combination of strategically implemented grazing, combined

PREDATOR CONTROL IS, HOWEVER, JUST ONE ELEMENT IN THEIR AMBITIOUS, STRUCTURED APPROACH TO RESTORING THE ONCE ABUNDANT WILDLIFE AND THRIVING ECOSYSTEM. RESTRUCTURING OF LAND MANAGEMENT PRINCIPLES AND PRACTICES HAS ALSO BEEN CRUCIAL.

THE LEGACY OF JAMES PURDEY & SONS LIES NOT ONLY IN THE FINE GUNS AND ACCESSORIES ADORNING THEIR LONDON SHOWROOM, BUT ALSO IN THEIR WILLINGNESS TO SUPPORT AND ELEVATE PEOPLE AND ORGANIZATIONS THAT ARE GENUINELY INVESTING IN A BETTER FUTURE.

with rotational muirburn, is "key to retaining and sequestering more soil carbon and enhancing biodiversity." Further, "the Glenwherry project is underpinned by sound scientific vegetation and habitat mapping to implement a grazing and burning strategy, which has resulted in a continuous, dense vegetation cover which will be resilient to climate change, have a reduced fire risk, retain biodiversity and sequester more carbon."

The most visually transformative change was ongoing during my visit, with the removal of a 50-hectare block of conifers that had been planted on deep peat and become entirely un-economic, while simultaneously crippling the immediate and surrounding ecosystem. Jim McAdam explained that "needle drop and shade created by the conifers resulted in highly degraded habitat with very low biodiversity and no peat growth." The site will be used to test regeneration methods, determining the best approach for future projects. Jim further explained that experience from other, similar sites showed that the plantation removal would quickly see improvements in peat accumulation and carbon sequestering as an active bog is allowed to re-establish.

As I came to the end of my two days with Alex, it seemed inconceivable that the landscape had been allowed to deteriorate so far. A string of poor, uninformed, ill-conceived landscape-wide measures had suffocated this place. It was heartening to see the level of collaboration between NGOs on the project, and the willingness to adopt management tools such as predator control. We don't have to look far to understand the implications of removing this hands-on management. The independent research and records bare evidence to a future without it, by highlighting the dire consequences of past mistakes.

The legacy of James Purdey & Sons lies not only in the fine guns and accessories adorning their London showroom, but also in their willingness to support and elevate people and organizations that are genuinely investing in a better future. By rewarding those who are willing to embrace collaborative, science-informed approaches to landscape-scale management, we stake a clear marker as to the community we wish to build. This community is the true legacy.

YOUNG GUNS

STORY BY *Jillian Lukiwski*

We walk behind our dog as he works into the wind. I shift the shotgun to my other hand to rest my grip and relax my hinges, and I find myself wondering what it might be like to carry an old gun — a true heirloom broken open over my shoulder, nicked up and notched, splendiferously engraved, heavy with legends and legacy, punchy with recoil.

I wonder what it's like to possess a wall tent that has dutifully kept the weather off generations of family. I wonder what it might be like to slip my arms into a heavy-weight, century-old wool coat laced with the dwindling scent of snow falling at first light. I wonder what it's like to grow up with rites of passage that revolve around weapons and food. I reflect on what it might be like to be a young kid given a set of ground rules to accompany an Ithaca model 37 with which to studiously pepper the covey of quail on the gravel driveway that leads from the family ranch out into open space.

I'm growing maudlin, as I hike behind my dog, over all the antiquated hunting-related apparatus I don't possess. Tools seem to be the face of tradition, the memories we can reach out and touch, the objects we press our faith into, the source of some superstition and luck. It's by using a tool of the hunting trade that we imbue it with story, purpose, history and worth. There's no mistaking it — I wear my lovely, covetous heart on my flannel sleeve. I wish we had old family hunting heirlooms, a sense of tradition that has been passed down to us. Alas, my husband and I have arrived in the world of hunting like squalling orphans left on a cold doorstep; we must find our own way.

We keep walking. The wind has picked up and the grass is groveling. The dog is working the air on the canyon rim now, and he pauses to gaze out at a sea of volcanic rubble before he follows his nose straight into hell. My husband and I exchange looks as we make our way down what we have termed a "chukar chute," a gap in the rimrock that allows bird

traffic to run upslope to the sage flats that flank the canyon. We came here the first time, long ago, by errant curiosity — which is how we arrive on the edges of most of the canyons we hunt. Our knowledge of land is slow to manifest and is the simple result of exploring time and space. As we learn and build a catalogue of information and understanding of the territories and animals we hunt, we've realized the greatest tradition to decorate family trees rooted in hunting legacy is the tradition of knowledge — knowledge of tools, weapons, land, seasons, animal behavior, and animal habitat. This trove of knowledge spans generations for some families and is what we envy most as hunting orphans. Instead of being lucky enough to learn by genealogical transmission and cultural immersion, we learn what we know by making mistakes, by stumbling into success, by carrying lessons forward with grit and grace and stubbornness. There is something tinier and older at work in us, too. It lies sleeping in our cells, in the coils of our DNA, so that learning is sometimes more like waking and remembering after generations of deep sleep.

The dog is pointing in a steep field of basalt debris. Boulders the size of basketballs, cars, and modest off-grid cabins lie stacked and wedged as far as I can see. I begin my traverse. The angle of repose sets rocks to teetering, and I wobble as quickly as I can across the slope. I scramble up and over and through while I try to keep my gun ready in my hands. When the chukar flush, I pick a bird, swing through, and pull the

——

YOUNG GUNS DON'T STAY YOUNG FOR LONG WHEN THEY'RE USED REGULARLY AND EARNESTLY. WE TEND TO FORGET THAT ALL GREAT THINGS HAVE SMALL BEGINNINGS, AND TRADITIONS ARE SIMPLY THE WONDERFUL CONSEQUENCES OF HEEDING AN ANCIENT CALL.

trigger as black rock shifts beneath my feet. The bird falls, and I fall too, having planted my boots on untrustworthy stone. I'm a tangle of elbows and knees; an ache flares in my hip where thinly clad bone met basalt. I laugh because it's more admirable to have a sense of humor than to cry, and I sort myself out. When I stand up, the dog is bringing a dead bird to me, and as I look down, I see a new, deep scratch in the stock of my gun. I feel a buzz of annoyance, and then I let it go. This is a young gun with many years of work ahead of it, and it's better to think about what a pleasure it will be to grow old with it in my hands here in the canyons with a lifetime of hard-working dogs. I don't want to be too precious about an inanimate tool that is intended to be my workhorse in the field. It's a scratch. It's a scratch that gave my dog a bird.

We arrive back at the truck as the world is turning golden. I toss my gear in the cab and look out at the sunset as the dog flops down in the grass and guzzles water. I decide it would be nice to come into this beautiful world on the receiving end of a family legacy, to be blessed with a birthright of knowledge, and to carry an old gun. But I'm able to recognize what an honor it is to carry a young gun, too. Young guns don't stay young for long when they're used regularly and earnestly. We tend to forget that all great things have small beginnings, and traditions are simply the wonderful consequences of heeding an ancient call. ⚕

THE ISLANDS

AND THE

WHALES

WORDS BY *Byron Pace*   PHOTOS BY *Derek Malou & Mike Day*

The battle drums of the north Atlantic Ocean groan loudly, stirring from the belly of warm currents pushing up to the Arctic, clashing unapologetically with the Norwegian Sea as these two mighty bodies of water meet the Faroes. The sprawling oceans are the sustaining lungs of this string of 18 major islands, breathing life into this seafaring nation. Myth and magic are embodied in the swelling waters. They offer up and take souls with equal indifference; these people are forged from the cauldrons of the deep.

The rolling waves harbor respect for what the ocean gives, and what it offered the forefathers of this land. Crashing whispers chant secrets along the shorelines, riling the soul and imagination to a simpler life, attuned to the rewards of land and sea. Early Norse settlers' lives flowed with the rise and fall of nature; the knowledge and skills they inherited were their greatest asset in this hostile, yet breathtakingly beautiful place. But these are not the islands of today. From plastic contamination to rising sea temperatures and the accumulation of mercury in the food chain, the Faroese culture, once so deeply at one with nature, faces a less-than-certain future.

The Vikings were not the first to arrive in the Faroes. Archaeologists have found early cereal pollen from domesticated plants from around 300 CE, but the current native population of the islands heralded from Viking explorers, landing circa 800 CE. The Faroese language evolved from Old West Norse tongue, and even today, their historic lineage is guarded as an essential element of who they are as people.

Culturally, the Faroese have held on firmly to their ties with the land, air and sea, and although modern conveniences and food imports have undoubtedly diluted the necessity of these old ways, there are few communities left that embrace natural harvest to the same extent. Most notoriously, this Danish territory is one of only five countries in the world that still hunts whales, an activity which sparks great controversy every year, and courts media attention from around the world. Interestingly this list includes the U.S.A., but only in Alaska, where limited numbers are hunted for native, cultural use. On the surface, this is a simple story, but as filmmaker Mike Day discovered, the web of underlying implications from this seasonal whale hunt encompasses international environmental issues.

The film Mike set out to make was focused on hunting traditions, but as with many great documentaries, the story which unfolds from spending time on the ground is what makes it come to life. The catalyst for venturing to the Faroes came from a previous documentary, *The Guga Hunters of Ness*. One of two legal gannet harvests left in the world, it was a tradition that had only been documented once before, 50 years previously. The only recorded gap where no hunting took place was during World War II. Obtaining permission to be present was met with resistance, something Mike would face again when seeking access from the Pilot Whale Hunting Association for his feature documentary in the Faroes. Eventually, Mike was granted rights to film, on the condition that he made his way to the island of Sula Sgeir independently. With his brother and a couple of friends, he skippered a sailing boat to the small island off the Isle of Lewis, and captured this historic hunt for guga, possible today only by special exemption from European regulations. Through the process of making this film, Mike established contacts that would eventually lead to four years of filming in the Faroes. His resulting documentary, *The Islands and The Whales*, has won global acclaim, boasting numerous awards including the HotDocs Emerging International Filmmaker Award, the DOC NYC Grand Jury Prize, and a Peabody Award, as well as being nominated for Best Documentary at the 2018 Emmy Awards.

Gaining acceptance as an outsider in the Faroese was Mike's first obstacle. He may have faced stormy seas on route to Sula Sgeir, but it took a hefty glass of schnapps and a sheep's sphincter on a plate before he was allowed into the heart of the Faroese community.

This may be a remote nation, seemingly a world away from the industrial growth of the continental mainland, but it soon became apparent that every facet of their cultural heritage was being affected by outside influences. One of the primary historical food sources of the Faroese was sea birds, which were much more consistent and guaranteed than whales. Today, for certain species, this harvest has entirely ceased. The drifting gulf stream and warming waters have pushed the food sources of many birds farther north following colder waters, further contributing to the severe decline in populations. Where 200,000 puffins were once hunted annually, none are now harvested. The remaining birds today rarely breed, the availability of sand eels too scarce to rear their young. Guillemot populations have also declined markedly, falling from 300,000 in the 1960s to less than 80,000 today. That decline is repeated for most of the species here.

In the documentary, a local taxidermist suggests that too many puffins were killed in years gone by. It is hard to know how much that can be attributed to the decline, or more accurately, how it affected the robustness of the population's ability to adapt to environmental changes. What's clearly evident, however, is that almost all seabirds have been touched by the reduced availability of prey species, and potentially the burden of plastic contamination in the ocean. Between 10 and 15 fragments of synthetic material can be found in almost every bird the Faroese harvest. These particles accumulate high concentrations of pollutants found in the ocean, including mercury and polychlorinated biphenyls (also known as PCBs, banned in the late 1970s but still persistent in our oceans). It is very possible that some birds may be dying directly from ingestion, or from resulting toxicity burdens.

One of the scenes that stuck with me from the documentary was the community harvesting of young gannets from the cliff faces around the islands. This was historically an important source of food right along the coastal settlements of the British Isles, but has long since disappeared from these

THIS MAY BE A REMOTE NATION, SEEMINGLY A WORLD AWAY FROM THE INDUSTRIAL GROWTH OF THE CONTINENTAL MAINLAND, BUT IT SOON BECAME APPARENT THAT EVERY FACET OF THEIR CULTURAL HERITAGE WAS BEING AFFECTED BY OUTSIDE INFLUENCES.

MODERN HUNTSMAN

rural communities. Unlike many other species in the Faroes, gannets have benefited from the warmer waters along the coast, as mackerel populations have continued to increase — their primary prey species.

In the cool, gray hue of failing light, weather-worn men marched along the clifftops, their lights flickering in the darkness. Slinging themselves toward the watery abysses below, an arm-thick rope supported each soul down the rocky faces, as the same woven fibres had done for 30 years. When Mike joined on the first evening, he became the first outsider to document the harvest. This old-world snapshot conjures an appreciation for the efforts and collaboration required to survive, along with an uncomfortable underlying feeling born from the rawness of dispatching juvenile birds from their nests.

———

IN THEIR SODDEN, CLARET HANDS, GRAPPLING HOOKS ARE DRIVEN THROUGH SKIN AND BLUBBER, DRAGGING QUIVERING BODIES FARTHER UP THE BEACH.

For people who rely on the bounty of nature, it is inherently in their interest to ensure the long-term proliferation of the resource. This may be in self-interest, but it is a powerful catalyst. It's not lost on the Faroese, that the historic harvests they once enjoyed may soon be confined to tales of old, as they observe the painfully apparent, precipitous declines of many species their ancestors had relied on.

Capturing the whale hunt itself was almost impossible to plan, and even positive sightings from fishermen going about the daily business didn't necessarily result in a successful pod beaching. The images conjured with the notion of whale hunting are of vast vessels and harpoons, which do indeed still exist in some countries, but this is not the story of a traditional Faroese whale hunt.

The primary targeted species in the Faroes is the long-finned pilot whale, which are the second-largest member of the dolphin family; the orca, or killer whale, being the biggest. Size varies between sexes, with males weighing up to 2300kg (5,000 lbs), measuring 6.7m (22 feet) long. The yearly average

harvest of 800 whales comes from the eastern North Atlantic ocean population of an estimated 778,000. This is regarded as sustainable, with the species currently listed of *Least Concern* by the IUCN. There is currently insufficient data to allow an accurate global population estimate.

The method used for hunting is known as a *Grindadrap*. This requires vast community participation and was once practiced all across the North Atlantic. It's a complex operation, drawing people from across the Faroes, as boats of all sizes join in to drive a located pod, herding the tiring pilot whales into an increasingly restricted area, before pushing them into the shallows of the shingle shoreline. It is without question the most iconic, yet harrowing sequence of the documentary, as splatters of blood-stained ocean swirl between the writhing bodies, the commotion and the people's elation and excitement palpable. In their sodden, claret hands, grappling hooks are driven through skin and blubber, dragging quivering bodies farther up the beach. The remaining members of the pod thrash in a helpless, contorted final effort as the last spines are severed. Slowly, the waters calm, people disperse, and the lapping, red wash of sea fades. The hunt is over.

This yearly harvest of around 500 tons of meat and blubber is shared among the community, with portions defined by complex rules of participation. This represents 30% of the total meat intake for the Faroes — a food source which would likely have to be replaced with imported protein, should the whale hunting ever be stopped.

The opposition to this has spawned from an increasingly unpopular global view of whale hunting as many species' populations continue to decline, and questions are raised on the grounds of animal welfare. It is unsurprising to find Sea Shepherd a persistent presence when the whale hunting season begins, determined to see all whale hunting stopped around the world. However, the story is much more nuanced and complicated than it first appears.

For a time, it seemed that whale hunting in the Faroes was dying out. The younger generation had lost interest in these old ways, and there was a feeling that this part of their culture would slip away with the passing of the older generation. With the arrival of Sea Shepherd and global pressures to stop the practice, this changed. In the words of one local, it "awoke the interest of our young people." In defiant retaliation at the notion of being forced to give up this historic element of their cultural identity, the number of those attending whale hunts began to increase. Cultural inertia is always hard to turn, and such efforts are rarely successful when imposed by outside agents. Quite possibly, the presence of Sea Shepherd breathed life into something that would have slowly been confined to history.

In the background of declining bird populations, plastic contamination and global pressures on banning whale hunting sits an underlying, opposing narrative to the cultural desire of the Faroese to continue harvesting whales: the high concentrations of mercury contained in whale meat is slowly killing them.

Impacts on our oceans from pollution and industry have been a topic increasingly brought to the fore alongside warming global temperatures. This includes elevated levels of mercury far above the background rates that occur naturally. Current trends indicate the concentration of mercury in our oceans will double in the next 10 years. The largest single source is the burning of fossil fuels, with coal being by far the biggest contributor today. The element of mercury itself is not as much of a concern as monomethyl mercury, which is formed from mercury deposits by the action of microbes that live in aquatic systems. In this form — a mercury atom attached to a methyl group — it becomes a bio-accumulative, toxic pollutant, which can build in the food chain in ever-increasing concentrations; first diffusing into plankton, then consumed by other organisms, which in turn are predated on through the complexities of oceanic food webs. As a result of this, there is a tendency for higher mercury concentrations in older, larger animals. Testing of whale meat by researchers at the University of Hokkaido in Japan, a country which still actively hunts and eats whale, showed an average concentration in whale livers of 900 times the government's regulated limit for safe consumption. While levels in the meat itself were lower, some 2.5 to 25 times the limit, the neurological and morphological effects of consuming contaminated whale meat have become very clear.

For 25 years, local toxicologist Dr. Pál Weihe has been testing mercury concentrations and monitoring the effects on the Faroese community. Although large-dose mercury poisoning had been well documented, there had never been a study looking at long-term, low-dose exposure. His research showed that by the age of 14 years old, cognitive impairments were being recorded in the population, with a doubling of mercury

levels relating to a reduction in childhood development, the equivalent of a month of cognitive learning. Children were being born with 40 times the background level of expected mercury in their system, with the older community members experiencing more than two times the rate of heart complications and Parkinson's disease — two symptoms associated with long-term mercury poisoning. Dr. Pál Weihe has spent most of his career trying to raise awareness of these health implications, but the lack of acute issues related to low-dose exposure had made it hard to convince the local communities to give up, or even reduce their whale meat consumption.

As we discover through the documentary, today there seems to be a growing acceptance among the younger generations that there are very real risks associated with eating whale meat. Umbilical cord tests on newborns have shown a large reduction in mercury, indicating that locals are beginning to understand the severe implications for their children's early development. This clash of cultural identity and acknowledgement of science is a new challenge for the Faroese, one they will have to wrestle with as they cling on to what makes them who they are in a world changing so rapidly. Most of these impacts are out of their control, even if they bear them more acutely than most.

The Islands and The Whales truly is a ground-breaking documentary, blending art and cinema with honest, authentic storytelling. It elevated Mike Day as one of the great modern documentary makers and showed the world how far-reaching and complicated the web of our actions can be. In the homes and communities of the Faroese archipelago, they are shouldering the burden of our historic global indifference to our impact on the planet. They are torn between grasping onto the fading, brittle fabrics which define them as people, and the very stark reality that they can no longer look fully to the ocean as their ancestors once did. ⩊

The Islands and the Whales *is available to watch online on the following websites:*

▷ *vimeo.com/ondemand/gugahunters*

▷ *facebook.com/intrepidcinema*

▷ *intrepidcinema.com*

▷ *vimeo.com/ondemand/theislandsandthewhales*

OF MEAT &
COMMUNITY

WORDS BY *Daniela Ibarra-Howell* PHOTOS BY *Guillermo Fernández López & Heidi Lender*

I fell in love with the Argentine countryside during the endless summers of my childhood. Its smells, its sounds, its infinite landscapes with bleeding horizons filled with nostalgia, and its captivating rituals lured me into an unlikely life path for a city girl. I learned at an early age that there were ceremonies across our lands that bound us in peculiar and irresistible ways.

Asado, meat slowly cooked over hot coals, is a pillar of the Argentine traditions. It is arguably the most valued currency of celebration — to honor work, dear friends, family, marriages, farewells. It is a gastronomic symbol and an emblem of the Argentine identity.

For centuries, when early European explorers visited these lands, they were astonished and even frightened as they observed "gauchos" — the cowboys of the Argentine grasslands — dressing full carcasses with nothing more than their simple *"facones"* (knives). Gauchos became experts in the art of organizing horseback expeditions to hunt wild cattle and cooking their meat — that otherwise would go to waste, as only salted hides were traded with Europe — over big open fires on simple crosses. It was the genesis of the legendary "asado." It's still done the same way: simply, with no extras apart from the occasional *"chapa"* (a piece of sheet metal) to protect the fire from gusts of wind.

Wood and fire, with their gifts of scent, warmth and trance, are central to the experience. Wood, hard enough to break an axe, is masterfully arranged and used to re-light the fire in the morning hours, then tenderly cared for as coals form, and glowing embers whiz and twirl up in pale blue columns of smoke. Heat is skillfully distributed by the *"asador"* until it colors the coals with an incandescent red, covering them in a velvety layer of white ash. Meat is never moved while it cooks — coals are.

Pride is paramount in every step of the ceremonial unfolding of this culinary art — pride for the revered skill, the watchful supervision, and the extraordinary patience that is required. Renowned chef Francis Mallmann reflects on this unique skill as one that is *"perfected during hundreds of Sundays directing a symphony of meat and fire."*

No outsider's advice is ever welcomed by an accomplished asador. Children's presence, on the other hand, is appreciated and accepted, as they delight in observing from an early age the dexterous moves of the virtuoso, along with the sensorial scenography that will remain imprinted in their memory forever. The loyal company of dogs is never missing, patiently awaiting alms, whether they be a piece of discarded fat or rawhide, or a bone.

Asado is a ritual so much more than it is a delicious meal. Beyond a dietary choice, it's a core of our culture and heritage. *Community* is the defining reward. No other food carries such ceremonial and uniting power for Argentineans.

During the long summer vacations on my family's ranch, and every weekend on our little farm outside the city of Buenos

Aires, asado roped in small crowds of our clan with a sense of anticipation, of promising rewards to come wrapped in slow and sweet Sunday glee.

Unassuming long tables were set by the women of the family, covering simple linen with bread baskets, large bowls of simple salads, and bottles of inexpensive red wine. They were, curiously, populated with perfect timing just before rounds of meat began circulating, served by the asador strolling around the table and deliberately selecting the piece that would land on your plate. Each round would take place in a predefined order and at a perfect tempo so that the temperature of the meat would be just right, every time. Guests were never hurried nor left waiting for too long. The meal would last for hours. A voice would arise from the table calling for *"un aplauso para el asador!"* (a round of applause for the asador). It would be terrible manners not to acknowledge such a feat of art with this customary and expected gesture.

And then, as slowly as it all started, the meal would wind up with plump peaches and *dulce de leche*, or caramel-coated flan and maybe sweetened espresso coffee as, one by one, people slowly departed. The children would leave the table to play, the youth to light a forbidden cigarette, the elders to take a siesta, and the women to clean up. We felt filled and fulfilled by the nourishing food, the lighthearted chatter, the passionate and unimportant recurrent debates during the *sobremesa* (the long after-meal time spent at the table discussing *futbol*, politics, or raising children). The day would

seamlessly and peacefully melt into an indigo twilight. We all felt enriched by the renewed sense of belonging.

But today more than ever before, a new kind of community is required for this tradition to deservedly live on — a community of stewardship. Not all meat is created equal, and for it to continue to be an emblem of Argentine culture, it must reflect deep care and humble reverence for the land and the animals. There is much more to consider than in those early days of wild cattle roaming the Pampas. We need to be much more mindful than we are presently, as industrial agriculture conspicuously erodes not only the soils and rich diversity of life in these grasslands, but also the deep indigenous knowledge and cultural understanding of how to manage land in harmony with its essence and rhythms. With feedlots now rearing their ugly head, disconcerted Argentinenans are struggling to recall what good meat is supposed to taste like.

As we pass down this notable tradition of "asado" to the younger generations in our quest to nurture community, I work and yearn to bestow upon them the more urgent and compelling legacy of profound love and homage for those landscapes that I became enamoured with during my childhood; to instill knowledge and skills for holistic stewardship focused on the beauty and complexity of the earth's inherent abundance and resilience. This is what will feed our children, and let them feast together, in community, around the table. ⚘

ENERGY [FT-LB]		
0	3433	
100	3110	
200	2809	
300	2529	
400	2271	
500	2033	
600	1815	

ZERO [200 YDS]		
0	-1.5	
100	+1	
200	0	
300	-4.9	
400	-14.2	
500	-28.3	
600	-47.7	

VELOCITY [FPS]		
0	3300	
100	3141	
200	2985	
300	2833	
400	2684	
500	2540	
600	2399	

INCHES

2
1
0
-1
-2
-3
-4

YARDS   0   50

PRESENTED BY *Nosler*   WORDS BY *Phil Massaro*   PHOTOS BY *Justin Moore*

A FAMILY TRADITION OF EXCELLENCE

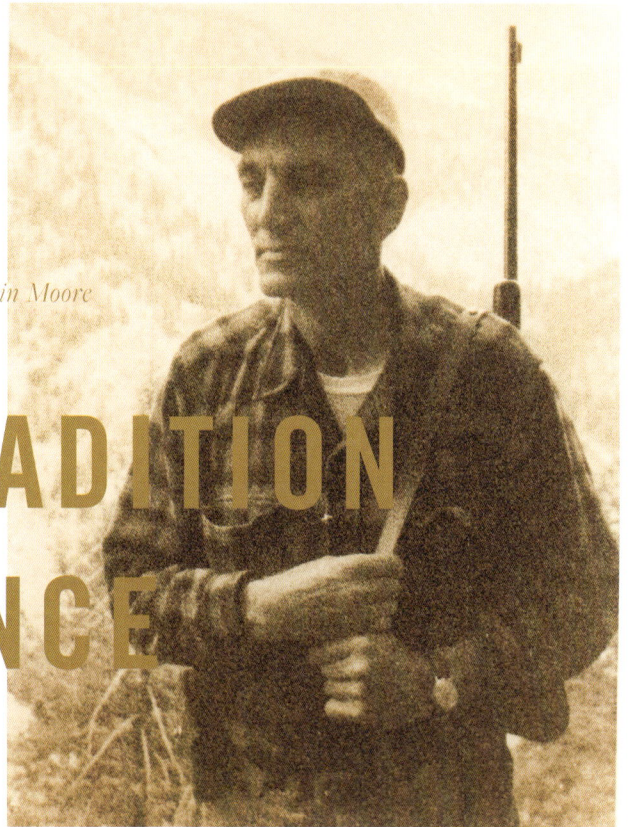

CALIBER	WEIGHT	VELOCITY	ZERO
26 Nosler	*142 Grains*	*3300 ft/s*	*200 yds.*

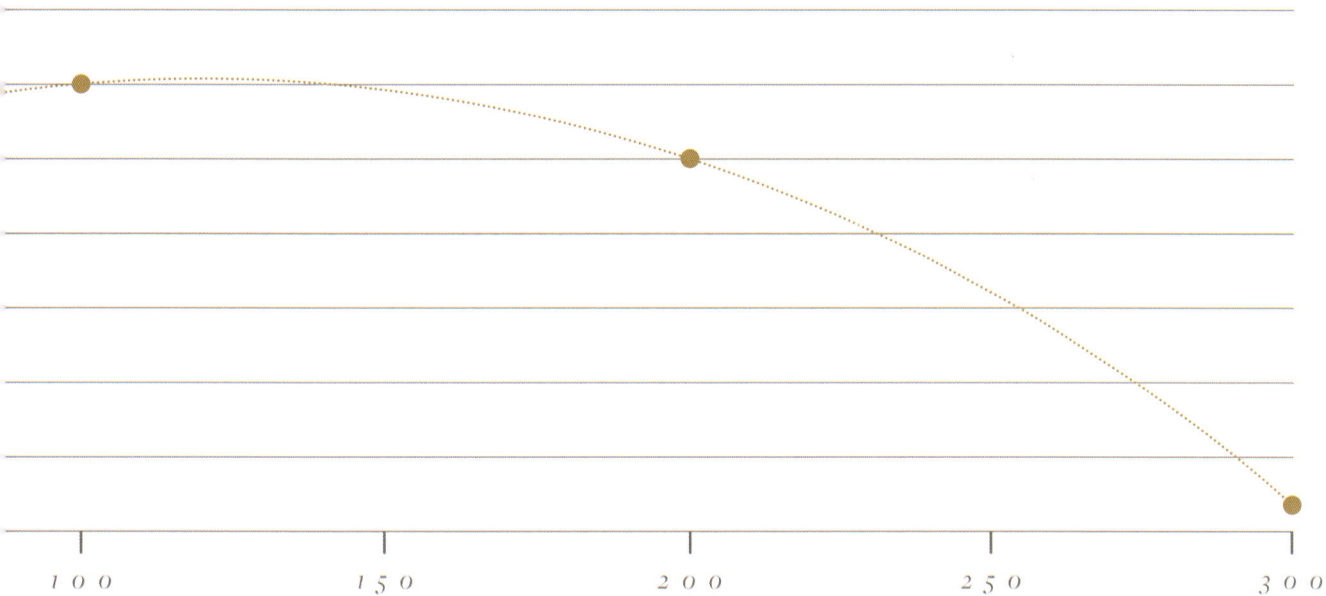

100   150   200   250   300

{ Nosler }

I stepped out of my truck into the inky blur of predawn light on a Thanksgiving morning, and it felt like the 15 degrees the thermometer had indicated. While the Hudson Valley had received a rain storm, the Catskill Mountains — specifically those locales above 2,000 feet in elevation — had been carpeted in snow, roughly two inches, perfect for tracking. I hadn't gone a quarter-mile down the logging trail when I came across prints from a doe and her fawn coming down off the hill to my right. Within another 50 paces, the huge track of what could only be a buck joined the trail, drifting slightly left and right like a heat-seeking missile.

She was obviously a hot doe, and I was no longer concerned about the 15-mph wind and blowing snow. With the tracks just minutes old, I followed on cautiously, a steely focus narrowing. This scenario had my undivided attention. Stopping before a small rise in the trail, the slightest glimpse of a heavy set of antlers caught my eye, disappearing behind a downed beech tree. The rifle came to shoulder effortlessly, and the instant he cleared the obstruction, my .308 Winchester sent a 165-grain Nosler Partition into his vitals. I soon stood over a beautiful eight-point buck surrounded by the idyllic Catskill Mountains, cradling a rifle handed down to me by my father. He had stopped hunting a couple years earlier, but I've carried on our Thanksgiving Day hunting tradition.

"There are big bears up there; load some Partitions for that hunt," he'd always say. Dad was, as usual, correct.

My dad and I are business partners, and have hunted all over the world together, so I can appreciate the trials, tribulations and rewards of a family business. In the hunting and shooting industry, many of the best companies either started out being or still are family run, and I can think of no better example of this than Nosler. The Partition, a flagship of the Nosler fleet, was the first bullet developed by avid outdoorsman John A. Nosler, the company's founder.

The Nosler story began in 1946, as John settled the crosshairs of his .300 Holland & Holland on the shoulder of a mud-caked bull moose in British Columbia. Much to his consternation, but to the benefit of the hunting world, the speedy bullet failed to penetrate properly, leading to a protracted follow-up. John wasn't going to tolerate this, and spent the next several months brooding, determined to build a better mousetrap.

The bullet that failed Mr. Nosler was the standard bullet du jour, and in fact the non-premium standard to this day: a cup-and-core design. It's simple and brilliant, using a jacket of copper (the cup) around a lead core. Upon impact, the copper jacket peels back, and the lead core deforms to create the classic mushroom. Under extreme stress, the jacket and core can separate, and can lead to penetration failures. This is exactly what happened to John Nosler

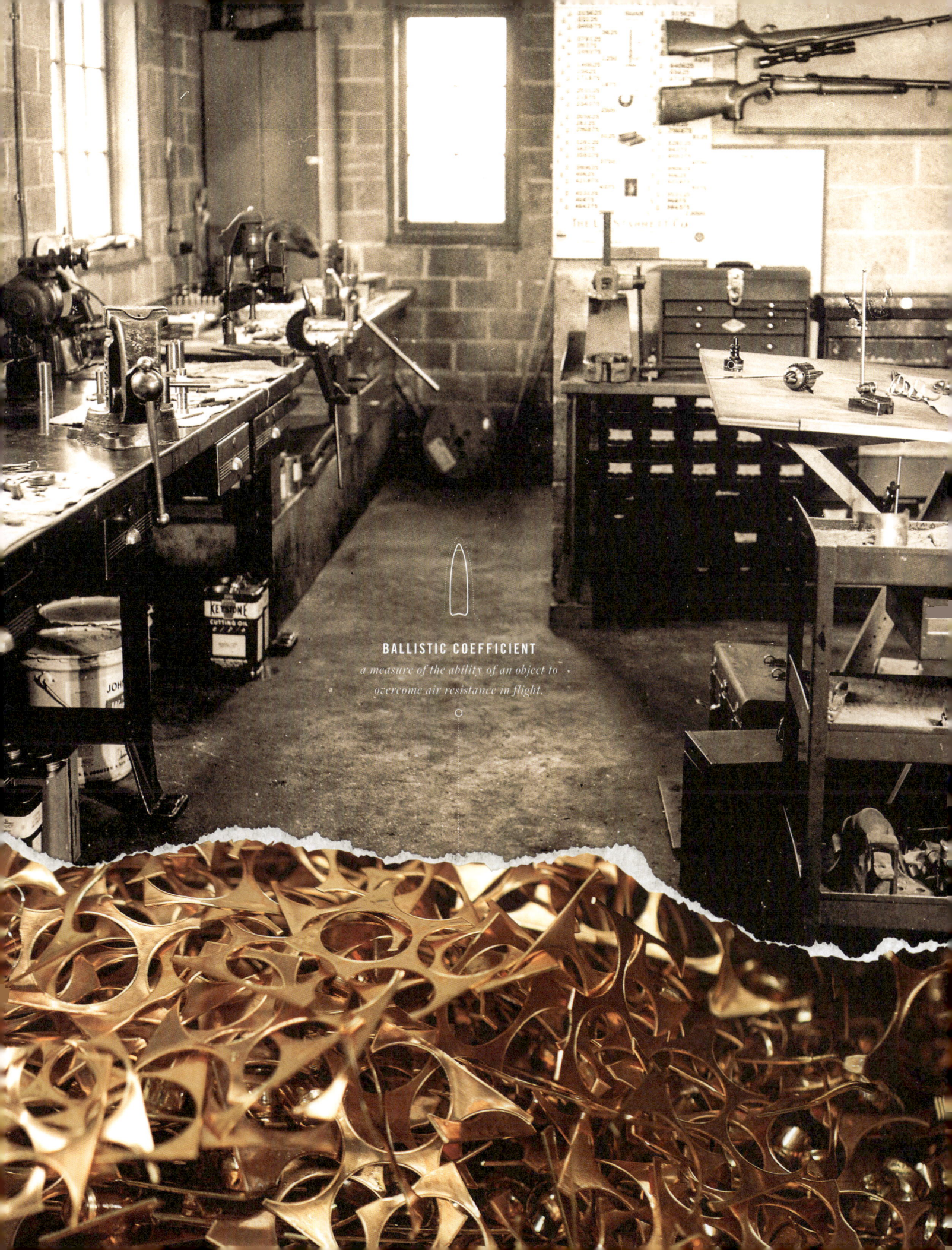

BALLISTIC COEFFICIENT

a measure of the ability of an object to
overcome air resistance in flight.

UNDER EXTREME STRESS, THE JACKET AND CORE CAN SEPARATE, AND CAN LEAD TO PENETRATION FAILURES. THIS IS EXACTLY WHAT HAPPENED TO JOHN NOSLER ON THAT FATEFUL DAY THAT CHANGED HISTORY, INITIATING HIS DRIVE TO BUILD A BULLET THAT WOULD TAKE ANY ANIMAL, OF ANY SIZE, AT ANY ANGLE. HIS GOAL — AS IS THE GOAL OF ANY ETHICAL HUNTER — WAS TO MAKE A QUICK, CLEAN KILL, AND TO MINIMIZE THE SUFFERING OF ANY GAME ANIMAL. A BULLET THAT DIDN'T DO ITS JOB FELL SHORT OF THE ETHICS HE HAD BEEN RAISED TO CONSIDER.

on that fateful day that changed history, initiating his drive to build a bullet that would take any animal, of any size, at any angle. His goal — as is the goal of any ethical hunter — was to make a quick, clean kill, and to minimize the suffering of any game animal. A bullet that didn't do its job fell short of the ethics he had been raised to consider.

A napkin sketch seeded his grand idea, which would be the catalyst for all manufacturers to scrutinize the terminal effectiveness of bullet construction. He would utilize a partition of copper across the middle of the bullet, preventing jacket and core from separating. In this way, the rear core would always remain intact, giving the bullet the ability to penetrate deeply into the vitals for a quick kill. He took his new design back to Canada the following autumn, and both he and Clarence Purdy took moose cleanly with one shot each, Clarence using his .30-'06 Springfield to take the first wild game with John's new bullet. The bullet was a success, and the Nosler Partition Bullet Company was born in 1948.

GEN ONE

John Amos Nosler was born in Southern California, in April 1913, the fifth and last child of Byrd and Perna Nosler. His father had been born on the Oregon Trail, and the family endeavored in a series of farming and ranching operations, from Colorado to California, as well as other ventures. Young John showed an aptitude for all things mechanical, fostered by his time spent alongside hot-rodded automobiles in an auto repair shop. He always had a penchant for the outdoors and hunting, with necessity playing some part in his hunting prowess.

His experiences with the .300 Savage, .30-40 Krag and .348 Winchester had vividly illustrated the issues involved with overstressing a cup-and-core bullet, and how longer bullets with a higher Sectional Density gave better

terminal performance than lighter slugs. These concerns and observations came from a man deeply invested in the morality of ethical hunting and the responsibility laid upon the hunter when harvesting a wild animal. The Nosler Partition design was revolutionary in 1948, and remains a hunting staple to this day. It has performed consistently, giving the desired expansion and deep penetration equated with quick, humane kills; the greater the upset bullet's diameter, the larger the wound channel, and the greater the destruction to vital tissue. The initial bullets were made from copper rods cut to length, drilled at either end, with molten lead poured into the cavity. This was a time-consuming process, which would eventually be adapted as production scaled up. As such, the early days were a small-scale, family-and-friends affair, and before long, the little shop in Ashland, Oregon was up and rolling.

After initially producing his Partition bullets on lathes (the first of which he built himself), he developed the revolutionary impact extrusion method, making his bullets more consistent and therefore more accurate. Production was slow initially, but as John made the transition to his bullet company full-time, he acquired the machines necessary to ramp up output. In an effort to raise the profile of his creation, John connected with some of the preeminent writers of the day, including Herb Klein (who took the Partition to Africa), Warren Page, Elmer Keith and Jack O'Connor, and before long, the Nosler Partition was enjoying unanimous praise the world over. For hunters, the Partition became the baseline by which all others would be judged. With popularity increasing, John soon expanded, moving the Nosler plant to Bend, Oregon. His son Bob, born in April 1946, would follow his father's footsteps and become an integral part of the company.

TERMINAL PERFORMANCE

the effectiveness of a projectile to disrupt material within a targeted object.

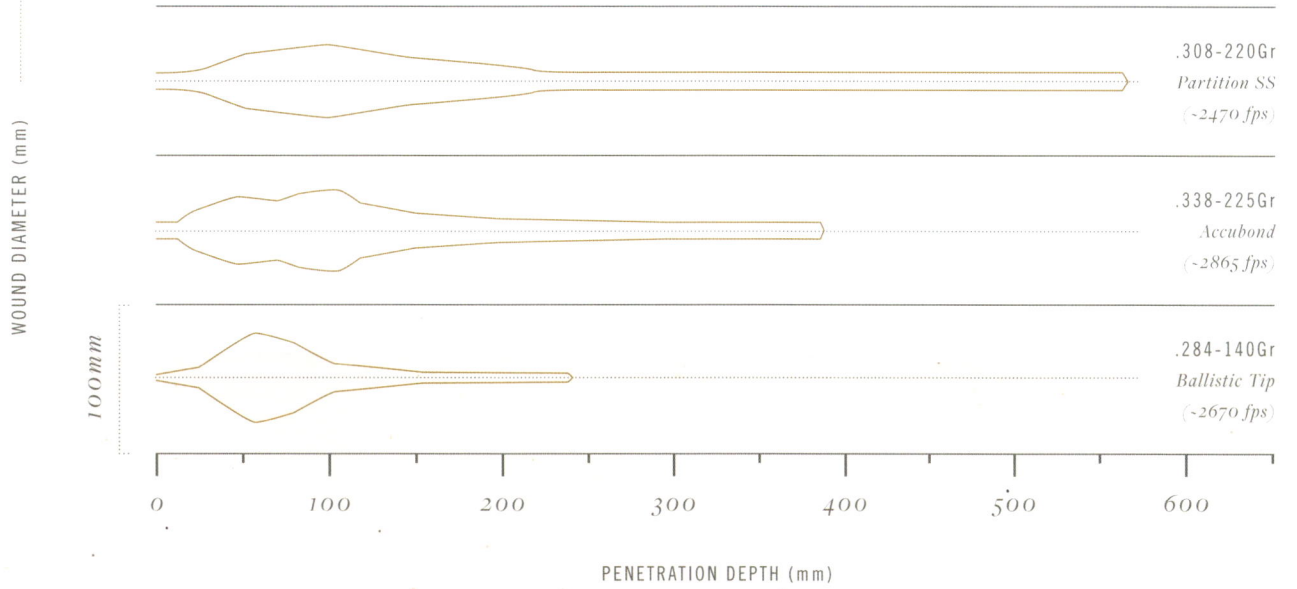

.308-220Gr
Partition SS
(~2470 fps)

.338-225Gr
Accubond
(~2865 fps)

.284-140Gr
Ballistic Tip
(~2670 fps)

WOUND DIAMETER (mm)

100mm

0   100   200   300   400   500   600

PENETRATION DEPTH (mm)

"I WON'T SAY I WAS GROOMED FOR THIS POSITION — I HAD THE CHOICE TO PURSUE ANY AVENUE I WANTED TO — BUT I WILL SAY I HAD TWO OF THE BEST MENTORS ANYONE COULD'VE ASKED FOR: MY FATHER AND MY GRANDFATHER," JOHN TOLD ME. "I COULDN'T FILL MY GRANDFATHER'S SHOES, AND I'M NOT THE MAN MY FATHER IS, BUT I'M PROUD TO BE ME."

John Nosler

Cal. .338
Gr. 300
SD. 0.375

Cal. 6.5 CM
Gr. 140
SD. 0.287

Cal. .243
Gr. 55
SD. 0.133

○ **SECTIONAL DENSITY**

*The ratio of an objects mass
to it's cross-sectional area.*

GEN TWO

From the inception of the company, John A. Nosler had taken on a partner in his business, Ray Wade; a pairing which without question helped facilitate the early success. But, Wade eventually wanted to sell his shares of Nosler, and the end of a long story is that the optics firm of Leupold & Stevens ended up owning Nosler as a subsidiary. During this time, John developed his second bullet, the Zipedo, which evolved into the Nosler Solid Base in the 1970s. The Leupold & Stevens years would hold some famous names — guys who I fondly recall from my youth. Chub Eastman, Gail Root, Bill Lewis; they would play an integral part in creating the Nosler we all know today, lending expertise in many different departments. By this time, the hunting and shooting world was beginning to embrace the premium bullet market, with manufacturers of loaded ammunition collaborating with premium bullet makers. Hunters now had more choice when it came to choosing their ammunition, and most importantly, the design of projectiles for their hunt. For the first time, real consideration was given to bullet construction, and the importance of understanding what was appropriate across varying species and circumstances.

The innovation at Nosler didn't stop there. Their revolutionary Ballistic Tip — an idea influenced by a Norma projectile with a round polymer ball at the nose — was also a huge success. This design saw an impact extruded bullet with a tapering jacket, and a sharp polymer tip at the nose to both initiate expansion and maintain the ballistic coefficient. It is fantastically efficient for rapid energy transfer, making it a perfect choice for deer, antelope and similar-sized animals, and today has been adopted in varying fashion by a number of manufacturers. The larger species are still best handled by John's Partition,

but the Ballistic Tip — if of proper weight — is hard to surpass. Bob's business acumen complemented his father's well. He was responsible for ending the financial relationship with Leupold & Stevens (though they remain on excellent terms), and in 1988, brought the company back under family ownership, setting the stage for the introduction of his son John and daughter Jill. This era would also see strong partnerships forged with both Federal and Winchester — both loading Nosler bullets in their line of factory ammunition — bringing the Nosler name to the masses, and allowing those who didn't handload their ammunition to enjoy the benefits of the Nosler line.

GEN THREE

John R. Nosler, the third and current generation of Nosler, fully understands the pressure of being in charge of such a prestigious company, and yet remains a down-to-earth guy. While I've been privileged enough to have met both Bob and young John Nosler at the trade shows, I recently had a chance to chat on the phone with John in a much more relaxed atmosphere. "I won't say I was groomed for this position — I had the choice to pursue any avenue I wanted to — but I will say I had two of the best mentors anyone could've asked for: my father and my grandfather," John told me. "I couldn't fill my grandfather's shoes, and I'm not the man my father is, but I'm proud to be me."

John has been on board for the most radical expansion of the Nosler brand, including the introduction of the Nosler AccuBond, AccuBond Long Range, RDF and E-Tip bullets, as well as the line of Nosler rifles, loaded ammunition and cartridges. As a matter of fact, he just completed the Grand Slam of North American wild sheep, and did it using the four new Nosler big game cartridges. An impressive feat for any hunter, anywhere, it must have carried all the more significance owing to the head stamp of the cartridges used.

"My dad, Bob, made a big push to diversify the Nosler name, without watering it down or cheapening it," John explained. In the tradition of John A. Nosler, the subsequent generations have the knack for recognizing the needs of the hunting and shooting community. The Nosler AccuBond is an improvement on the Ballistic Tip concept, in that the polymer tip helps to keep the bullet's meplat, or nose, consistent and resistant to deformation in the magazine. Further still, the markedly thicker jacket is chemically bonded to the jacket, slowing down the expansion, which allows the bullet to penetrate deep into the vitals before losing momentum. The bonding, the polymer tip, the boat tail and the accuracy all help to make the AccuBond a bullet capable of handling the high-impact velocities of a magnum cartridge, yet still expand at long ranges when the bullet's velocity drops off. To some, this may feel a little technical, but selecting the right bullet is crucial, and without question, the ethical hunter has a responsibility to understand, to a certain degree,

how to choose the appropriate bullet design for the quarry being pursued. The AccuBond is a wonderful bullet, and along with its excellent terminal performance, it produces tiny target groupings from a number of my rifles.

I asked John a little more about the diversification of the company, and how this complements the core of their business. "We are also very proud of our component brass cases, and the Nosler series of loaded ammunition. We took a big leap when we offered our line of ammunition, as we have been known as a component bullet company since the late '40s. We have a great partnership with both Winchester and Federal, who load our bullets, and we didn't want to compromise those relationships in any way."

Now, I can attest to the fact that the Nosler component brass offers a quality hard to match; it comes out of the box ready to go, and doesn't require any of the prep-work associated with some other brands. When I loaded my .280 Ackley Improved ammunition for a safari to Namibia, I reached for Nosler

cases; the accuracy and consistency was phenomenal. I've also come to appreciate the quality of Nosler's factory ammunition, from the varmint loads to the deer, bear and elk offerings, right on up to the safari ammunition for large bore rifles. Their Partition is a great choice for big game animals, and the Nosler Solid — a lead-free, non-expanding bullet — is a perfect choice for backup shots on dangerous game.

Nosler has also embraced the global movement toward lead-free ammunition, both for big game and varmint hunting. Nosler's ExpansionTip is a lead-free copper-alloy bullet, with an O.D. green polymer tip over the patented $E2$ cavity. The tip is used to initiate expansion upon impact, driving the sidewalls outward, expanding the bullet for optimal performance. Comparing a homogenous copper alloy bullet to one of the same weight with a lead core, you'll find the former much longer than the latter. Copper is lighter than lead, and so to achieve equivalent weights, a longer projectile is needed. The E-Tip will tend to run at middle-

of-the-road weights for caliber, and all the reports show that this bullet has fantastic penetrative qualities and performance. Staying with the 'green' mentality, Nosler also offers their Ballistic Tip Varmint in a lead-free configuration, giving the same frangible jacket and explosive expansion as its lead core counterparts.

We shooters and hunters have a wide field of cartridges to choose from, so it was a risky proposition when Nosler announced their own line of proprietary cartridges. "We were slightly concerned about how they'd be received, but by the time we released the .28 Nosler — second in the series — we knew we would be okay," John explained. The Nosler big game cartridges are based on the rimless .404 Jeffery cartridge, with the walls blown out to maximize capacity, and shortened to fit in a standard .30-'06-length receiver. There are currently five, spanning from the 6.5mm 26 Nosler to the largest, the .338-caliber 33 Nosler. In addition, an AR-15 designed 22 Nosler completes the lineup.

In finishing up my conversation with John, he emphasized the importance of the people who make Nosler what it is today. "The Nosler of 2020 is like one large family unit. I'm blessed to work with my father, mother, sister and two brothers-in-law, but our team — those people who we rely on daily — are like family to us; they believe in the Nosler brand, and take their jobs very seriously. We have done our best to assemble the dream team. Guys like Jeff Bailey, Zach Waterman, Pat Mundy, Mason Payer, Mike Lake and Jeff Sipe, and there are others. We all share the same vision," John proudly stated. When I asked John what he'd say to the new shooter or hunter who asked why they should buy Nosler products, he paused for a brief second, and rather than recite some preconceived mission statement, he gave it to me straight. "We want our customers happy, and if they're not, we'll do what is necessary to make it

right. Nosler isn't the cheapest, but it represents the best value out there. There is no 'good enough' at Nosler; we strive for the absolute best."

Lastly, I asked what I thought to be an obvious question: would any of his children be following in the family footsteps? "Well, my son Robert, named after my dad, has the same engineering mindset my grandfather had, and at 10 wants to get into reloading. If he wants it, he'd certainly be a natural fit." Personally, I'd like nothing more than to see a fourth generation of Nosler continuing the tradition, and I know the Nosler family feels the same way.

For generations, the Nosler name has been synonymous with hunting. My dad introduced me to both the Partition and Ballistic Tip, and they became an integral part of our personal hunting traditions as we reloaded our ammunition. Today, I've happily brought the E-Tip and AccuBond into my lineup. As a hunter and shooter, I'm grateful for a family as dedicated to their craft as the Noslers are, and I look forward to the continuation of their tradition for innovation. John Amos Nosler's hard work, sweat and focus has been handed to his son, and in turn to his grandson, but each has a healthy respect for that which has come before, and each has made an indelible mark on the company's history as well as the shooting industry. From a brilliant sketch on a paper napkin, to one of the most innovative ammunition companies in existence, the Nosler product line will continue to help hunters around the globe make memories and put food on the table.

John Amos Nosler left this life on October 10, 2010 at 97 years old, but he still walks among us. His gift to the hunting tradition lives on in his children, grandchildren and great-grandchildren, and every time a hunter or shooter sends a Nosler bullet down their barrel. 🦌

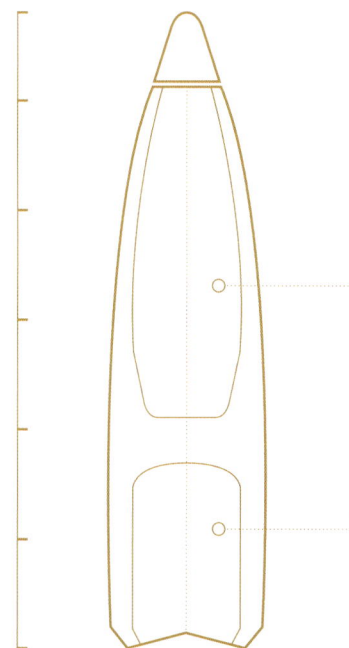

WHEN I ASKED JOHN WHAT HE'D SAY TO THE NEW SHOOTER OR HUNTER WHO ASKED WHY THEY SHOULD BUY NOSLER PRODUCTS, HE PAUSED FOR A BRIEF SECOND, AND RATHER THAN RECITE SOME PRECONCEIVED MISSION STATEMENT, HE GAVE IT TO ME STRAIGHT. "WE WANT OUR CUSTOMERS HAPPY, AND IF THEY'RE NOT, WE'LL DO WHAT IS NECESSARY TO MAKE IT RIGHT. NOSLER ISN'T THE CHEAPEST, BUT IT REPRESENTS THE BEST VALUE OUT THERE. THERE IS NO 'GOOD ENOUGH' AT NOSLER; WE STRIVE FOR THE ABSOLUTE BEST."

Image used with permission from Mike Kenny. Knoydart Keeper, circa 1890

THE FATHER OF MOUNTAIN HUNTING

STORY BY *Sam Thompson*

"William Scrope (1772 - 1852) was an English sportsman and amateur artist, known as a writer on sports..."

As far as Wikipedia introductions go, I find that a modest one. The whole article totals less than 300 words, and mentions nowhere that this man probably played a more important role in creating opportunities for hunting in wild places than anyone else in history.

William Scrope avidly fished for salmon on the famous River Tweed in the borders of Scotland, and while he was there, became friends with a number of notable Scotsmen including Sir Walter Scott, the acclaimed novelist and poet. His time in esteemed literary company, and a passion for salmon, spawned his first book, *Days and Nights of Salmon Fishing in the Tweed*. Highland Scotland at this time had a very different relationship with and standing in the world than it does now, still recovering from the 1745 Jacobite uprising, where Highland clans rallied behind the exiled Stuart Royal family. While we know that Scrope was a keen sportsman of all kinds, enjoying fox hunting and bird shooting, there are no records as to what drove him to try his hand at deer stalking, which at the time was practiced mostly by local men and the few Highland lairds that still resided in Scotland — little more than a food-gathering exercise. In the late 18th century and well into the early 19th, the land north of Edinburgh was seen as the frontier of the civilized world, in much the same way as Western America. Scrope was keen for adventure as well as recreation.

He arrived in a landscape scarred by the Highland Clearances, where large numbers of Gaels had been evicted from their homes (generally to coastal villages, North America and Australasia) to make way for larger scale farms and better economics for land owners. In the case of Glengarry, a location mentioned extensively by Scrope in his seminal work *The Art of Deerstalking*, published in 1838, the chaplain (and later Bishop) Alexander Macdonell led families away from Scottish shores to settle in Glengarry County, Ontario. Whether Scrope was unaware of this going on in the background or he consciously omitted mention in his writings is unknown; perhaps there is irony lost on the modern reader in his prose of 'untouched' land in which 'you find not a dwelling.'

The politics of history aside, there were two things that drew those with disposable time and income away from the civilized south of England and its cities at this time: the landscape and the deer. This was the era of fox hunting in Britain, where gentlemen and women followed a huntsman and a pack around the hedged and cultured English countryside. Top hats, cravats and stately homes aplenty, it held none of the intrigue that the Perthshire forests did to Scrope. Forests, in this case, were the Gaelic term nearly forgotten now, meaning a barren and empty land, not necessarily involving trees at all.

Old Ronald + dog

Image used with permission from Euan MacDonald

THE POLITICS OF HISTORY ASIDE, THERE ARE TWO THINGS THAT DRAW THOSE WITH DISPOSABLE TIME AND INCOME AWAY FROM THE CIVILIZED SOUTH OF ENGLAND AND ITS CITIES AT THIS TIME: THE LANDSCAPE AND THE DEER. THIS WAS THE ERA OF FOX HUNTING IN BRITAIN, WHERE GENTLEMEN AND WOMEN FOLLOWED A HUNTSMAN AND A PACK AROUND THE HEDGED AND CULTURED ENGLISH COUNTRYSIDE.

While Scrope stalked and explored various parts of the Highlands in his time, the majority of his experience and writing focuses on the Atholl Estate in Perthshire. About 80 miles north of Edinburgh, comprising four deer forests, it amounted to some 190,000 acres. Hunting had long been a part of the estate, with records of deer drives carried out as early as 1529 during a visit by King James V. Accounts at the time talk of hundreds of tenants making a line over four miles long to surround over a thousand deer and drive them to the waiting royalty and peers of the realm. In July of 1822, Sir Walter Scott wrote a letter on behalf of Scrope, introducing him to the 7th Duke as a prospective sporting tenant. The letter is still kept in the archives at Blair Castle, the home of the Duke of Atholl to this day.

———

EDINBURGH, 9 JULY 1822

My Lord Duke,

I take the liberty to intrude these lines on your Grace at the request of Mr Scrope of Castlecombe, an English Gentleman of family and fortune, who has been for many years my neighbour in Roxburghshire during the fishing season. Having become an offerer to your Grace's Agent for some ground which he is desirous to take, chiefly with the purpose of shooting, he naturally supposes that if his proposal should be agreeable in other respects, your Grace may desire to know something of his personal character. From the acquaintance of many years I am able to say that Mr Scrope is not only a perfect Gentleman, and incapable of indulging his love of sport otherwise than as becomes one, but that he is of highly cultivated taste and understanding as well as much accomplishments.

Trusting that your Grace's goodness will excuse this intrusion, I venture to add my respects to my Lady Duchess, and have the honor to be,

My Lord Duke, Your Grace's most obedient humble Servant,

Walter Scott

———

Top: *Atholl Keepers in the mid 1800's.*
From the Collection at Blair Castle, Perthshire

Bottom: *Return of the deer stalkers, Sir Edwin Henry Landseer, 1827.*
With thanks to owner Dr. Raymond Matte in Sherbrooke, QC, Canada.

In 1823, Scrope took residence in Bruar Lodge at Atholl, and gathered a small army of locals to assist him in his quest. From the lodge, with his caravan of local men and boys hired as porters, hawks, dogs, fishing rods and guns, Scrope traveled and hunted his way between tented camps around the forest for the next decade. In this way, and with the assistance of some local foresters, he learned the skills of a deer stalker.

Though sometimes accompanied by friends from farther south, Scrope often hunted on his own and always without a guide. To him, the attraction in this newfound pursuit was in his own skill. Working with nature was foreign to Victorian gentlemen for the most part, but something Scrope found vital. Recording his escapades became the basis for *The Art of Deerstalking* and the inspiration for Queen Victoria and Prince Albert to visit Atholl and then purchase Balmoral Castle years later, so Prince Albert would have his own land to hunt in the same fashion. Mixed with stories of the hill, and detailed descriptions of deer, stalking techniques and deer forests around the Highlands, the literary collection of these escapades made a formidable guide book for other hunters seeking adventure.

Soon others followed suit, intrigued by these wild lands of mountains and deer. Grimble, Chalmers, St John and others joined the Lords, Ladies and Dukes that took a new interest in the wild Highland hunt, renting and buying estates of their own to make sporting paradises. The late 19th century saw countless estates turn into deer forests, with grander and grander lodges being built all over the highlands. This period, known as "Balmoralism" after Queen Victoria's creation of Balmoral Castle in 1853, threw hunting into the center of Scottish culture. For the gentry of London, Paris, Berlin, Moscow and New York, heading to Scotland in the autumn in pursuit of stags, grouse shooting, and fishing was the most fashionable pilgrimage one could make.

While it's easy to look back on this period of hunting history and wonder how it applies to the pursuit we see today, this change in hunting culture was significant. These were men and women who first championed fair chase hunting, and were the first real sportsmen as we see them today. Previous to this, sport hunting was always a matter of game being chased toward waiting hunters or the hunter coursing the game on horseback. Deer stalking was the first form that championed not strength or speed, but guile and cunning, being at one with nature rather than trying to better it. Scrope extolled the virtue of imitating the animals around him; the antelope, eel and greyhound are all related to the competent deer stalker by Scrope — just as they could be today.

The ethics of pitting the hunter directly against their quarry without assistance soon spread into Europe, where hunting chamois in the alps followed a very similar form. It then made the jump over the ocean to North America, with the great fathers of the North American Model of conservation bringing the ethics of the noblemen to the American public with the Boone & Crockett Club. In Scotland, the legacy of the Victorian patronage lives on too, but the stalking has changed. Scrope and his original group of compatriots were lucky in the luxury of being able to spend entire hunting seasons in the mountains, but the people who followed them were not.

Royalty and captains of industry had other things to do beside learning the techniques and assays of the deer stalker, and so they employed local men to guide them in their hunting season and look after the deer populations through the rest of the year — hunting predators and poachers with equal resolution. Clad in uniforms of tweed, with patterns unique to their estate, these armies of gamekeepers built pony paths through the mountains to aid extraction of harvested deer, bolstered populations by introducing animals from prized blood-lines, and honed the craft of understanding and managing deer.

Some things pass, and some things remain. There are few gentlemen who still stalk deer in the Highlands without a guide, and the term Deer Stalker is now used to denote a professional deer manager and guide, with the traveling sportsman called the guest. Our management ideas have changed too, with a focus now not on carrying the largest number of deer, but instead the optimum carrying capacity of the limited land, with a focus on making our environment and hunt as sustainable as possible. Without the deep pockets of industrialists and nobility in many places, stalking now has become a commercial business that pays for employment and conservation in these otherwise unprofitable wild places, open to anyone able to travel and pay.

Scotland's game laws exist without a tag system and with limited government intervention. We are allowed to manage our cull numbers and herds as the landowner sees fit. With the vast majority of owners honouring the traditional principles of fair chase and responsible management, this system operates with some debate and disagreement, which is inevitable when there are many different management objectives.

Thankfully, our management practice of selection has remained. In Scotland, the most honour and pride has always been placed in shooting not the largest animal, but the eldest or the one with the weakest genetics — a trophy of the poorest animal. Particular emphasis is placed on the shooting of 'switch' stags; an animal that grows antlers without tines — historically referred to as 'murder' or simply 'killing' stags. At the rut, these are the animals most likely to kill or maim the better stags of superior genetics and fitness, so they are the least wanted in the herd. The shooting of good stags is actively frowned upon, and the decision of the Deer Stalker is always final. Woe betide the guest who shoots a larger stag than he is told to.

While most estates have changed hands many times since Scrope put pen to ink, the average estate in the upland red deer range is still estimated at 14,000 acres, allowing some measure of landscape scale conservation to flourish. Private ownership often means large injections of money into conservation and improvement programs — work that would likely be cripplingly expensive if funded by the government. Very few upland estates manage to break even year over year, let alone turn a profit, and so our conservation and land management relies on estate owners and visiting sportsmen who pay to come and stalk deer. Often surprisingly cheap, this

means that deer stalking now is more accessible to the public than ever before. It's possible to go stalking in the Highlands for as little as 200 pounds for a day.

As wildlife management changes, constantly evolving with the latest science, environmental changes and political pressures, it is perhaps strange that many of us in Scotland still champion a system such as our own. Maybe there is an element of clinging to what we know, but the benefit to this voluntary principal of management is that it is entirely flexible to local pressures and conditions.

The Deer Stalker of today is a blend of many roles. He is a hunter, a trapper, an ecologist, a guide, a foreman and often more, but the best deer stalkers are the ones who have mastered those skills writen about by Scrope in his book so many years ago. As Scrope did, they aim to learn and understand deer and how they move, considering the conditions, the landscape and the effect that their actions today will have on the herd tomorrow. The experience given to stalking guests in the modern era is, of course, different from those of the early years (the Scotland of those days was possibly more comparable to Tajikistan today) but the stalking remains the same — man working with nature, to harvest a worthy and challenging adversary. ⚐

SIBERIAN DAYS

WORDS BY *Jack Evans*   ILLUSTRATIONS BY *Dani Vergés*

Some of the most important human knowledge cannot be researched. It must be encountered.

Before they were two of Denmark's foremost scientists, Rane and Eske Willerslev spent their youths living voluntarily in the cold expanses of Siberia as hunters and trappers. They bared themselves to a harsh and beautiful life for reasons once known only to themselves--and to each other. The identical twins were brought to the edges of survival, by choice and by vision.

The challenges of the tundra opened the secret doors in their minds to the incredible discoveries each have made of who we are as a species. More than books, more than data, it was hunting, trapping, survival and friendships in the wildlands of the farthest East that brought revelation to the Willerslev twins. But there are mysteries, still, to be uncovered. We sat down with them last summer to find out how the brightest insights are borne of wonder, risk and immersion.

RANE

Imeet Rane Willerslev outside the National Museum of Denmark, a 17th-century mansion among the canals of Copenhagen. He greets me excitedly, and we head up a maze of stone staircases. By the time we reach a palatial dining hall, his office, the stories have already begun.

"So we are hiding in the grass, and the translator just looks at me all crazy-eyed and points and says, 'Poachers—run!' And it's like I've never run faster in my life!"

He's recounting a recent work trip to Uganda.

Before becoming the Director of the National Museum, Rane was an anthropologist, a professor and, before all that, a fur trapper in Siberia. Though born in Denmark, he's spent years of his life living with indigenous hunter-gatherer societies, drawn almost helplessly to the raw tundra's world of revelations. Immersions in Siberia that began when he was eighteen have laden him with questions: How do these remote societies thrive in the most desperate physical conditions? How does their belief in animism, in the realm of spirits, keep them so purposefully alive? When they talk to moose in their dreams, and hunt them with success the next morning, what are they really seeing?

At the height of our conversation, he leans in, telling me this story:

"I was out in Kamchatka, Russia, with this Chukchi reindeer herder, and we are walking along the shore when he suddenly stops. And he picks a small stone up off the ground, and he's completely stunned. His mouth is open. He is completely made a child by this stone. And I watch him, but then we go on walking. The next day, we wake up and I see that he's sewn it into his belt like an amulet. So I ask him: 'What is this?' And he says: 'This is my second heart. And I know that because when I saw this stone, my heart started beating so wild, so fast. If my first heart stops beating, my second heart will go on.'"

We stare at each other, wide-eyed.

"I mean, how to understand that?" Rane shouts. "How do you begin to comprehend something so different as that?"

What the Chukchi man himself sees is one of the great mysteries for Western society. Rane, in his lifelong efforts to relate to hunter-gatherers, has provided modern anthropology with its most intimate illumination of this animist worldview and revolutionized the study of human-animal relationships along the way. It's not because he's the sharpest or most articulate. It's because he began to dream of moose after years of surviving on the tundra; because he nearly died when he ignored the advice of shamans. It's because he immersed in the lifeways of others, lost relationships, fought depression, trusted his visions and straddled two worlds. The raw, demanding, inexplicable life of a subsistence hunter does not balance with the rational, socialized home life of Denmark. Rane's contribution has been as a translator between them.

At 49, he is still irrepressible.

"Basically, in the beginning, my brother Eske and I were driven by adventure, which they laughed about at my department when I started anthropology. But I think that's the drive of science, it's the drive of curiosity, it's the drive of everything! It's like, man, there's this world out there that is unknown — Hell, *I would like to get to know it!*"

ESKE

Eske Willerslev and I meet in a crowded coffee shop outside Copenhagen. It's a summer weekend, so he's free from his work as the Director of the Centre for Geogenetics at the University. The cafe's a noisy, come-and-go type of place, but I notice a few customers linger around us—overhearing Eske's stories.

He speaks of recovering ancient Greenlandic ice mummies and sharing councils with Aboriginal Australians. In the course of the conversation we discuss the entire migration of early humans out of Africa like it's a film script. The stories fill the space, and one rolls into the next as Eske lays out vast maps of explanations and questions.

"I'm fascinated by how the differences between people created who we are. Both in terms of time and space — I mean, how did we get the distribution of humans we have today? How did we get the similarities between Siberians and Native Americans culturally? How did we get the similarities genetically? It's really a question of understanding 'Who are we?' as modern humans, right?

As a geneticist, Eske is a pioneer in the study of ancient DNA. He was the first person to sequence an ancient human genome, and the first to obtain ancient DNA directly from ice cores of permafrost. His research on megafauna has changed the way we imagine their extinction. His work continually rewrites history, refining our understanding of the human past.

Eske shares the tone of urgent, excited curiosity with his twin brother Rane, as well as the fixation on great mysteries.

"We obviously have a lot of shared history, with the early expeditions, both of us living as trappers, and then genetically we are identical, right? For those reasons, a lot of our thinking is very similar to each other's. I mean, he chose a humanities angle. I chose a natural sciences angle. But the questions we've addressed are very similar."

The questions they've addressed have the same origin, too. Throughout their youth in suburban Copenhagen, they dreamed of becoming explorers. At the first opportunity, upon turning eighteen, they headed to Eastern Siberia. That was where the inspiration flooded in.

ESKE WILLERSLEV

I'M FASCINATED BY HOW THE DIFFERENCES BETWEEN PEOPLE CREATED WHO WE ARE. BOTH IN TERMS OF TIME AND SPACE — I MEAN, HOW DID WE GET THE DISTRIBUTION OF HUMANS WE HAVE TODAY? HOW DID WE GET THE SIMILARITIES BETWEEN SIBERIANS AND NATIVE AMERICANS CULTURALLY? HOW DID WE GET THE SIMILARITIES GENETICALLY? IT'S REALLY A QUESTION OF UNDERSTANDING 'WHO ARE WE?' AS MODERN HUMANS, RIGHT?

Eske

ESKE: As a child, I really just wanted to be a Native American. You get a bit older and realize you can't do that, but I still wanted to find some place where there was still *wilderness*. So Rane and I started making expeditions, first a trip to northern Scandinavia, to the Arctic, with some friends when we were thirteen. The others turned around but we kept going, and every year we went on these trips around Scandinavia with the whole idea, from my point of view, to prepare myself to become a trapper

RANE: The drive for all of this basically comes from these imaginations in childhood. It was built up by my brother and I in this bubble world — none of our friends nor our environment encouraged it in any way. We mutually created this fantasy about becoming explorers. The most wild place that you could imagine then was the Northwest Territories in Canada. The big trip was supposed to take place after we finished high school. We would take one year off and then go to Canada.

But at that point, Gorbachev was in power in Russia and the Soviet Union suddenly kind of ... opened. Suddenly there was this possibility, theoretically, that we could enter northeastern Siberia, which was completely unknown to the Western world.

There was very little literature in English, too, almost none. But there was this book that became very important for us, which is called *The Yukaghir and the Yukaghirized Tungus*, by a Russian guy named Waldemar Jochelson.

Jochelson was a Communist exile at the end of the 1800s, under the Czar. Because he had nothing to do there in exile, he started studying these indigenous peoples in Siberia. Then he became part of Franz Boas' big project called the Jesup North Pacific expedition, which had fieldworks going on both in Eastern Siberia and in Alaska. The idea was to try to find the connection between Asia and the Americas. This very small group, the Yukaghir, were interesting for Jochelson because they were living only as hunters when pretty much everyone else in Siberia had become pastoralists.

We found this book, and we knew we wanted to find the Yukaghir.

ESKE: For all kinds of reasons, Jochelson speculated a possible relationship to Native Americans, so I already started thinking about this. We went to the Russian embassy and they said no, forget about it. Then we went to this Russian-Danish friendship union, some kind of Communist thing in Denmark connected to Russia, and they said no, forget about it. And then, in this kind of suspect bar in Copenhagen, I met this guy who was buying seeds from people around Lake Baikal, in Irkutsk. I talked to him about our idea and he said, 'I think I have the contacts who can do this.' So we paid him some money; our childhood savings were basically being transferred to Russia, and it turned out later on it was some pretty dodgy stuff. It was some kind of mafia operation. My brother and I didn't have much more money, so we got a couple of other guys to join us.

RANE: We put an ad in the Danish newspaper and ended up picking two guys who were really wackos. One was a forester whom we later found out was a member of a very radical right-wing party, of course, and the other was a former lieutenant in the army. Then we got two Russians to join. One was a trapper from Irkutsk, a very charming guy actually with this huge beard. He was a professional hunter so he had a rifle and kind of became the leader of the expedition. And the other one was a professor of religion from Irkutsk University who just wanted to go to the wilderness and die because his wife had left him. We would take the Trans-Siberian Railroad to Irkutsk, and then would be flown to the Omolon River, where we'd be put out in the mountains to canoe to the Lena River and get picked up there.

ESKE: I can see now that already when we did the first expeditions, I had this scientific mind. We both did — I mean, we were never interested in being the first to go to a mountaintop or something. It wasn't a sport expedition. We were interested in collecting woolly mammoth bones, you know, megafauna bones. It was an amazing experience. I mean, we didn't meet any Yukaghir on this trip, but we were picking up ethnographic materials, fossils, incredible stuff.

RANE: The maps were completely unreliable; there were supposed to be villages, and there was nothing out there. We meet one group of reindeer herders near the Arctic Ocean, and on the second river we don't meet anybody whatsoever. When we are picked up after these three-and-a-half months, the pilot says the Soviet Union has collapsed! At that point, they don't know if there will be a civil war. The two Russians were completely in shock, because for Russians it was unimaginable that the Soviet Union would disappear. But that was the beginning.

The brothers were entranced. Over the next four years, they kept returning to Siberia to meet the people and gather the bones of ancient megafauna. Rane had plans to study anthropology, in Denmark, to more deeply investigate and publish what they'd witnessed in the tundra peoples. Eske, meanwhile, took up biology.

ESKE: The questions that rose in my head were about how you get this diversity of people in northeastern Siberia with all these different languages, these different lifestyles. What is the relationship to Native Americans? Why did the megafauna, the mammoth, the bison, the wild horses die out? I mean, today, you have very few big-bodied mammals in these parts of the world. During the Ice Age it was like the African Savannah. So these questions are exactly what I've been working with afterward, right? It really defined my line of research.

RANE: During canoe journeys I got really interested in the native people. When we met them — and that was rarely — I always sat down and tried to talk to them. Eske, though, was more interested in all the mammoth bones that we collected on the shore banks, so the differences in approach were already established at that point.

A year after the expedition I dropped out of university — completely disillusioned. Anthropology was in this postmodern crisis where everyone's saying that indigenous knowledge is just a Western invention, and the teachers think I'm ridiculous with this Yukaghir and hunter-gatherer obsession.

The next expedition we made was to Kamchatka, in '92. Then in the winter of '92, I wanted to return to Kamchatka to marry a Chukchi girl I'd fallen in love with, but I don't have the money to fly there. So I took the Trans-Siberian Railroad to the northern Altai Mountains, where I lived as a hunter — first with a group called the Shors and then with some Russian poachers. I lived for six months with them, and I actually learned quite a lot about hunting! But then Eske gets a telegram out to me …

He said, "You have to come back, we are going on a big expedition to the Kolyma River. We've got the permissions, and a film crew will be coming along."

And this time, we find the Yukaghir.

The Yukaghir are hunter-gatherers in the truest sense. They live in the coldest human settlement in the world. They eat from moose, and trap sable to buy hunting equipment. In their small society, every resource is shared evenly throughout the group. There is no hierarchy. Even the most successful hunters are wary of accumulating wealth — angering the animal spirits, as they describe it. Their complex and ever-evolving belief in spiritual relationships is the basis of their survival and knowledge. Both Rane and Eske began a lifelong education in the Yukaghirs' principles.

ESKE: We went to where Jochelson had reported the Yukaghirs at the Kolyma River. The most exciting person we met there was a guy called Nikolai Nikolaivich, who was the last survivor of the Korgodon group of Yukaghirs. They had basically died out. Nikolai was moving to Nelemnoye, the only settlement of the other band of hunters, the forest Yukaghir.

RANE: It's the most intimate meeting I've had with native people. And it's weird because we have been waiting for this for so long, you know? But it's also as if they have been waiting for us. It's like they feel that their relationship to us might be of great importance. It's very ... sort of ... *full of love* between the Yukaghir and Eske and me.

We get these very close relationships to certain individuals, like the old woman Akulina, who becomes my grandmother and sews all my reindeer clothing when I go to live as a trapper there. We go on this expedition for three months and become very close with them, and Eske stays all winter to trap with them.

We can see that their economy has collapsed completely. During Soviet times, every industry that could generate foreign cash had special support. So the fur companies were subsidized by the state, and a fur trapper was making more than a medical doctor in Moscow. They were flown out by helicopter into the wilderness where they would trap for almost seven, eight months a year. They'd return their furs and have a plan to get groceries and supplies — everything was actually working quite well during Soviet times. All of that disappeared.

It's replaced by another monopoly, but now it's called the *Sakhabult*, and they're buying furs at these fixed low prices and never delivering supplies. They're corrupt all the way. So the idea comes to create this alternative for them; I want to create this nonprofit so the Yukaghir can sell their furs directly to the Danish fur auction house, which is the biggest in the world, actually.

I returned to do fieldwork as part of my PhD and lived for a year with the hunters. No Westerner had lived as a hunter like this. Of course, you can find descriptions of anthropologists living with some communities and going hunting now and then, but this was about living intensely *only as a hunter*, as the men there do. They had never experienced someone who came to live their way of life and actually help them. So I began trying to create this fur cooperative project. It completely shaped everything that's happened since.

———

IT'S THE MOST INTIMATE MEETING I'VE HAD WITH NATIVE PEOPLE. AND IT'S WEIRD BECAUSE WE HAVE BEEN WAITING FOR THIS FOR SO LONG, YOU KNOW? BUT IT'S ALSO AS IF THEY HAVE BEEN WAITING FOR US. IT'S LIKE THEY FEEL THAT THEIR RELATIONSHIP TO US MIGHT BE OF GREAT IMPORTANCE. IT'S VERY... SORT OF ... FULL OF LOVE BETWEEN THE YUKAGHIR AND ESE AND ME.

Rane

Rane began travelling between two worlds — the anthropology studies he had returned to in Denmark and Britain, and the Yukaghir settlement of Nelemnoye 4,000 miles away. He would carry on for years, trying to establish the nonprofit fur trade between Yukaghir trappers and the Danish buyers. Meanwhile, Eske stayed behind for an immersion in the trappers' existence.

ESKE: This is the first event where I almost lost my life.

Regular temperatures in the winter are minus 40, 50, 60 degrees Celsius, and we were flown out there in a helicopter and dumped with some guns, dogs, tea, and the rest we basically had to get for ourselves. And I tell you, I was in top shape because we had been on the expedition, and in the beginning I was so tired that I couldn't eat.

It was all so fucking brutal. I mean it was wonderful in the sense that it was a very simple way of life — sleep, kill, eat. That's it. All the normal worries you have disappear. But there, an individual life is valued very little. I was pushing my limits and we were taking risks every day, man. I mean, one day we came back to the cabin and one of our dogs was eaten by wolves. There was just a tail lying there in a pile of blood …

At one point, we needed to get some meat, so I went out moose hunting. It was -30 C, early in the winter, but there's so little precipitation there that the snow was still patchy. I lost my track. I couldn't find the camp. It became dark and I realized I had to spend the night out there.

And you know, I've almost *tried* to lose my life on some occasions, but this was a situation where it was a very slow death I was facing, so I really had time to think about it… and it's exactly as you hear from old people who are dying. Suddenly, family relationships, relationships to your girlfriend—those kinds of things become important. Your career, all that, it doesn't matter. I came to the conclusion that I'd led my life completely wrongly. I thought I'd be really

afraid because I'm not that brave, but I wasn't afraid. I was just very sad.

I didn't have much fire, not much wood, and it became so cold. What happens first is you're freezing, you're shaking, but then it becomes completely warm. You feel like you want to take off your clothes. And then you become tremendously tired, I mean to a level that is indescribable. I knew that if I fell asleep then I was probably gone, so I had to keep awake, thinking: *just ten seconds* of sleep, ten seconds … But it's just so dangerous. Still, I managed, and the other guys were out looking for me. We found each other the next morning, firing shots in the air.

I should have been back by Christmas, but the guy who was supposed to send the helicopter went bankrupt, so he didn't even send one. I remember we had run out of petrol for our lamps, we hadn't had success with hunting for a while so there wasn't enough meat, we were running out of tea, and I was just sitting there Christmas Evening with a cup of boiled water, and I was just crying.

I'm glad I did it, but it was a *very rough experience.*

———

AND YOU KNOW, I'VE ALMOST TRIED TO LOSE MY LIFE ON SOME OCCASIONS, BUT THIS WAS A SITUATION WHERE IT WAS A VERY SLOW DEATH I WAS FACING...

Eske

A Chukchi hunter from the Anadyr region of Chukotka. Based on a photo by Casper Dalhoff, taken on expedition with Rane Willerslev in 2004.

Rane's efforts to establish the fur cooperative were effectively a well-intentioned attempt to work around the Russian State monopoly. In the middle of the project's development, the police confiscated a stockpile of sable furs and approached Nelemnoye to arrest Rane. The village came together to rush Rane into the wilderness. He hid there for nine months, facing the harshest reality of survival possible. He wrote a memoir of this time entitled On the Run in Siberia, and in it recalls his hungriest, most despairing moment, facing death, when he penned a letter to his brother. It reads:

Our dad impressed on us from an early age that the desire for knowledge is the most important thing. You sought it through biology, and I through anthropology. And we both sought it in the Siberian wilds. But the actual goal of our strenuous journeys has not been science but just each other. For your sake, I wanted to research the Yukaghirs. For my sake, you had to find the mammoth's DNA. Only people who do not understand what it means to be identical twins would call it mutual competition. Whether or not we ever see each other again, the two of us are really all there has ever been.

Rane survived that winter, learning that the Yukaghirs' every "superstition," ritual, animal communication and dream premonition, were indispensable to survival in the desolate landscape. This time of desperate flight became an immersion in the lifeworld of animism, where rivers, forests and moose all have humanlike "shadows," spirits that must be respected and spoken to. As a subsistence hunter, learning from his Yukaghir teachers over the months, Rane encountered the strangest, most surprising phenomena of their ways.

RANE: The ideal hunting technique among the Yukaghir is this one where you can hunt the moose by imitating it. First, you go to this sauna built of sticks and get all the human smell out of your body. Then you go to sleep and dream with this small figurine, the half-man-half-moose, which is a replication of your ... we would call it soul. They call it shadow, which is your spiritual doppelganger that travels to the moose spirit, who is a woman, and has sex with her. The next day you go outside and make the track and the moose comes close by. You start imitating it.

It's basically a technique where you move your body from side to side, you have skis that are covered underneath with leg skin from a moose, and you can imitate the sound. From our rational perspective, we would say: "Okay, he moves to imitate the moose so that it thinks he's another moose, and therefore, he can kill it." From their viewpoint, the animal is seeing itself as a human, you know, a person, choosing to come to the hunter. When I first saw it I was puzzled by it, because it worked. I mean, when I saw Old Spiridon — who is like the master of moose hunting — do it, he took control over the moose. It was almost as if it was hypnotized. I was told how he once got a moose to run around the camp and then collapse in front of the fire. I've seen him doing it in the tundra.

In the animist worldview, everything outside yourself has intentions, you know? Even with the mushrooms that the Chukchi pick to get high — they say, 'The mushroom chooses if I am going to pick it, it's not me choosing the mushroom.' It's amazing. Learning these things is not about knowing yourself. It's about knowing the world. It's not like yoga or meditation or something where you try to find meaning by going inside yourself. Here you find meaning by reading the landscape.

When you're hunting this way, animals become persons or potential persons because ... it's weird, but even though everything is animated in principle, not everything that is animated chooses to interact with you. If you imagine going into a crowd of people, not everyone will look at you. Not everyone will relate to you at that moment. But the moment someone relates to you, there's a different type of relationship going on. So I think one has to understand the hunt as if a certain constellation creates an encounter between hunter and prey.

I actually ended up becoming really good at it, but it really changes your perception of the world. I mean, they said I would see dancing people in the forest and that kind of stuff, and I didn't. But this thing about the dreams where, you know, the spirits are coming ... this whole hunter's logic completely became a part of me.

———

"BY TRANSFORMING HIMSELF INTO THE IMAGE OF THE MOOSE, HE COMES TO SEE THE WORLD AS THE ANIMAL SEES IT. HOWEVER, THE DANGER OF UNDERGOING A COMPLETE TRANSFORMATION IS ALWAYS PRESENT, SO YOU HAVE TO BE VIGILANT WHEN YOU TRANSFORM YOURSELF INTO AN ANIMAL. THERE ARE SEVERAL ACCOUNTS OF HUNTERS WHO NEVER RETURN TO THEIR ORIGINAL HUMAN FORM BUT GO ON LIVING WITH THE ANIMALS."

Rane Wilerslev, On the Run in Siberia

Rane was able to return to Denmark, over a year later, after a Yukaghir representative appealed to the Putin administration to clear his arrest warrant. He carried a heavy sense of failure from his naivety with the fur project. His girlfriend had left him for another man. "Not only am I exhausted and lonely," he writes in *On the Run*, "but I go around with an agonizing sense of having neglected something vital: love." He also carried incredible insights into the Yukaghirs' animal relationships. Thus, like Eske, he embarked on the most difficult part of the journey — coming home. The brothers each had to reconcile two disparate existences. They had to speak their truth to a world of Western academia that shuns spiritual sensibility and demands hard proofs for all knowledge.

RANE: Writing my PhD became kind of necessary, because you have to turn your experiences into a narrative as a way to make sense of things. It's a real struggle to connect it, though. I mean, I came back to Cambridge to just sit there, like a monk, and I was very depressed pretty much the whole time.

I remember when I was walking in the street and just saw a piece of string in the road, I would pick it up and put it in my pocket. I was just so accustomed to using everything, you know? Every tin can. And these spirit visions kept coming ...

It was important that Eske and I had each other, because we kind of convinced each other to keep doing these things. The biggest challenge was that we were surrounded by a world that wanted to pull it apart. And it was difficult to keep up, because who was going to believe and support it?

If you are really committed to something — and we were really committed to that type of life — then you can get the greatest, most amazing wonders and experiences, but you also pay a price on the other side.

ESKE: All this is a matter of challenging yourself in order to challenge your own worldview. I mean, in the end, I would say I became at least almost crazy out there. Sometimes you're going along on your skis and it's completely silent. Because the trees are a larix species, they lose their needles in the winter. It's just a dead landscape, with these endless sticks in the snow. You're alone and it completely does not sound right. And then, I mean, I could hear birds singing in the spring in Denmark. And I look around and I see glimpses of green Danish forest and I just think: shit, man. This is not good.

So when I came back from life as a trapper, I had real problems adapting. You go from this extreme where it's all about survival, to here, where if you walk outside there's a sign that warns you: "Sidewalk ends in five meters, please be careful." Everything's so secured. I remember sitting in a genetics exam thinking how pointless it all seemed. I thought about going back to Siberia. It was a life-defining moment, because I knew if I went, I would probably never really return to Denmark. Or I could stay here and adapt. I chose the latter, but ... I was even facing suicide. I was just really far out. I mean, I completely lost purpose in life, for a year or so.

But I decided to finish my studies. During my masters, I completely kind of ... fell in love with science.

———

IF YOU ARE REALLY COMMITTED TO SOMETHING — AND WE WERE REALLY COMMITTED TO THAT TYPE OF LIFE — THEN YOU CAN GET THE GREATEST, MOST AMAZING WONDERS AND EXPERIENCES, BUT YOU ALSO PAY A PRICE ON THE OTHER SIDE.

Rane

Surviving the return home, Rane completed his PhD, a totally original integration of Yukaghir animist vision into the rigid theoretical doctrines of anthropology. His work was the first to study these beliefs in an entirely respectful way — treating the perspective of the animist hunters as unquestionably legitimate knowledge. He couldn't have done so without living it. The work, collected in his book Soul Hunters, is an essential text in the emergent field of human-animal anthropology.

Meanwhile, Eske made a series of discoveries that helped explain the extinction of the great Eurasian mammals, then some that allowed for the testing of ancient human genomes. He, too, began to answer his earliest questions, and in the following decades traveled from Siberia to Montana to Australia, testing genetic samples from ancient and living human bodies alike, assembling the map of how humans moved and changed over the millennia.

ESKE: I've been back to Siberia on multiple occasions, taking sediment DNA. One of the first things I did was discover that you can take sediments, permafrost, and ice cores, and you can actually retrieve the DNA and find out what animals and plants were living there right back in time. So I've been back taking sediment cores all over. I've also been working with Native Americans in different places in the United States to understand that side of the human relationship — you also need the American part of it. But we were also in Australia, in Southeast Asia, in Africa, assembling that big picture from my methodology.

We did the first ancient human genome back in 2010. That was from the oldest human remains from Greenland, which were 4,000 years old. This is kind of that approach that we have then used all over the world, anywhere we can.

It's been super interesting with the Native Americans, the Aboriginal Australians, because there's a lot of ethics that connect to this. There is still massive resistance to genetic research among indigenous groups. It's understandable. I mean, science has treated them like shit, completely. Many scientists have tried to engage with these groups because genetically they're super unique and important, and they carry this deep knowledge that is also indispensable. But

there's rightfully a tremendous skepticism of Western scientists coming into their groups to perform research.

There, it has been a major benefit for me to have been living as a trapper. In meeting these indigenous peoples, we have very easily found common ground. Having this hunting experience and bush background means that we can talk about things that we both have in common, that we're both passionate about. That makes a huge difference.

I've come to the conclusion that this line of work has to happen with the endorsement of the indigenous groups. I mean, ethics is about taking into account the people today that might be affected by your result. There, I think I have used a lot of my experience from Siberia.

And from this research, we can see now that the story, genetically, of the inhabitation of Siberia is very different from what we thought.

The Yukaghir, as it turns out, are genetically far removed from Native Americans. There were actually several waves of human migration across Russia toward the Americas. Eske not only pioneered the technical means for obtaining the DNA that rewrote this history, but also excelled in bridging the gaps in trust between cultures, bringing a deferential respect to societies with entirely different perspectives, values and knowledge. He tells the story of an ancient human body found in Spirit Cave, Nevada that he sampled after obtaining personal permission from the Paiute-Shoshone tribe. His research proved that the man was, as the tribe expected, their ancestor.

Eske: I went to the reburial ceremony for the Spirit Cave Man, and a lot of scientists say that these reburials are just a way for Native Americans to get political attention. That's totally wrong; it's like burying your mother. It's the same intensely emotional feelings that you might not be able to understand because you're burying remains that are 10,000 years old, but you have to acknowledge them and respect them. That's exactly where your mind expands, when you are part of this. It's what the fieldwork does. If you just get the samples shipped to your lab, you will never understand how these people feel.

Rane: There is a difference between *knowing* and *understanding*. I can know that there are 5.5 million people in Denmark, it's a fact, but that doesn't mean I can understand them, too. To understand them implies that you invest something of yourself into that relationship with them.

I'm still trying to understand: What is rebirth in these societies? What beings are living; what are dead; what are animals; what are humans? It's kind of a never-ending exploration, and there's no way that my method can absolutely prove what they think or believe in. But I can certainly experience, as close as I can, an indigenous hunter's perspective by living with him and doing what he's doing, month after month, year after year. That might not be looked upon as *scientific* knowledge by a hardcore scientist, but it's certainly knowledge. And it's important knowledge.

This is the gap in which culture evolves and life is lived, and you can *only* get into that gap by investing yourself in the relationship with people, not studying them through questionnaires or statistics. The greatest advantage of anthropology is its intersubjective foundation, where you go out and live with people and you *take it in*. We use concepts that the natives have developed to destabilize *our* worldview.

What drives me is a real potential for our society to learn from these people. We cannot adopt their ways in a one-to-one relationship, but I think the fascinating thing is the radical *otherness* that we can use to rethink our own relationships with nature and in our societies. We need this radical otherness to reinvent ourselves.

———

OFTEN, HUNTERS THEMSELVES CANNOT DESCRIBE THE LOGIC OR CAUSALITY OF THESE THINGS. BUT I HAVE LEARNED THAT THE INTIMACY BETWEEN HUNTER AND PREY CREATES A TYPE OF KNOWLEDGE. IT'S NOT FACTUAL KNOWLEDGE, BUT IT'S A TYPE OF INSIGHT YOU COULDN'T GET WITHOUT THAT RELATIONSHIP.

Rane

Rane and Eske's lives have been a near-constant pursuit of self-reinvention and the risking of their comfortable perspectives, as well as their safety and sanity. What they've brought back to the West's understanding, though, is incomparable.

ESKE: What is so beautiful about going out there is that you are challenged and you are changed. It means you become much wiser, not only for your science but for your story. Who you are as an individual is so important for the research you're doing.

RANE: I've still had difficulties communicating all of this. Because I've tried to explain shamanism and animism and the belief that the world is full of spirits, journalists will often ask me if I believe in the supernatural. That question is kind of absurd to me, because for hunters it's not a question of belief, you know? It's like a technique to make things happen.

I have a tree at my summer house in Sweden with the skull of a bear I killed on it. I give presents to it when I go hunting up there — little hanging vodka bottles and colored bands and that kind of thing. If someone passed by they'd probably think there was a witch living there, but for me I use it as a technique, just like the Yukaghir hunters do.

I'm not trying to test if it's right or not. Often, hunters themselves cannot describe the logic or causality of these things. But I have learned that the intimacy between hunter and prey creates a type of knowledge. It's not *factual* knowledge, but it's a type of insight you couldn't get without that relationship.

For the Yukaghir, only what you have realized yourself, what you have actually practiced, tried out, counts as knowledge as such. So survival is about getting these experiences that create a kind of backbone on which you can trust your personal judgment.

There was a very interesting case where I was out hunting with this old Yukaghir man, and at that point I had become really skilled at reading moose tracks. We pass this track in the snow, and he says: "Can we, should we, try to run this moose down?"

I look at the track and I see that this is a completely agile, fresh moose, and I say, "No, we can't do that."

And he says, "Wrong."

I look again and I say, "No, this is fresh."

And he says, "Wrong." And so this goes on until the conversation becomes completely absurd.

I finally say, "Well, okay, you are older than me, maybe you see something I don't."

And then he laughs and says, "Don't be sad, I was just testing you. Remember that only you know, only you know what is right."

Perhaps this is the meaning of the beach pebble that the Chukchi herder picked up — his second heart.

As Westerners, we seek out and adopt the beliefs of others. We learn grand theories of how the world works, and we rely on facts, though we may not have witnessed them in action.

The Chukchi man called the stone his heart simply because he felt a link between them. Without the need for proof or the confirmation of others, he believes only and totally in what he senses. Rather than speculating on causes and effects, reasons, he takes meaning from the world as it comes to him. His heart can relate to a stone with no further explanation beyond its beating. It's not the scientific method, but it is belief, and it kept the Willerslevs alive in the wilderness. It is absolutely a part of the answer to the great question of who we are, and what we're capable of experiencing.

Curiosity took Rane and Eske to frontiers of the human experience, where the wilderness and the wild others educated them. Commitment kept them seeking, trusting, and needing their own knowledge. Sacrifice made it all real, made it felt, and made each of their discoveries deeply certain — personal. Like a right and left brain, with a shared, courageous heart, Rane and Eske have ventured into the wilderness with a ready embrace of whatever comes. They still let themselves be surprised. Can true discovery come any other way? ⚘

CULTIVATING

PERRENIALISM

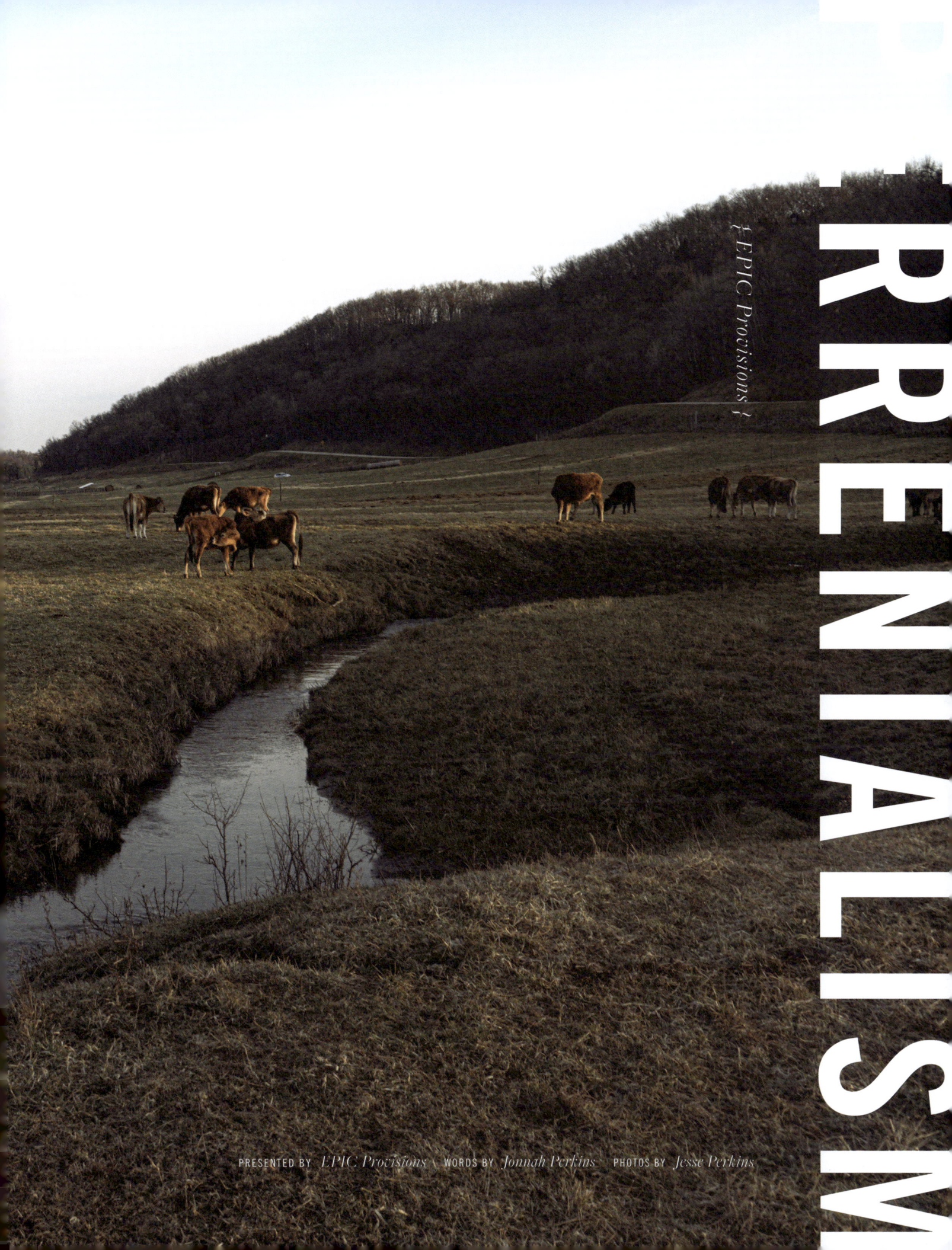

{ EPIC Provisions }

PRESENTED BY *EPIC Provisions* \ WORDS BY *Jonnah Perkins* / PHOTOS BY *Jesse Perkins*

Around the same time that humans began domesticating the wild auroch in the Near East, glaciers from the last ice age were retreating from the Upper Midwest. Vast tracts were chiseled into the windswept landscape that is recognizable across the Dakotas, Minnesota, Iowa and Wisconsin. Roughly 24,000 square miles of land were left untouched by continental glaciers, leaving behind a tangle of bluffs, forested ravines, and fertile river valleys.

Agriculture in the Driftless region of Wisconsin has a fraught history. Wetlands have been filled in, streams rerouted, and forests clear-cut to make larger contiguous tillable acreage, first for wheat production, and more recently for corn and soy. Today, thankfully, there is a growing movement away from monocropping in this region and toward holistic grazing that utilizes the nuances of the landscape instead of fighting against them. The evolving traditions of multigenerational farmers are paving a way for the return of agriculture that mimics wild biological processes, not only improving our environment, but fostering a system that supports independent farmers and rural communities.

In an economic climate where our food system is shaped from the top down with federal subsidies incentivizing commodity grain production, we're left with some big questions. Can farmers really make a living on grass-fed beef production? Can the grass-fed/grass-finished model produce enough beef for the American appetite? And there's the more existential question: can regenerative agriculture help save us from ourselves?

Richard "Dick" Cates of Cates Family Farm in Spring Green, Wisconsin, is a pioneer in the small-scale agriculture movement that has been taking root in the Midwest. In this geologically unique region, coldwater streams emanate from springs in the cracks of the bedrock. There are no natural lakes in the entire Driftless area. The pattern of rising and falling water tables has been challenging crop farmers for decades. In the late 1980s, after attending a lecture about managed grazing, Dick and his family realized that their farm could be more productive with a system that worked with the contours of the land.

"We said, that's what this farm needs. This land can grow grass, and through managed grazing it can grow even more grass on the same acreage. Over time we realized that this land used to be an extension of the Eastern Tallgrass Prairie; an oak savanna populated with grasses and oak trees. Wild ruminants helped keep the landscape open by grazing, with fire also playing a role as architect of the land. We realized that's what this landscape was meant to do. It really wasn't made for arable farming. It's not a plowable farm. So, managed grazing has been a method that's worked for the landscape," Dick explains. The Cates 110-acre farm is divided into 35 paddocks, with herds rotated daily, allowing for each pasture to rest for four weeks so grass can re-establish.

The concept of holistic, planned grazing seems to contradict itself. If humans are supposed to let the herd dictate where they graze and when they want to move, then what is the farmer's role in this system? Daniela Ibarra-Howell, CEO and Co-Founder of the Savory Institute, is a leader in the global movement to restore grassland ecosystems through holistic, managed grazing. She explains the importance of stress and recovery in grass ecosystems: "In what are called brittle environments with seasonal humidity, if plants don't get grazed properly year after year, they become stagnant and they start accumulating plant material that becomes a liability to the plant. So those plants either produce below their potential, or they die off. If they are over-grazed, ruminants will eventually kill their roots."

While this explains why it is important to manage when and where grazing livestock moves, we need to understand how nature facilitates these patterns in wild, self-managed scenarios. Dick Cates articulates how holistic planned grazing is a natural process, yet requires management. "This is a biomimicry of the way grasslands in any place on planet Earth are managed by the genetics of the large mammalian herbivores that graze those landscapes. They move in herds

according to various pressures, whether that be drought, fire or predators. Grasslands across the globe have survived and thrived through that movement. So what we're doing is mimicking that movement. Grasslands are a biome of movement. European agriculture took that movement out of the equation. When I talk about managed grazing, we're trying to do what was done in nature on our grasslands. We don't have the wolf or other predators which push the herd, but we can come and open a gate."

Human ingenuity has been trying to replace natural rhythms in our food production for centuries. If we pull back the curtain of biology, we can see webs so intricate that agronomists and food scientists are finally accepting their wisdom as laws of nature. With so much of our food production coming from systems that have been designed to strip away biological variables, it is daunting to imagine a return to diversity in a production-scale system. But this is the very work being done on holistically managed farms, small and large.

Margot Conover, EPIC Provisions' Senior Sustainability Analyst, works with ranchers through supply chain facilitation and by supporting their operations via consumer outreach, so the farmers can focus on being productive while taking cues from the natural habitats in which the farms are

located. "In any given place in the world, there's never just one thing growing or living there. There are always many species layered on top of each other — plants, animals, fungi, infects, bacteria — all kinds of little creatures interconnected and doing a job within that ecosystem. I think that's what's really exciting about holistic management and biomimicry. It looks to ecosystems for guidance on how to structure the farm system. The farm is an ecosystem, and right now, in the dominant agricultural paradigm, farms are treated as factories where maybe you have two or three crop rotations, or all the animals are totally sequestered from any other species. You would never see that in nature at all."

The realization that humans are a collaborative part of nature, and that we cannot slam our ecosystems into submission, is the great humbling lesson of our modern regenerative movement. This production philosophy can be applied to any micro-region, varying in implementation depending on the natural landscape.

Seven Seeds Farm, also in Spring Green, Wisconsin, was established in 1872 and has seen many faces of agriculture. With the strong tradition of a small, diversified dairy farm at its roots, Seven Seeds Farm followed a similar trajectory to the anthropogenic molding of the Midwest. As the viability of the family dairy operation fell out of favor for more profitable corn and soy production, many farmers sold their dairy herds, tilled over family gardens, and streamlined their time by removing hens, hogs, and open pollinated orchards. In the 1970s, Nixon-era Agriculture Secretary Earl Butz urged farmers to "get big or get out" and plant "fence row to fence row." This commodity mindset dried up diversity on farms across the nation, and locked farmers into an input program of biocides, engineered proprietary seed, and fertilizers, often owned by singular, vertically integrated, multinational seed companies.

In 2007, Seven Seeds Farm began to transition their rolling ridgetop farm from a monocropped system into a regenerative operation, with several production channels bringing the farm simultaneous revenue streams while building the soil biome. Restoring perennial root systems to the windy ridgelines that cover this region has worked to hold topsoil in place. In heavily tilled fields across the Driftless, sandstone rock that sits beneath the surface has started to poke through, as though an ancient voice from the past is calling out with an ominous message. Sandstone formations date back 450 million years, to an era of vast seas that covered the region. These seas eventually retreated, creating layers of sediment. Over the millennia, flowing water carved rock faces, creating steep valleys and buttes, and topsoil formed through biomass accumulation, making this region rich in grasslands and forest. Margot Conover of EPIC Provisions explains that what took tens of thousands of years to create

is being lost in a short period of time: "If you see naked soil when you're driving through an agricultural area, just picture that 50 percent of topsoil on the planet has been lost in the past 250 years. We used to measure topsoil in feet; now we measure it in inches."

Starting with 14 head of cattle in the first year, Seven Seeds has grown their herd to 170 Murray Gray cattle, 150 hogs, and 1,500 meat chickens and laying hens on roughly 500 acres of owned and rented pasture and tillable land. Seven Seeds Farm's biodiverse system stacks multiple enterprises that work together to create more productivity. Michael Dolan, along with his wife, Chloe, is the 27-year-old owner and part of the seventh generation to care for this land. He says that multispecies pastures go beyond farm production. "Our chickens tend to follow the cattle when they're on rotating pasture. They're great at keeping the fly larva population down for cattle. There's a lot of symbiotic relationships between these species on our farm, and they occur because of our diversity. In our culture now, food systems are very segregated and very confined. That's the opposite of what we want to do on our farm." Unraveling the biological partnerships that work together in nature has a dark side that presents in a cascading chain of consequences that are mitigated through more and more inputs.

We know that our great ruminants evolved to eat grass, so it's important to understand why our food system has interrupted what ranchers, shepherds and hunters have always known. Savory Institute's Ibarra-Howell shares the origin of our concentrated animal feeding operations (CAFO's). "Grain surpluses caused by government price supports provided an opportunity for grain feeding to become a standard practice in the beef industry. That's how it all started. Finishing (young) cattle were confined and fed grain, growth hormones, and other supplements to push their weight up as quickly as possible, along with antibiotics to keep them from getting sick — acidosis, for example, is a big issue. The result was a faster cycle and more consistent meat product, more like a factory, but it carried tons of unintended negative consequences for human health, animal health and welfare, and for the integrity of family farms, entire communities and the ecosystem. This artificial system for finishing cattle is designed around efficiencies of scale, not health of land, animals and people. It is fuel-based and it's subsidized, and it carries a big carbon footprint."

Ibarra-Howell's work through the Savory Institute aims to disrupt this system through advocacy and education for farmers and consumers, as well as supply-chain innovations from grassroots producers up to corporate-level distribution. With the great riddle of whether American grasslands can support our nation's beef consumption, Ibarra-Howell points to an analysis of USDA-sourced data on the hypothetical increase in nationwide stocking rates if all beef production were to undergo 100% conversion to being grass-finished. She says, "It's totally doable. If the study is right, it would mean a 30% increase in stocking rates on grasslands. We know with holistic planned grazing we can easily double our carrying capacity. But these animals need to be managed properly for regenerative outcomes, not just put on grass." While we probably won't see grass-fed, grass-finished beef used exclusively on fast food menus anytime soon, our individual buying choices are creating the momentum that propels the regenerative movement forward.

AS FARMERS, WE ALWAYS SAY THAT IT'S IMPORTANT TO UNDERSTAND WHERE YOUR FOOD COMES FROM, AND TO KNOW YOUR FARMER, BUT THE BIGGER PICTURE IS TO UNDERSTAND THE FOOD CHAIN AND KNOW HOW IT INTERACTS WITH OUR CHOICES INDIVIDUALLY.

Eric Cates, the second-generation beef farmer who is following in his father's farming tradition, returned to the family business after a career in alpine ski racing. Living a life split between Western mountain landscapes and summers on his family's farm has given Eric a zoomed-out perspective on the separation that most people have from their food. He points out that knowing how our food is produced can shift the entire way we eat. "It's pretty easy to be blind to a lot of things and just walk down an aisle and throw things in your cart and go on with your life. But the decisions we make all have background stories, so it's important for consumers to know this. As farmers, we always say that it's important to understand where your food comes from, and to know your farmer, but the bigger picture is to understand the food chain and know how it interacts with our choices individually." When we take a hard look at how we are connected to these greater systems, we can start to see which path we are perpetuating.

Our current food paradigm separates us farther and farther from the farmers growing our food. This design, where products change hands multiple times before they reach the buyer, drives down the farmer's margins and incentivizes breeds chosen for production rate first and foremost. Considerations of flavor and quality fall a long way down the list. Through the Cates Family Farm's direct-to-consumer model, Eric can talk firsthand with his buyers about their meat. "Jerseys are from the dairy industry and put on meat in different areas of the body from our Angus cattle. They have a really unique flavor profile and they do really well on grass. I always remind people that in the dairy industry, Holstein is the volume animal, but Jerseys have this innate ability to turn grass into delicious, creamy fat, and you can see it in their meat. It's got a slightly gamier flavor to it, on the spectrum of venison and elk; it's a deep reddish purple, and the fat is much more colorful, but they take longer — 30 to 36 months." Eric reminds us that this attention to detail only works because that is what his buyers want. Regeneratively produced products will initially pass the costs on to consumers, but the investment back into the land and the community will ultimately offset the hidden costs of conventional agriculture, which are evident in our chronic diseases, environmental damage, and wildlife habitat loss, as well as the shuttering of small towns across the country. Although the bill comes down the line, it is still paid by the consumer.

The change that is created through the circular economy of diversified agriculture is the path to creating the sustainable opportunities that farmers need to thrive independent of national market influence. Ibarra-Howell of the Savory Institute explains how the health of a farm circulates through the entire community. "When you don't have that choice, even if you want to buy from a farmer, you can't because they're producing for commodity markets. But when you have a choice and you can invest in your own local farmers, instead of leaving, that money stays circulating in the local community, creating a more resilient, productive and healthy community. The moment you start exporting everything, the value of that community is extracted, from a point of view of money, from a point of view of tradition, from a point of view of health, and from a point of view of intimacy with each other." The hollowing out of rural communities that has consolidated our economy and devastated local businesses can be reversed through a return to holistic agriculture practices. Dolan of Seven Seeds Farm explains that the buying of his products ripples out to the rest of his community. "If you're supporting me and my family working on the land and trying to make a living from farming, you're also supporting a local family butcher. We're bringing back money and wealth to these rural economies."

While the concept of relying on managed grazing to return carbon to the earth is entering mainstream dialogue, it's important to remember the Pandora's Box that was opened when we took the mechanical plow to oceans of native grassland in the 1920s. Dick Cates counts soil-based carbon as a mineral that has been extracted. "The great wealth of the American Prairie was the fact that carbon had been stored for millennia and now is released from an organic form into a CO_2 form. It allowed microbes and plants to grow. That carbon has left us. We've mined in a sense, just like we mined oil or we mine coal. We mined stored carbon."

As if the information were hiding in plain sight, new research has shown that the very animals we pulled from their evolutionary habitats to fit into our feeding systems have the potential to sequester the carbon that we have unlocked through extensive soil disruption. EPIC Provisions is seeing measurable environmental improvements on one of their supplier partner ranches, White Oak Pastures, creating a movement that aligns regenerative producers with the national reach of EPIC products. Conover explains how we can use regenerative grazing to reverse environmental damage. "For every pound of meat White Oak Pastures produces, they're sequestering 3.5 pounds of greenhouse gas equivalents. Conventional beef — raised on a feedlot and grain-fed — is emitting 33 pounds of greenhouse gases per pound of meat produced. So that's not just going to net zero emissions, but beyond net zero to create a positive climate and a positive environmental impact. It really opens this opportunity of thinking about how humans can be beneficial actors in the ecosystem. So that's a really big, exciting new frontier that we can break into."

With wide-open opportunity to use our food production to double down on carbon capture, both on a national level and in direct-to-consumer models, Seven Seeds Farm is going beyond grazing and animal cohabitation and has introduced the principles of Silvopasture on their land: the integrated approach of trees and pasture for erosion control, animal nutrition, and diversification of revenue streams.

Dolan says that investing in trees on pasture serves many purposes. "In 2015, when I came back from college, we planted 12,000 fruit and nut trees on our soil berms. Mainly chestnuts, hazelnuts, apples and pears that will provide food and shelter for our livestock — and food for us." While Seven Seeds already cultivates organic grain feed for their hogs and chickens, Dolan is excited about the nutritional profile that his animals will benefit from as his trees mature. "When you look in comparison, chestnuts are very similar in nutrition to

corn, and hazelnuts are very similar in nutrition to soybeans. If we can raise those crops perennially, we could make a really big difference."

At a time when the average age of the American farmer is 57, the greatest shift in the way we value soil, carbon sequestration, and the local economy will be a movement championed by farmers like Eric and Michael. The generational transition of a small family farm is a victory that pushes the needle of agriculture away from consolidation. Dick Cates talked about what the future may hold: "Not in my lifetime, but maybe Eric's lifetime, I believe that farmers who do the right thing will glean an income from taking care of our ecological goods and services; elements which don't have a market value at the moment — carbon and phosphorus that's retained in the soil, or keeping a trout stream clear. At some point, I think we will be paid for those things, and this kind of agriculture is poised to do that very well."

When the Cates started grazing steers in their valley in the 1980s, the Lowery Creek that flowed through their pastures was a Class 2 trout stream, dominated by brown trout, which tolerate warmer water. Through managed grazing, their stretch of the Lowery Creek has become a prized coldwater Class 1 trout stream, also supporting native brook trout. Department of Natural Resources conservation specialists in the region have noted that the Cates Family Farm region of Lowery Creek now supports heritage brook trout genetics that date back to pre-European settlement. When food production is taken in the context of our natural world, we can turn back the clock.

It's three miles as the crow flies from the windy ridgetop of the Seven Seeds Farm, down the valley floor to the Cates Family Farm. In the mysteriously perfect dance between the slow hands of geological time and the rapidly cycling birth and decay of soil microbes, we can hear echoes of all of the great animals that have lived and died in the tiny piece of earth that connects these two farms. In the evolutionary timeline of our intervention between ruminants and their native habitats, our age of destruction has been small, but not trivial. In a lofty bow of compassion, the gentle creatures that we've treated as beasts have shown us a way back. ʬ

A Eulogy of Golden Leaves

WORDS BY *Tyler Sharp*   PHOTOS BY *Danny Christensen*

As I took my first steps onto Hungarian soil outside of the Budapest airport — swaying slightly from the mixture of fitful sleep and disruption of circadian rhythm that accompanies international travel — a cold and damp mist hit me in the face. It was early November, with fall and winter wrestling for control of the weather. It seemed like winter might win out.

Then, jarring me from my daze, a Land Rover with Italian plates pulled up, the window rolled down, and a deep, booming Danish voice yelled, "You gonna stand in the rain all night or do you want to go hunting?" Danny Christensen — an accomplished photographer, chef and art instructor in Milan — has been an online friend for a few years now and has contributed to the last three issues of Modern Huntsman, yet this was our first meeting in person. He flashed a big grin, belying his otherwise rough countenance, then gave me a bear hug, and we threw my bags into the Rover already full of adventure supplies. Strangers once, friends before, brothers now.

To document some of the hunting traditions of Europe, Danny had charted a course over the next three weeks that would take us through several countries and regions to experience the history of local hunting, yield some adventure, and hopefully provide table fare as well. But before we could tell stories about Hungarian hunting traditions, we had to

actually learn about and experience them ourselves. Based in Budapest, our friends at the International Council for Game and Wildlife Conservation (better known as CIC), introduced us to Mr. Péter Gőbölös, the CEO of Gyulaj Forestry and Hunting Estate, which is a forestry and game management area that totals about 70,000 acres across several properties and is considered one of Hungary's crowning historical hunting estates. Mr. Gőbölös honored us with an invitation to visit, and we happily obliged.

Driving onto that property felt like moving through a postcard, with endless views of thin-trunked trees midway through shedding their autumn-hued leaves. We were given a brief, but thorough historical tour detailing the land management ethic practiced for over 200 years, the result of which has been enjoyed by a long and prestigious list of patrons. Danny and I flipped a coin to see who would hunt for the fallow deer in the morning. Fate, it seems, was in my favor, so I was to wield the rifle.

Driving onto the property gets like moving through a portrait, with endless views of thin-trunked trees mixing through shedding their autumn-hued leaves.

We entered the boat before dawn, and the fog hung thick and heavy with no whisper of wind.

We entered the forest before dawn, and the fog hung thick and heavy, with no whisper of wind. As we walked in the dark silence of the woods, mist enveloped us — the only sound was the muted rustle of trodden-upon leaves, made softer by the dampness of morning dew. This forest was old, and I sensed its wisdom. Our guide Petar, dressed in the dark, solid earth tones that are customary of the region, said nothing because he didn't need to — we are both hunters. After nearly an hour, we suddenly paused to listen, he nodded to the northwest, and we began our stalk.

We strode deeper into the forest, silently. Our breath hung in the cold air, and the dull gray of a shrouded dawn slowly bloomed, revealing inky shadows whose movements were cloaked through a bastion of ancient trees. After some time, we stopped to glass. In the distant grove, blurred shapes started to take form in our binoculars, though still obscured by the fog. We crept farther, and waited. The wind still slept. We sensed it before we heard it — in the distance, a herd moved into view, grazing across the meadow. All was as it should be.

Petar made the slightest shift in his stance, an almost imperceptible perking of the senses, and I followed his gaze to see a pair of antlers lift above the mass of brown-furred bodies. He signaled with a nod, *that's the one*. I chambered a round as quietly as I could, eased the rifle onto the shooting sticks, and waited for a clear glimpse of his broad shoulder. The forest seemed to hold its breath.

My shot rang out, breaking the silence of the scene with a powerful echo made suddenly dull as it resounded off the crowding mass of arboreal bystanders filed rank upon rank, then all went quiet again.

The herd moved on. To them, perhaps, it was thunder, a falling tree, or some other weather of the world. The wind picked up and leaves began to fall again, seeming to shower our approach like a commemorative procession. We found the fallow buck lying in a bed of soft earth with hues of faded orange and brown now tinged with the deep, rich red of congealing blood — you could hear its slow pooling across the ground as it was sponged back to its terrestrial source.

We stood in silence. There were no whoops or hollers, no high fives or back claps, just reverence and awe for a beautiful beast whose life had now left the forest but also joined it. The

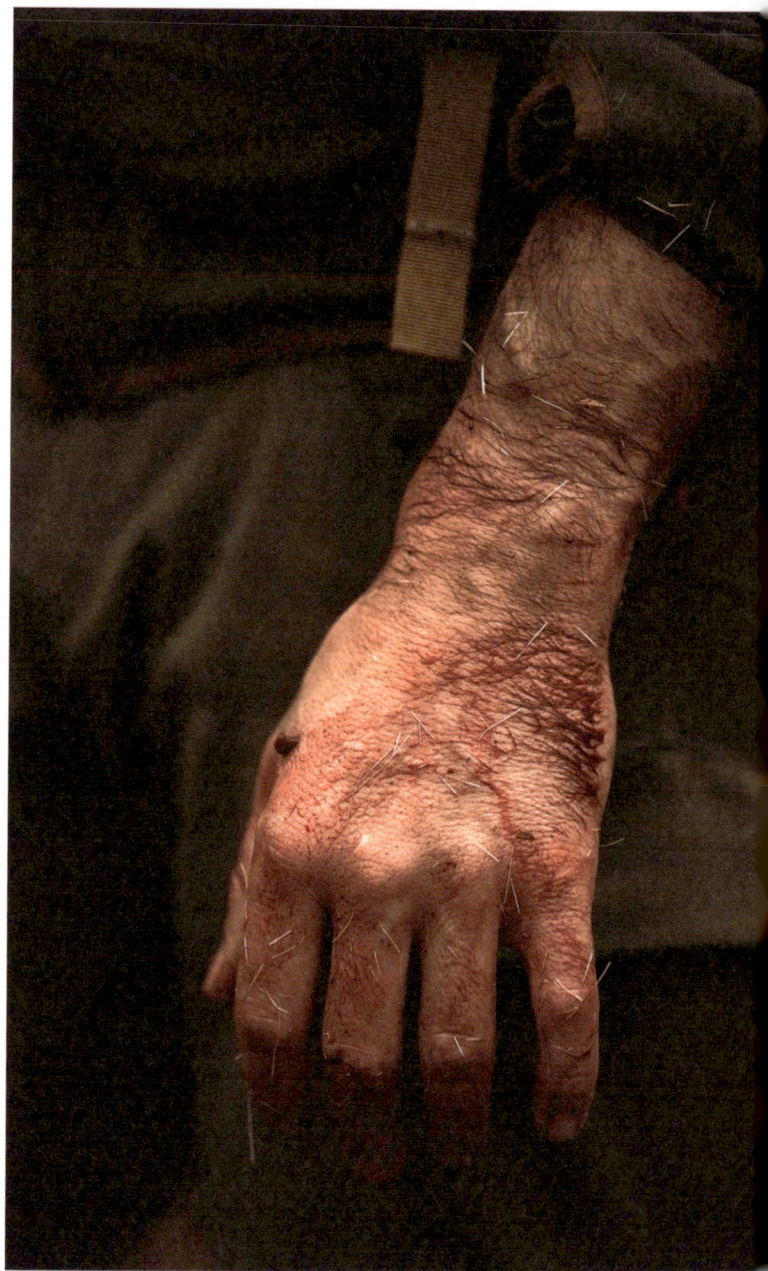

wind sighed, and the silent reverie was broken by the snap of a branch. Then, in a show of great respect, Petar removed his hat, placed one leafy bough over the buck's wound, and another in its mouth — one final morsel for the journey ahead.

Then he walked over, shook my hand, kissed my cheeks, and said what translates from Hungarian to, "hail the hunter," as he placed the last branch in the right side of my hat. The circle was complete, in both action and symbol.

For those who hunt professionally or in some management sense, there may come a point where you don't feel the emotional impact or the gravity of the situation — taking a life to sustain another — but this was not the case for me. Being halfway across the world in an ancient Hungarian forest, enveloped in a gray mist, and participating in a sacred ceremony led to a new and profound sense of respect and appreciation for the act, and tradition, of hunting. Revelation often comes unlooked for, and despite having witnessed rituals before, I've rarely been the reason that one was carried out. We all have ways of giving thanks, some more introspective than others, but I'd been part of *their* ritual, and just like so many generations before, made offerings of appreciation for the sacrifice within *their* mythology. Perhaps it was the otherworldly aura of the morning, but to me, it felt profound.

I laid my hands on the magnificent deer, then traced the abstract contours of antlers largely foreign to me — contours that would become a map of experience, of emotion, in the years to come. I made a cut across the soft white belly fur to remove the organs, the steam of fleeting life rose, and the blood of respected prey warmed my numb, stiff hands — a primally familiar sensation, comforting even, like a scarlet-tinged glove of our forgotten humanity that quickly dries and cracks in the cold morning air, the flakes falling earthward, connecting us back to who we are, what we are.

Now it was time to celebrate, or so I thought. We returned to the lodge, and on the crest of a green hill they placed the fallow buck, and encircled him with golden oak leaves. Then the initiation began.

I was congratulated by a few others, and politely asked to stand within the ring of leaves. Petar and another guide then

began playing a clear ringing tune on their hunting horns, heralding the end of the hunt, and homage paid. Mostly.

They asked if this was the first fallow buck that I had killed. Being that it was, and that I'm an honest man, I said yes. I was then told to kneel down and lean over the fallen deer with my hands on the ground — in short, on all fours. They cut a switch from a nearby tree, and after repeating traditional words that welcomed me into the ranks of successful fallow deer hunters, added that it required tribute for taking a life, then struck me with a well-placed and well-practiced lashing across an area that rhymes with ass.

While I've certainly had worse licks when I was a sharp-tongued and rebellious boy, being on my hands and knees in front of what were in effect cultural ambassadors while getting whipped and having my photo taken was, needless to say, humiliating. It's even humiliating to write this, knowing that a fair amount of strangers will read it. Certainly, it wasn't made any better when I looked over at Danny to see his ear-to-ear grin, which was briefly covered as he snapped yet another photo. He was having a great time.

But the word humiliation is derived from the same root as humility, and while it was a few moments of unease, perhaps that is something more of us should experience in hunting. I was humbled before the forest for the taking of a fallow buck's life, and this was my penance. I believe that most of the time respect is earned, but sometimes respect can be required, even demanded, in this case practiced through ritual as it has been for so many Hungarian hunters before me.

I was told I got off easy, and I agree that I did. Several men regaled tales of shooting their first fallow buck, and how they had the living hell whipped out of them by brothers, uncles, fathers and grandfathers. It's part of the tradition. To the Hungarians, killing a deer is a serious matter, and whether you come from there or not, appreciation should be given and ceremonial tribute paid for the life taken. I couldn't agree more.

Shortly after, as I stood amid a eulogy of golden leaves with a healthy dram of palinka in my hand, we toasted, then feasted.

WE STOOD IN SILENCE. THERE WERE NO WHOOPS OR HOLLERS, NO HIGH FIVES OR BACK CLAPS, JUST REVERENCE AND AWE FOR A BEAUTIFUL BEAST WHOSE LIFE HAD NOW LEFT THE FOREST BUT ALSO JOINED IT. THE WIND SIGHED, AND THE SILENT REVERIE WAS BROKEN BY THE SNAP OF A BRANCH. THEN, IN A SHOW OF GREAT RESPECT, PETAR REMOVED HIS HAT, PLACED ONE LEAFY BOUGH OVER THE BUCK'S WOUND, AND ANOTHER IN ITS MOUTH — ONE FINAL MOUTHFUL FOR THE JOURNEY AHEAD.

As I stood amid a eulogy of golden leaves with a healing
drum & polisher in my hand, we toasted, then pivoted.

After the hunt, we had a diplomatic mission to embark on, which is becoming more and more of a focus with Modern Huntsman. To increase overseas collaboration, we've been working closely over the past year with CIC Director General Tamás Marghescu and his team to define shared conservation goals and promote cultural understanding. They had arranged a meeting for us with Dr. Zoltán Kovács, State Secretary for International Communication and Relations in the Cabinet Office of the Prime Minister, to discuss the "One with Nature: World Hunting and Nature Exhibition" — a three-week-long event slated for the fall of 2021 that will present hunting traditions and host panel discussions and cultural exchanges to showcase the benefits of sustainable use of wildlife resources internationally, as well as explore solutions for the global conservation challenges that we all face. It was an especially proud moment, to think that what

began as a humble print publication has now led to high-level discussions of cultural ambassadorship with foreign dignitaries, and we left on a high note, basking in the stately ring of our new moniker, "the Modern Huntsman delegation."

Our final engagement was an educational program that introduced local schoolchildren to various aspects of Hungarian hunting — including falconry, dog handlers, horn playing and a display of fallow buck antlers from recent years — which was taken in with wide-eyed enthusiasm by both the students and us. Coming from a country with a much less established hunting tradition, it was very refreshing to see the enthusiasm and pride in which these historical practices were demonstrated, and we all left a bit more cultured and learned.

we basked in the stately ring of our new moniker, "The Modern Huntsman Delegation."

Rare Blend

INTERVIEW BY *Danny Christensen*   PHOTOS BY *Tyler Sharp*

After formal farewells, we headed west toward Lake Balaton, a famed Hungarian summer destination — though it was decidedly not summer outside — to visit a German transplant named Florian Zaruba, the CEO and estate manager of the Kristinus Winery. He and Danny forged an online friendship through a shared passion for hunting and cooking wild game, and thus an invitation was extended for us to come visit and expand our cultural horizons. Apart from producing award-winning biodynamic wines, Florian is blending regenerative agriculture with hunting, wild cuisine, and local culture, offering a rare blend of experience in what is often a rigid tradition.

With him and his partner Lazlo as our immaculate hosts, we would spend the next five days learning about their passion for and innovation with winemaking, hunting for a variety of species across pristine, idyllic Hungarian countryside, and of course, drinking a lot of wine. On our last night, we sat down with a few bottles to discuss Florian's background, the challenges he faces, and what he hopes for the future as he follows a path that mixes old traditions with new.

MH: *First, what's a Bavarian German doing in Hungary? Tell us about the journey that led you here.*

FLORIAN: When I was a teenager, I figured out that I was gay and I did not feel welcome in hunting and agriculture. Even in Germany, it was a big topic and not really tolerated, especially in this part of society. So I turned to marketing and advertising — a more tolerant industry, but not my passion. That led me to a time of change in my life, when I had a sense of ... destiny. I was struggling with my job, or maybe with my whole life. I was focused too much on monetary success, and became more and more unhappy and burned out. Finally, I crashed with my company and also in my relationship. I questioned my life. Where was the wrong turn?

I decided to be a forest engineer, to combine my passion with my job, so I would never again have to work in the literal sense. I wanted to go back to my roots and visit my dreams from my childhood of hunting and working in agriculture. Things became clearer when a hunting friend from Bavaria brought me to Hungary. They had a hunting house in a red deer habitat. That's also how I met with the winery, six years

ago. So I applied at the Kristinus winery and eventually became the general manager.

MH: *Are you from a bloodline of farmers and hunters? Tell us about some of the hunting traditions you were raised with.*

FLORIAN: Well, kind of. When I was ten, I learned how to hunt with birds of prey. It is a very traditional way of hunting. I had a golden eagle, and at that time that was as big as me! In this pursuit, you have to be one with nature, because your "weapon" is an animal. You are a real team — bird, dog and falconer. Falconry has been a tradition for thousands of years in many parts of the world, and still is.

I learned to play the parforce horn, which is what we play here as a signal before, during and after the hunt. I also learned the traditional signals of wooden stocks — Jagd Brüche. Before mobile phones, hunters had secret signals made out of wooden sticks to communicate with other hunters, messages like where they had seen which animal, where it was going, or where a shot had landed.

In general, I can say traditions in Hungary are very similar to those in Austria and Bavaria. We have a common history and common kings who were great hunters. The traditions are very respectful; you learn to see the prey as a gift, as a creature of God. It doesn't matter if you believe in God, what matters is that the animal has a value like yourself. It reminds us to see "meat" with greater respect. For me, hunting is always done for food. It's a cultural value. I don't agree with killers and trophy hunters.

MH: *Take us back to your most memorable hunting experience.*

The first prey I hunted with a golden eagle was a fox. I was 11 years old and very scared! Not of the kill, but of the eagle — it was his first fox too, and there was a chance for the eagle to be injured or killed by the fox. After he flew from my fist, I started running after him, and when he caught the fox I still had 300 meters to run. I was functioning like a machine. When I arrived, the eagle was holding the fox perfectly on the neck and head. I claimed the fox quickly and was very proud — the first prey kill for both of us.

MH: *You are a gay man, and you have been lucky to meet your partner through your life and work here. How do you feel people in general, and especially the local hunting community, have reacted to that? Are they accepting?*

FLORIAN: Yes, I am lucky to have found my love here — he has the same interests and passions. He is a winemaker and hunter too. Do people accept this? More or less … Agriculture and hunting are often very conservative fields, so we mainly avoid this topic, especially in rural Hungary. It's not always an open-minded community here, especially when it comes to social issues like this. On the other hand, my partner and I have a 100-hectare plot of land of our own with nothing around us, so we don't give a fuck about what others are thinking. I had to learn this as well — if you are more self-confident, it's less of a problem. But I would be lying if I said it isn't still hard or uncomfortable. I hate to have to explain, make excuses and be judged on who I am, so I don't anymore.

MH: *Hungary has a rich history of winemaking, but you're taking a new approach. Tell us a bit more about the biodynamic approach to production.*

FLORIAN: Making biodynamic wine is all about respecting and working together with nature. The winery is a self-sufficient circle; it relies on healthy and strong biodiversity. You don't need anything from outside for the farming process. The goal is to strengthen what you are farming to keep it healthy, so you do not have to fight diseases with chemicals, antibiotics and pesticides. We produce our own natural fertilizers, mainly from cow manure, like farmers have done for thousands of years.

It has a lot in common with hunting for meat. Hunters don't like meat to be mass-produced, fed with proteins, chemicals and antibiotics. Sometimes I think people forget that they eat what they are feeding to animals. They forget how to treat the animals and plants.

Industrial agriculture is moving away from nature and quality to an industry about cost and profit. But is this really what we want as farmers, and especially as consumers? If most people saw how many chemicals food was contaminated with, they would not buy it. Eighty percent of the winemakers use a huge list of chemicals — it's legal, but it has nothing to do with a natural product anymore.

Biodynamic agriculture is a philosophy. You want to give the soil back better than it was when you began working it, and you want to produce healthy, sustainable and delicious food. This includes making sure that animals have an appropriate life, with only "one bad day," like in hunting. With the animals producing fertilizers, we are self-sufficient.

MH: *How has your vision been received locally and in the wine community? Is there opposition toward your new take on the tradition of winemaking? Tell us about any challenges you face, and why you think it's important to be on this new path.*

FLORIAN: It's time for a change. Our winemaking is a revival of what was done 100 years ago. Sure, the kind of work that can be done today is cleaner, we have better techniques, but chemicals are not needed to produce wine or other agricultural products. But this has been normalized for a long time, and the lobby of a multi-billion-dollar chemical industry is a strong one. Many people doubt our way, but we think it's the right path forward.

MH: *You strive for a deeper understanding and balance through wine production. Do you feel the same way about food? Is it important to you that you also eat wild game?*

FLORIAN: Besides that it is delicious and healthy, it is the most appropriate way to eat meat. A hunter who is not eating the prey is not a hunter — with the exception of those regulating game stock, like predators.

MH: *You are doing something unique with your work at Kristinus Winery — a place to stay, dine, enjoy wine, and hunt. What do you hope to accomplish, or what sort of legacy do you hope to leave behind with this blending of old ways and new?*

FLORIAN: Honestly, what makes a good hunting experience? It doesn't matter if you are hunting alone or with a group — afterward, it's the best to have a drink and good food together and share the experiences of the day. That's what we try to provide here — a chance to make friends, go hunting, and enjoy good food and wine.

Apart from the experience, I hope I can really contribute to a change in agriculture and create awareness for the climate situation. I want people to understand that this change can make things better for them personally — better environment, better quality of water, food, wine, et cetera. If I can motivate others to follow this lifestyle and show that it's enjoyable, I will be happy! It's not something to view as circumstances out of our control; it's a chance to be better.

Transylvania Travelogue

Story by Tyler Sharp & Danny Christensen

It was dark when we crossed the border into Transylvania, and darker still when we pulled into the winding valleys that skirted the feet of the Carpathian Mountains.

Arrival in a Land of Legend

Tyler

As we arrived at the lodge of our host, Silviu Marinescu of SS Wild Hunts, the wind whipped through the canyons, howling; the trees swayed to their very roots; and the veiled moon peeked through the clouds to reveal the jagged teeth of the cliffs that loomed over us. It was a fitting introduction to a land of such legend, one that I'd dreamed of since hearing nocturne tales as a child. But Silviu's hearth was warm, his hospitality grand, and the exotic local foods spread across his table quickly warded off the chill of a strange and mysterious country still cloaked by darkness.

The jagged teeth of the cliffs loomed over us.

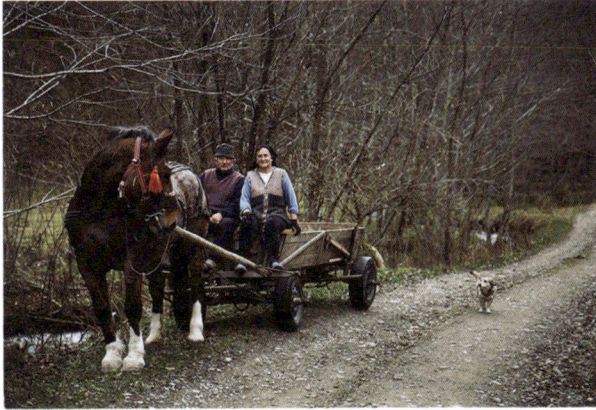

Danny

On our approach to Romania, Silviu sent us some pictures that were a reminder of the natural connections still tying the rural people to the land there. In one, a farmer holds a domestic sheep's head while he slits its throat, the man's face showing some of the same pain of the animal.
He's embracing the sheep as he kills it.

On the long road into the mountains, we drove past an old couple on a horse-drawn carriage. A little dog ran alongside them. The scene reminded me of photos of my great-grandparents in Denmark — that country has changed, though. The couple smiled at us as we passed, and Silviu told me that he once visited their little farm. It was without electricity and had a beautiful garden in the middle of pristine mountains. The old man told Silviu then: "I am the luckiest man alive, I have everything."

"I am the luckiest man alive, I have everything."

The Driven Hunt

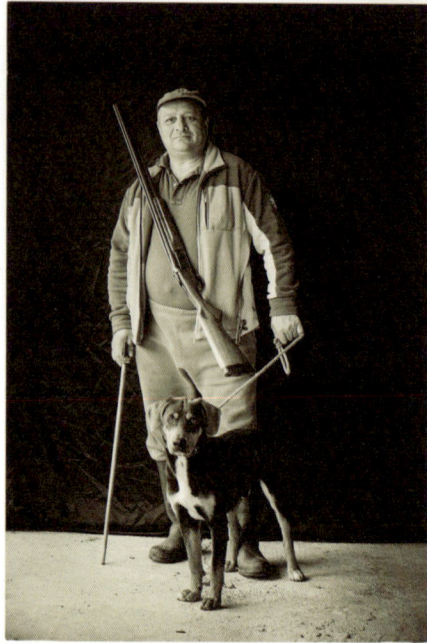

Tyler

With the sunrise came our introduction to driven wild boar hunting. The locals greeted us with the sort of respectful skepticism typical of the rural reaches of the world. We split up, encircled a large, wooded valley, and started converging from opposite ends. I felt I was halfway in a dream as I sat amid tall, thin trees that reluctantly let their last orange leaves fall under the coaxing of a persistent morning breeze. Branches creaked, leaves whispered, and the sounds of barking hounds muffled the fragments of Romanian shouted across a now-bustling forest. There was one boar, but it got away, and the group came back empty-handed.

When we broke out the beers, the hunters warmed to our cause, and agreed to let Danny take their portraits. In our makeshift studio, they proudly displayed prized guns, dogs, and as much bravado and prowess as can be shown in one moment of time. Transylvanian Hunters.

There was one bear, but it got away and the group came back empty-handed.

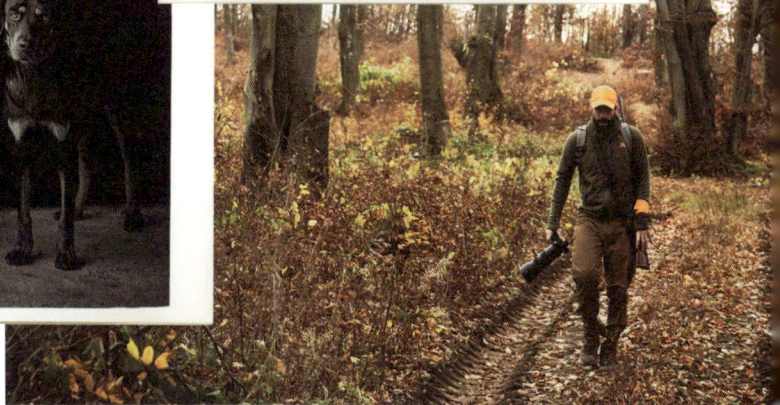

Danny

I heard the distant barks of the dogs bouncing up through the valley. The sound spiraled, louder and louder. Shots rang out, followed by distant shouting. When everyone came down from the mountain, there were scores to be settled. A beater was very upset — a close encounter with a giant wild boar had almost cost him his life when one hunter missed the beast. The arguing rose, back and forth, until enough cigarettes had been lit to start calming the nerves.

Transylvanian Hunters

The Elusive Red Stag

Tyler

Red stag proved the most elusive quarry, and we must've hiked 25 miles or more looking for them through silent groves. We found imprints of recent beds, but the giants had moved on. On the last night, a mist crept across the elbows of the mountain as the sun started to sink. As the fog reached the knoll we were watching from below, a magnificent stag stepped onto the trail, displaying his gargantuan antlers for a brief moment. He lowered his head, and I got into a shooting position, readying the crosshairs for an unobstructed shot.

My heart pounded, and I exhaled, and started to squeeze the trigger in anticipation, but the fog billowed in, lowering the visibility of the scene with a maddeningly slow gradient. When it dissipated, he was gone, like a ghost in a mist, and the image of his massive antlers in the crosshairs is still burned in my retina. While we saw a few others, none presented a shot. That was him, and he gave us the slip. But it left an addictive spark that will smolder until I return.

He was gone, like a ghost in the mist.

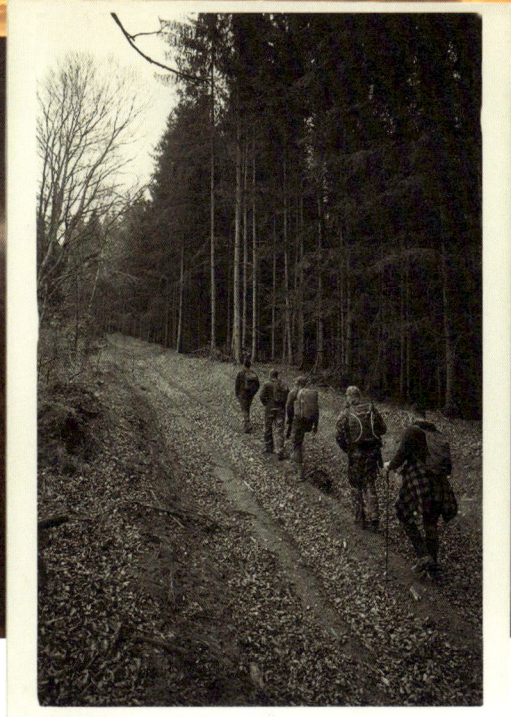

Hunting stag left an addictive spark that will smolder until I can return.

Danny

Silviu spun a story that the beasts in the Transylvanian mountains are so big that they can barely fit into their skin. News had arrived from loggers that they had supposedly spotted the giants. We arrived at daybreak, and the clouds and sun were dancing in a way that I had never seen before. The birds fell silent, and the mountains flexed their muscular silhouettes against the fiery sky.

Fighting, sliding and crawling through the dense forest, we spotted fresh rubs on a few young trees. We pursued them to a small clearing. The animals were there, with an enormous stag leading the herd down a little ravine. I struggled to steady my aim as a fog approached. The stag wove in and out through trees toward the edge of the forest ... and then was gone. I waited for his return that never came. Octaviu tapped my shoulder, and pointed to the left where Tyler and Marian were, close by the spot where the herd had been swallowed by the forest. We had been hunting the same stag from different sides of the valley. Shooting that deer would have been a fantastic experience and, most likely, the end of my valued friendship with Tyler.

Search for Chamois

Danny

It was my turn to hunt for chamois, and the hike was long and tough to get to their domain. As we broke through the trees, the first light revealed a vague shine of the ice-glaze on the mossy rocks beneath my feet, and I instantly slipped and fell off of them. We hiked to the highest point, but found no sign. On that outcrop, we glassed for chamois and shared the moment, as hunters. We checked one last area: shit, shit, and more shit. Chamois shit and bear shit, scattered all over, made it clear that the goats had been forced out of the area by big brown bears. At least we had palinka.

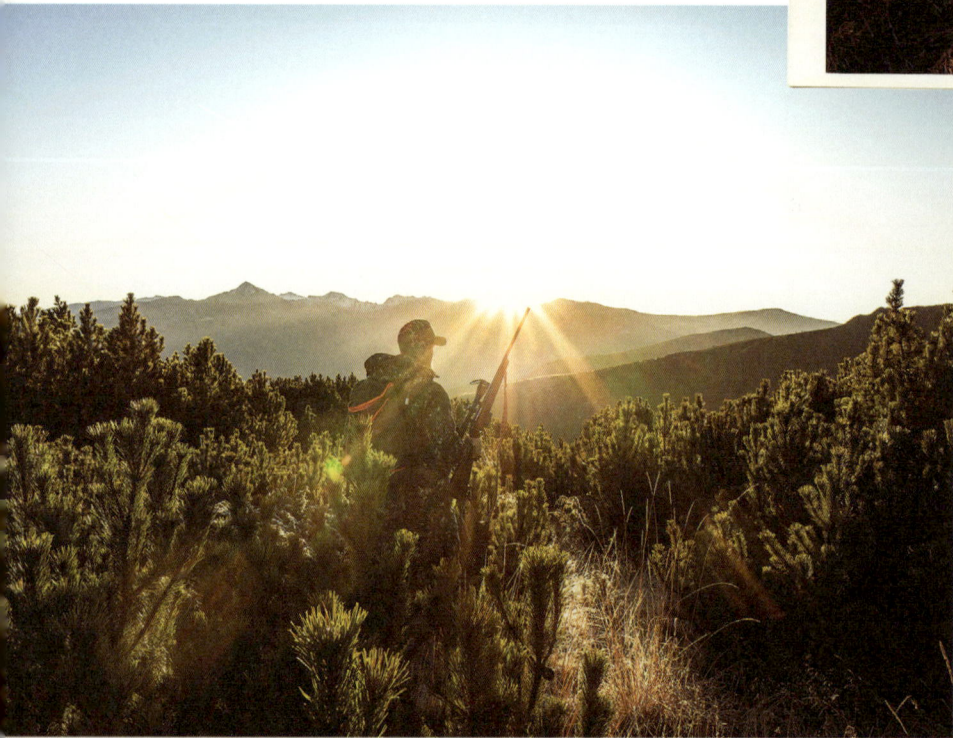

We hiked to a whopping alpine region to find chamois.

Right habitat, no luck.

Tyler

We hiked to a skyscraping alpine region to seek the nimble cliff goats called chamois. It was a clear but frosty morning, and as the sun crept over the distant peaks, its rays danced across a frozen, crystalline ground. Danny hiked an adjacent ridge with a forest ranger, but they saw no chamois. Right habitat, but no luck. The winds were gale force and a chill set in as we glassed the valley. Cold was countered with palinka, the potent plum liquor, which seemed to be as necessary a hunting tool as any. The hike down was much more cheerful.

Wild Boar

Danny

It was getting dark as we drove down through the secluded valley. I was told to get ready. Past the bend in the road, we would meet the low spot that the boars descend to, feeding on the lush vegetation in old river beds. Down on all fours, I crawled, carefully peeking ahead. There were two massive wild boars on the edge of the forest, so I picked the bigger of the two, and sent a bullet into the vitals. My aim was true, the death was clean, and together we celebrated success on the last day of the hunt.

A different kind of love enveloped me. It felt ancient and eternal, reminiscent of a time when one lived off, with and by the land, where you simply took what was necessary — where homemade high-octane plum wine and old rain boots were all you needed.

One hundred and eighty pounds of boar meat fed my wife and I through the winter. Meals shared with loved ones are always a pleasant reminder of when time stood still, or instead went back to the only future worth living. One with nature, a simpler one, as the luckiest man alive.

Danny took a massive pig back to Italy.

We had learned the ways of Transylvanian hunting, been in the lairs of the beasts, and made new friends in high places.

Tyler

On our last foray, we got caught in a torrential downpour that seemed to signal the end of autumn, and the onset of winter. Danny had one final chance for a wild boar, so he belly crawled through the mud to pursue them, and I sat in the jeep with Octaviu, smoking cheap cigarettes and conversing in broken Spanish about what hunting in Montana was like. Danny was successful, and would be taking a massive pig back home to Italy. Though I was going home empty-handed, I count it as a very successful trip, gaining a week of unforgettable experiences in some of the most mystical mountains I've ever seen. We had learned the ways of Tranyslvanian hunting, been in the lairs of the beasts, and made new friends in high places. ⚔

Red Pepper Wild Boar Stew

RECIPE BY *Danny Christensen*   SERVES: *4-8*

INGREDIENTS

2 lb / 1 kg wild boar meat cut into cubes, plus some boar bones

Lard (can find at butcher)

Smoked fat (or bacon/pancetta)

1 large onion

5 large red bell peppers

4-5 cloves of fresh garlic

Late autumn sweet tomato puree/sauce. If you don't have the puree, add some brown sugar

Salt & Pepper

Smoked paprika, Hungarian if possible.

Caraway seeds

Bay leaves

Fresh thyme

Brandy

Red wine

Beef stock

8 oz / 250 ml organic tomato purée

INSTRUCTIONS

There are two ways to do it: cast iron pot over the open fire, or in the oven. If cooking over open fire, you have to add some stock from time to time. If using an oven, you just need one cup of stock reduction.

1. Sweat the peppers: Char the peppers over an open fire or on a gas stove flame *(alternatively, grill in the oven on the top shelf with top broiler only — watch and turn when blackened)*

2. When charred, move to a large bowl and cover with wrap or a tight-fitting lid. Let rest for 10-15 minutes.

3. Gently peel off the loose skin and de-seed the peppers, saving only the meat.

4. Melt the lard at high heat, adding the smoked fat and boar meat.

5. When everything starts to caramelize, add the brandy and flame it. Keep flames until the liquid begins to evaporate.

6. Remove and store the meat.

7. Reduce to medium heat.

8. Add to the pot smoked paprika, caraway, salt and pepper — one teaspoon each — and fry for a couple of minutes.

9. Add tomato puree / a teaspoon of brown sugar, followed by the chopped onions. Fry them till soft and translucent.

10. Add peppers, and stock.

11. Cook for 10 minutes, then blend to smooth sauce with hand-blender.

12. Add the meat and a few bay leaves to the sauce.

13. Now, if you are cooking in the oven, just put the lid on or cover with tin foil and cook at 400F / 200C for 3-4 hours.

14. If you have time, slow cook at 250F / 120C for eight hours.

15. The best way is, of course, to cook over an open fire, for flavor and for the soul of the chef.

16. If over an open fire, remove the lid, keep the flame small, turn frequently, and add stock as you go along. For an expedited version, put the lid/tin foil on.

17. 30 minutes before the finish, crush the garlic and mix with salt, fresh thyme, and a bit of olive oil.

18. For the last 15 minutes, add 1 healthy glass of red wine — Zinfandel or Pinot Noir are both good.

19. Add the garlic mix.

20. Taste and add salt & pepper as preferred. For a little heat, use crushed dried chili and let cook for minimum 30 minutes before serving.

21. Serve with a glass of red and a thick piece of toasted day-old bread.

LEARNING FROM DAD

WORDS BY *Kate Watson*   PHOTOS BY *Jeremy Koreski*

There is something wildly romantic about being a guide today. It is an escape from the hyper-convenience of modern society, from the tyranny of a nine-to-five. There is a picture painted into the psyche of our young minds that guiding offers a life of innate freedom, of adventure, of fulfilling passion. Perhaps this fantasy was always here though, as society progressed in the ways of modern times. Perhaps there were always some who looked westward, into the mountains among the wild and into the frontera of what we call public lands here in Canada: Crown Land. Perhaps this notion of seeking the simple, yet complex mosaic of nature was what created guiding, cowboying and thus conservation movements.

I fell into guiding by looking through that same lens, through the lens of my father, but perhaps he did the same when he was my age. I grew up knowing him as a logger, business owner, and hunting guide, as president of a chapter of the Guide Outfitter's Association, as a builder and someone full of gruff and ogre-ish backwoods character. His stories bring anyone to tears from fits of laughter. He is outspoken, with an extraordinary ability to formulate a well-educated and skillfully worded argument. At times, he comes off as a wildlife managerial zealot, but at his core he is a harmless combination of pious dedication and appreciation of our wild spaces and their inhabitants. My father checks all the boxes of an old-timer outfitter trying to work in today's modern political environment without the finesse of delicate tact.

In the 35 years my father has been guiding professionally, there have been detrimental changes to the global landscape; wildlife populations have plummeted, stressors are reshaping ecosystems, activist groups and intentions have been created or altered to fit modern needs, and resource-based industries that were once sustainable have changed practices. We have become inundated and numbed by statistical shock value numbers surrounding these modern changes regarding conservation, but numbers are not always as persuasive as a captivating campfire story from a man who has spent over 50 years traversing what he considers his backyard.

Meet my father, Ken Watson, a straight-shooter, who is as famous for his hysterical stories as he is for his fearlessness to ask hard-hitting questions to those in positions of power.

KATE: *When we were growing up, you didn't want us telling people that you owned and operated a hunting lodge, so I used to tell friends that you owned a wildlife nature camp. Do you think if it becomes generally more accepted, future generations could view it differently?*

KEN: I think we should just all keep it low profile and quietly go about our own business. I don't post hunts on Facebook; I don't even know how to post on Facebook. That's more about bragging. If people don't like hunting, that is their opinion. I am not going to shove it in their face to cause an altercation — I think people appreciate that in the end. That's something more young people could practice. People are just tooting their own horns every day on social media, and I don't want that. I just want to keep to myself. That's why I don't even like doing these interviews, because people take bits of stories and run with it. You can't even have a candid conversation.

KATE: *Did anyone in your family hunt? How did you learn?*

KEN: No, my dad was a farmer and didn't hunt, so I learned on my own. It's something that is in your soul; it's in your makeup. I started with a BB gun my dad bought me when I was ten, and figured it out as I went. I loved fishing, though; I sold worms at the end of my driveway for 35 cents a can. Each held a dozen, and I would make between $75 and $100 dollars a summer — that's a lot of worm digging. I would ride my pedal bike, and eventually my motorbike, to the lakes and creeks, balancing my rod between the handlebars. I would catch anything I could: rainbows, course fish, bull trout. I was fishy — still am fishy. I borrowed my dad's canoe, and my parents would drop me off with my pole and the boat, and they'd come back hours later to pick me up. I still have that canoe; I have it stashed in some trees when I guide for moose. But if you go all the time, you learn pretty quickly in the field. I used to tell my mom that there was no school for my class, and my four sisters would walk to the bus stop and I would just go tromping through the forest with my BB gun or my fishing rod. I'd come home and she'd ask why my sisters had school and I did not. There was definitely school those days, but I'd always rather go hunting.

KATE: *How'd you get into trapping if your parents weren't hunters? There is relevance in this, today, with people trying to get into hunting when they don't come from that background.*

KEN: I took a night school trapping course in grade eight at the local college. The neighbour kid, who was 16 at the time, was taking the course too, so he drove me. My dad was fine with it because he thought it kept me out of trouble, and when I started making money they liked it even more. When I was in grade 10, I made $1,700 selling furs to Hudson's Bay Company, which was Ontario's Trappers Association then. I saved my money in the bank and bought a Chevy short box three-on-the-tree pickup when I turned 16 so I could go even more.

I would skin my rodents and furs in the basement; one of my sister's bedrooms happened to be right there too. She wasn't a fan, especially when I would sometimes nick the scent gland. My mom would be digging through the freezer and find my furs wrapped in plastic. She'd scream, "Kenny-boy what the hell is this?" It was no use telling her, because she'd get so pissed off trying to find dinner and moving my furs or animals. On one of my first dates with your mother, I asked her to come check my trap line. She came from a non-hunting

and farming family too, but she ended up having to pack a beaver out — she got used to it after a while, but I don't think she ever liked it. I trapped until I went to college for three days and decided it was not for me, so I started working full-time at 19.

KATE: *How did you get your start as a guide?*

KEN: I wanted to check out a new lake to fish, but I took the wrong turn and ended up at what looked like a cabin. It was actually a hunting lodge. The owner offered me flies that would work on the lake, and when I got back he was gone, so I stuck them into a post. I went back a second time and he offered me a job to start guiding for him — I guided for 20 years before I bought the lodge from him.

KATE: *How has guiding changed since you started?*

KEN: There is definitely fancier gear and clothing today, which helps for staying out there longer. All we had was wool, and that's still all I use. Wool is silent, like a mouse pissing on cotton. That's what you want out there. When we first started, we had boonie bikes, which were one of the first three-wheelers out, but now four-wheelers and 4X4 trucks can get you anywhere. Unfortunately, guiding has changed in the sense that big industry has expanded so much into our forests. There aren't many spaces left without roads. You wonder why we have so many predators right now. Well, they're making highway systems for them. Moose numbers are drastically dropping and an iconic species, caribou, has been red listed. That has all changed.

KATE: *You were asked to serve as President of the North-Central Guide Outfitters Association chapter. Had you ever wanted to take on a role like this?*

KEN: I was busy and didn't think I could take on a role of that size, but I also saw the problems and I saw how I could help, so I accepted; I wanted to evoke change. I'm not a people person — I can be, but not around people who don't listen — so it's frustrating to explain the importance of putting value on our wildlife when industry leaders do not want to participate. It's disheartening that outfitters aren't taken at face value. It's like the government thinks we all have agendas when we just want wildlife. When we reported in 2008-09 that there was something wrong with our moose populations, we were told three years later, in 2011, that they were going to prove us wrong and do a moose density survey. Guess what their numbers came back as? They couldn't find the moose either — they were down 50% from the last survey. What we're left with is a species that has evolved for a millenium in boreal forests now trying to figure out how to survive in a clear cut. They're struggling to adapt to this.

IT CAN'T JUST BE ROCKS OR TREES OUT THERE. WE CAN'T JUST KEEP TAKING, AND IT'S TIME TO GIVE BACK. WE HAVE TO PUT VALUE ON WILDLIFE. IF WE DON'T, THERE WILL NOT BE ANY LEFT. HOW DO YOU LIVE WITH THAT? ALL WE HAVE TO DO IS NURTURE WILDLIFE AND SAVE HABITAT. THIS USED TO BE A DIFFERENT WORLD, AND HOPEFULLY WE CAN LEAVE IT HALF AS GOOD AS IT WAS.

So they started collar projects to study the problem, but they never pulled the necessary levers that would shift the downward trend. Most of the time we're handcuffed by government, and industries like forestry, to give concrete proof, on paper, on why and how. Until we put a value on wildlife, it is not going to get better. There are few places in the world as beautiful and diverse as British Columbia, but at the rate we're logging and shutting down hunts while ignoring science, we won't have this anymore. I served for eight years, and I am glad I did.

KATE: *What are some of the most memorable moments from your guiding career?*

KEN: There are easily more good memories than bad. I am so proud of our guides; they're incredibly talented people. That's the best part. Well, that and working with your mother. I think that is my favorite guide story, seeing how much your mother puts into this business when she's not a hunter. She constantly makes sure people are comfortable and has fully immersed herself into cooking wild game, and into this lifestyle. Working with the pups has also been pretty cool. It's awesome to see their little hearts and tenacity. If people only had half the amount of heart those little dogs have, the world would be a better place. There's also nothing better than coming down a mountain with a pack string of horses and meat behind you. Good people, good horses — that's living right there.

KATE: *Any last things you want to say?*

KEN: It can't just be rocks or trees out there. We can't just keep taking, and it's time to give back. We have to put value on wildlife. If we don't, there will not be any left. How do you live with that? All we have to do is nurture wildlife and save habitat. This used to be a different world, and hopefully we can leave it half as good as it was.

KATE: The same dogged determination to follow that deep moral compass rules over me. I started guiding with my father, taking fishing trips together and learning the sticks on the river, but long before that I was understanding how to work with clients, learning to cook in the lodge, on the river, and even drafting letters for my dad to industry leaders and Members of Parliament. I would type as he paced the room telling me what to say, almost Churchill-like, only a little more Western. From a young age, I was taught the importance of speaking out against corporate malpractices and how to serve wildlife. This will be my seventh year of guiding, and even though I've been working as a guide for one fifth of the time as my father has, I've witnessed mass changes in the rivers and the wildlife we see.

Along with the necessary skills passed down through our generational lineage, our forefathers and mothers have passed down a devotion to protect our wild lands. We've been handed a responsibility through their dedication and through our privilege of being able to enjoy wildlife. We need to better what they have fought for; we need to keep science-based conservation at the forefront of our psyche and our political agenda. I believe I have a responsibility, an obligation to help ensure outdoor resources exist for my future child to pass the torch to another generation. We pride ourselves on promoting our province as the cultural epicenter of wilderness, with forests that stretch hundreds of thousands of kilometers and rivers that flow with the sounds of wild waters through unseen remote lands. Let's be the generation that carried on the tradition; let's be a generation worthy of men like Ken Watson.

WORDS BY *Aaron Gulley*   PHOTOS BY *Jen Judge*

The Old Women

*Five Korean grannies with painted-on eyebrows and perm-fluffed hair are preparing to walk into the frigid East China Sea. It's a raw morning in the wind-lashed village of Hado, on the eastern coast of South Korea's Jeju Island. I've come to visit these **haenyeo** (literally "women of the sea") for a lesson in the art of freediving.*

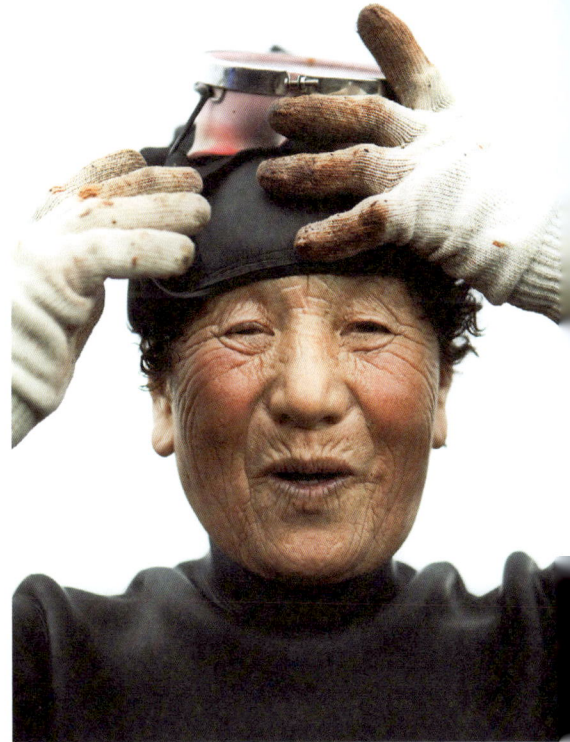

of the Sea

A cold drizzle has me on edge, but the ladies seem not to notice. "Don't you want to dive with us?" one sweet 72-year-old asks. The truth is, with rain ratcheting up and water temperatures hovering around 57 degrees, I can't think of anything I'd rather do less.

For the women of Jeju, diving is life. They dive to harvest abalone, conch, octopus, urchin and seaweed. It's work that's reserved for women, which I'd read stemmed from a historical legal loophole that exempted husbands from paying taxes on their wives' earnings. The truth, I'd find out, is bleaker. The women of Jeju took up diving as early as the 17th century to support their families because their sailor husbands were frequently lost in the treacherous seas. It's possible that the work also fell to the women, much the way it did among the ama pearl divers of Japan, because, with slightly higher levels of body fat, they could better endure the cold waters. Jeju still has about 5,000 working haenyeo, though the trade is dwindling as young girls gain access to education and easier livelihoods. The women still diving, most of whom are over 50 years old, are emblematic of Jeju's past, where life was a struggle against the harsh marine environment and people did what they had to do to eke out an existence.

"Jeju is known for three things," my guide and translator, Sunny Hong, told me on arrival, quoting a local maxim. "Strong winds, strong rock, and strong women."

I'm up against them all in Hado, where I realize that I'm going to have to get wet despite my misgivings about the conditions. As the five haenyeo trudge into the inky water, I wrestle with my wetsuit, which feels as difficult to don as an octopus costume. By the time I'm suited up, the old gals are emerging from the sea. The swells are rising, one tells me, and it's no good for harvesting shellfish today, though I notice that each woman carries a small net of crustaceans they've gathered. The women motion for me to follow them into their stone warming hut. Once they've built a fire, they press whole fresh abalone into my mouth and feed me spoonfuls of urchin roe. The haenyeo may be tougher than walrus hide, but they're still grandmothers at heart.

I ask the women about their work. Yoon Bok-hee, a pudgy 70-year-old who identifies herself as the head of this unit, tells me that they sell the seafood they harvest to a cooperative, which in turn sells to restaurateurs and fish

"JEJU IS KNOWN FOR THREE THINGS," MY GUIDE AND TRANSLATOR, SUNNY HONG, TOLD ME ON ARRIVAL, QUOTING A LOCAL MAXIM. "STRONG WINDS, STRONG ROCK, AND STRONG WOMEN."

markets both domestically and abroad. There are small units of 15 to 20 women like this one all over the island; Hado has seven such groups. The women work at depths between 15 and 70 feet without any breathing apparatus, partly because they began diving before such innovations and partly as a limit on how much each can take. They dive approximately 150 days each year, according to the tides, and spend between four and six hours in the water each shift. Most suffer from headaches and ear problems, and all of them say they know at least one woman who died while diving. The work is so grueling and treacherous that, according to one timeworn expression, "It's better to be born as a cow than to be born as a girl on Jeju."

I ask if they make a decent living. "We don't need to dive anymore. We have plenty of money," Yoon

Bok-hee tells me as she cleans her mask. "But we like to come here and be together. It's our community. Our children tell us not to dive anymore. They want us to come take care of the grandchildren. But that would be like a jail sentence. Our life is here, on the ocean."

This is the paradox of today's hunters and gatherers. Faced with the conveniences and structures of modern life, once-fundamental pursuits are becoming superfluous, skills and knowledge lost. But even as society shrugs them off and admonishes their pursuits as arcane and frivolous, these haenyeo seem to remember that diving is more than just the basic pursuit of food. The visceral act of striving to exist in the elements binds us to the natural world, and doing it collectively underscores and defines our humanity.

The women, who are unrecognizable from their seagoing selves after they emerge from the showers with rouged cheeks, primped hair, and Louis Vuitton bags, tell me to return to dive with them in a few days when the forecast is better. On the appointed date, the weather is even more ominous, a cloak of cold mist hanging eerily over the island. But at the stone warming hut, 15 stout old women are prepping their gear, oblivious to the freezing drizzle. "You can't choose the weather," says one of the divers, 64-year-old Kim Doo-soon, explaining that the haenyeo were often forced to work in spite of the conditions, since their livelihood depended on it. "Before, we had to dive if we wanted to eat."

I follow the grannies — several of them in their 70s — down an algae-slick concrete path to a rocky point where we put on our fins and clamber in. My hands go instantly numb and the cold stings my face despite my mask and hood. The women kick out into the black maw of surf, and I fall behind trying

to adjust my gear. By the time I catch up with a small cluster of divers, we're over half a mile offshore and I'm winded from exertion. The haenyeo bob in the waves, laughing and chatting as they hang on to the personal floats attached to beanbag-sized nets they've each dragged with them.

Kelp shrouds the sea floor in a thick carpet of crimson and thrusts up toward the daylight in ropey vines that sway and surge with the waves. The haenyeo kick down 50 feet to the seabed and plunge into the thick foliage to root around for their quarry. Each carries a J-shaped metal hook in one hand, which they use to prize abalone from the rocks with a sharp twist. One minute passes, sometimes two, before they finally stream back to the surface. As they crest the rollers, they let out a massive exhalation of carbon dioxide in a stiff, shrill squeal. All young haenyeo girls are taught this breathing technique, called *sumbi*. I rarely see a woman ascend without at least one or two abalone, and their nets begin to sag. They only stay above water for a minute or two before flipping over and repeating the process. It looks as easy as plucking tomatoes.

I try finning down with them a few times, but by the time I reach the bottom, my lungs are burning and I have to kick back to the surface. I give up and observe, and after an hour of inactivity I'm trembling from the cold. I wave goodbye to the women and fight the waves back to land, where I steal a hot shower in their women's-only bathhouse.

Warm again, I sit down with my umbrella to wait. I snack on rice and seafood rolls called *kimbap* and huddle against the wind. The day stretches on, past the sun's zenith and into the afternoon, and I'm flabbergasted the women are still out in the icy water. Unlike many delicate grandmothers back in the US, these old women are as robust as many Olympic swimmers. One irony of our existence today is that as technology makes life easier, it also makes us softer and less self-sufficient. When the day comes that there are no more haenyeo, not only will we have lost this wild and stalwart culture but, as a species, we will be one step farther from being able to exist in our natural world.

Finally, around 3 p.m., some six hours after they went out, the haenyeo begin floating in one at a time, their nets bulging behind them. Some of the hauls are so substantial that it takes two or three women working together to drag them from the water. With their harvest safe, the haenyeo scrabble from the icy froth and totter over rocks that glisten like polished onyx, tiny black sea creatures from a bygone age coming ashore. ⚊

INSTAGRAM CONTEST WINNERS

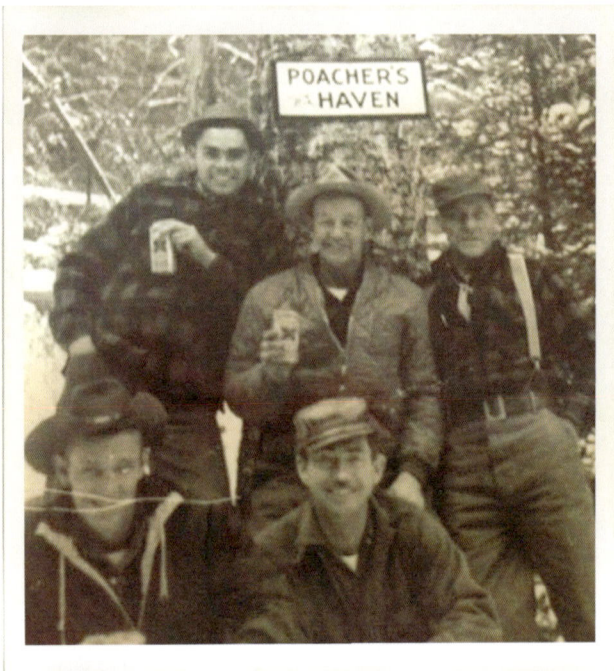

1. MARGIE NELSON | *@margie_nelson*

This band of brothers (by other mothers) hunted through the 50s and 60s together. They had wall tents, corrals, a fire pit and everything you could possibly need for hunting camp. This was vacation for the beer truck driver, the store owner, the railroaders and the mechanics of their era. They had a comradery with each other and the hunt. Their sense of humor was of none other and their skills were impeccable. I would love to go back in time to see them all in their glory again ... my grandpa (leaning, far right) and his posse. Men's men!

3. WES KRUEGER | *@Whatsupdoc1*

Exhausted hunters returning to base camp after a long and grueling but successful bighorn sheep hunt in the Ute Indian Territory of Utah.

2. KEN WENSEL | *@wenselken*

Sled dogs patiently waiting in Whitefish, Montana.

CONTRIBUTORS

PHOTO BY *Jean-François Lagrot*

AARON GULLEY
@aarongulley
www.aarongulley.com

CHRIS DOUGLAS
@chrisdouglasphoto
www.chrisdouglas.photography

DANI VERGÉS
@dani_verges | @slowartworks
www.slowartworks.com

DANIELA IBARRA-HOWELL
@savoryinstitute
savory.global

DANNY CHRISTENSEN
@theurbanhuntsman
www.theurbanhuntsman.com

ELLIOT ROSS
@elliotstudio
www.elliotstudio.com

FABIO PURROY
@fabiopurroy

FILIP ÖRNERKRANS
@fornerkrans

GLORIA GOÑI
@glogoni
www.gloriagoni.com

GUNNAR GUÐMUNDSSON
@hunting_iceland
www.huntingiceland.net

GUILLERMO FERNÁNDEZ LÓPEZ
@guillermo_ez

HANS BERGGREN
@hansberggren
hansberggren.squarespace.com

HEIDI LENDER
@heidilender
www.heidilender.com

JEAN-FRANÇOIS LAGROT
@lagrotjf

JEFF MOORE
@jeffmooreimages
www.jeffmooreimages.net

JEN JUDGE
@jenjudgephoto
www.jenjudge.com

JEREMY KORESKI
@jeremykoreski
www.jeremykoreski.com

JESSE PERKINS
The Wilds

JILLIAN LUKIWSKI
@thenoisyplume
www.thenoisyplume.com

JOHN DUNAWAY
@abstractconformity
www.abstractconformity.com

JONNAH PERKINS
@_jonnah
jonnahperkins.com

JUSTIN MOORE
@dangersoup
www.dangersoup.com

KATE WATSON
@katywat
katewatsonflyfishing.com

PAUL KING
@dirtlord
www.paulkingphoto.com

PHILIP MASSARO
@philmassaro
www.philmassaro.com

RANDY NEWBERG
@randynewberghunter
www.RandyNewberg.com

RYAN HOLM
@ryan__holm
www.ryanholmphotography.com

RICK HUTTON
@rhuttonjr

SAM THOMPSON
govha.co.uk

SHANE MAHONEY
@conservation_visions
www.conservationvisions.com

THANK YOU TO OUR

SPONSORS

FOR VOLUME FIVE

DON'T MISS OUT ON

VOLUME SIX

MODERNHUNTSMAN.COM/SUBSCRIBE